For Merie,
lovely to *know* you,
Cynthia

C. Redfern (signature)

Seasons of the Soul

A Memoir

Cynthia Redfern

iUniverse, Inc.
Bloomington

Seasons of the Soul
A Memoir

iUniverse books may be ordered through booksellers or by contacting:

iUniverse
1663 Liberty Drive
Bloomington, IN 47403
www.iuniverse.com
1-800-Authors (1-800-288-4677)

ISBN: 978-1-4759-5634-4 (sc)
ISBN: 978-1-4759-5635-1 (hc)
ISBN: 978-1-4759-5636-8 (e)

Library of Congress Control Number: 2012919315

Printed in the United States of America

iUniverse rev. date: 10/16/2012

Cover Design by Andrea Bayly

THIS BOOK IS DEDICATED TO MY GRANDCHILDREN,
SO THEY MAY KNOW OF THEIR GRANDMOTHER'S LIFE.

Preface

I had never considered my life unusual. As I lived through the various twists and turns it took through the years, I just accepted that that was the way most people's lives unfolded—that everyone has his or her various trials, joys and tribulations. While this is true to some extent, I began to gather, from the comments I received, that my life was far from the norm. Comments such as "If you wrote down what happens in your life they would make it into a soap opera" (this from one particular co-worker). Then again (from another friend): "Chris is so stressed she doesn't even know she is stressed," to which I replied, "Well, I guess I don't have to worry about it then."

Although I did not take these comments seriously at the time, with the passing of the years I began to realize that perhaps there was some validity to these sorts of comments I'd received. After talking with other people about their own lives, I finally came to the conclusion that yes, I did have an unusual life and a story to tell.

The following pages are the result of my musings.

Acknowledgments

There are many people who have encouraged me in writing my autobiography. Many thanks must go to my dear friend Anne Cowling, who was the first to point out that she thought my story had appeal and that I should write it. She has encouraged me every step of the way. Secondly I must mention my friend Beverly Perks for her enthusiasm about my project, and of course my children, who have had faith in me, as well as provide me with interesting subject matter. Then there is Tom Eriksen, my friend and companion in Chittagong, who told me, "You should write a story about your life," and last but not least, my dear friend John McCaw, who has been the one constant throughout my whole life. Thank you, John.

Prologue

It was one of those moody, misty days that occur in either early spring or late autumn. The kind of day that sets a person to thinking about the "could have beens" and the "what ifs," all of them uncomfortable to a person's peace of mind. After all, it is so much easier to carry on with the day to day of one's routine little life rather than delve into the more uneven paths of old memories. Then there is the question of what is real memory and what imagined—you know how it is with us oldsters—sometimes the "wished for" becomes the "was"!

But this was one time that the long-ago voices would not be stilled by my becoming immersed in just one more load of laundry; today they would be heard and heeded. Maybe even analyzed if my mood became too grim. So I gave in (albeit a little ungraciously) to the *thinking*! Hmm, took a little getting used to, this thinking thing. You know, I soon began to realize that my life was not just a continuous thread of changing events, but, in fact, was a conglomeration of different lives, if you will, with the only common denominator being that these lives were all lived (consecutively) by one person. Oh dear, was that person really me?

So long ago; so far away ... the season of "life just begun" in the soul of a child.

1.

Life Just Begun (the Child)

Whenever I think back to that little house where I was born, the image in my mind is always of a day full of warmth and sunshine—wearing cotton dresses, pigtails flying as the child skipped through the day in an aura of warmth and joy. Reality was the "now" of this small, personal universe. The global reality of war, and the implications thereof, was the purview of the attendant adults and as yet had left no shadow on this one little soul. So how does it all begin? When do we leave behind the security of our joy in the moment and allow our souls to succumb to the scars of the events that form our lives?

My life began on a night in December 1940 when the sky was lit with the flares of antiaircraft guns and the air was full of the sounds of destruction. I emerged into this world at the hands of the inimitable Nurse Brown, who arrived on the scene complete with her tin helmet firmly on her head, and I was immediately and unceremoniously shoved under the bed (at the hands of the aforementioned inimitable)! Only in retrospect, and then only in moments of rare introspection, can I imagine the strength of will it must have taken for the mother giving birth to handle her fears. Fear for her three boys huddled in the bomb shelter at the bottom of the garden, and fear for her long-awaited baby girl—that her life would not be taken so soon after beginning by one of the many bombs creating destruction around the house where this little miracle of birth had just taken place. The air-raid wardens stationed around the house bravely kept their own vigil. What must their thoughts have been on this night of chaos and destruction? Where were their own families as these men protected the environment of this little soul, so unaware on her emergence into the world of anything but the urgent hands of Nurse Brown placing her in the dubious safety of the underside of the bed. Would their homes still be standing when this night of madness ended? Would their loved ones be there, eagerly awaiting their arrival when they returned? Would their personal world still be intact? Questions! Questions for the adult I had become that would never be answered, gratitude needing to be given that could never be received.

So I grew and thrived in a world full of love and caring, unaware that this was a world out of step with the accepted norms of humanity. The cadence of the sirens warning of approaching enemy aircraft and the need to head for the bomb shelter were just a part of the life into which I had been born, as was the "all clear" denoting that (at least for the time being) the very real threat of obliteration had passed. As yet my tender age protected me from the psychological and emotional havoc these sounds must have wrought on the adults in my life. Or did it?

At the bottom of the stairs that led up to the bathroom and

the bedrooms, and just inside the front door, was a row of coat hooks that were used for hanging up the gas masks so common in all households. So, what—isn't that what coat hooks were for? Being very young I had a Mickey Mouse gas mask, and oh what fun it was to put it on and blow, causing the flap to move up and down, making a delightfully questionable noise! In memory, every day was summer, every day free from rain. Now I know without a doubt this is just an "oldster's" imagination. Since when did it not rain almost every day in England? How we idealize our memories and mould them to our need for comforting thoughts.

In this land of constant summer, I ran carefree with my friends as we indulged in all the wonders that life had to offer us. Oh, there were so many things! My best friend was Pamela, and in Pamela's garden grew an abundance of flowers, the best of which were the nasturtiums. You see, these particular flowers attracted caterpillars by the dozen. So with the use of an old tin tray to mark the boundaries, Pamela and I would have caterpillar races. Pamela's mother was very kind, and when offered a treat I would always remember to say, "No, please" and "Yes, thank you." Now this was perfectly logical to me, but looking back, probably confusing to Pamela's mother. However, I digress, so you must forgive this old lady if her reminiscing sometimes runs off on a tangent.

In our garden was a swing that my father had built for me and upon which Pamela and I would sit at the same time, facing each other with our legs sticking out in opposite directions. This worked well until one day we decided to put a kitten on our laps between us, "So it could have a lovely ride." Unfortunately this was not up the kitten's alley, so it showed its disapproval by vomiting profusely all over her unthinking benefactresses. Well, we should have asked first! After all, the kitten much preferred being pushed around in the doll's pram, even if it did mean enduring the indignity of being dressed up and covered with a blanket. Having been born into this world where materials for supplying children with toys were scarce, I was unaware of the effort it took for my father to build my swing and doll pram, or that my mother lovingly stitched my dolly clothes from scraps of fabric that were salvaged from garments too heavily worn out to be reworked. Neither did I know until many years later that the beautiful little playhouse at the bottom of the garden had once been my father's aviary and that the birds had all died from the shock of the bombing. This causes me to ask myself, Did the passing of so much time between the enjoyment of my "things," and the later realization of what effort it took for my parents to try to give me a normal life in this terrible war, detract in any way in my mind from the enormity of their sacrifices or just how much these sacrifices spoke of their love for me? Once again, gratitude needs to be given that can never be received.

By three to four years of age I was already starting to show the strongly independent trait that, in later years, I would need to survive with my spirit (for the most part) still intact. There was the three-wheeler bike, you see. My father had made it from parts he had scavenged, and it was painted maroon. Well, the pavement outside our house had an incline, so I decided to pedal as fast as I could down the hill. Fortunately (or not), a strategically placed lamppost prevented me from flying over the curb and onto the road. This old lady still has a scar below her right knee as evidence of the piece of wire that just happened to be hanging out in the vicinity where I ended up in a heap! Oh, and incidentally, the tricycle was fine. My adventurous spirit also took me off on an excursion all by myself—and without my mother's knowledge.

Looking back, I judge that my wanderings took me about

three miles out down the country lanes, where I was caught in a sudden thunderstorm. The angels must have been watching over me that day as I was found by four workmen who took me into the work hut where they were sheltering from the storm. What joy! The men had lemon tarts with which they thoroughly spoiled me. Mmm, how I remember those lemon tarts. They were very special, you see, because they were bought! This brings me to thinking how, over the decades, the mores of society have changed. Today a wandering child, at least in this part of the world, would not be at risk of a bomb but of the more sinister possibility of abduction, rape or murder. Today our children cannot, for their own safety, be allowed to be so innocent. No longer can small children accept candy from a kindly stranger or play outside with their friends without a designated adult watching over them. Gone are the days when they could walk the distance of even three or four houses by themselves to visit and play with a friend. There is always the fear of abduction. This is now a world that is once again out of step with the norms of society but for a very different reason than the world of my early years. Then again, can we even trust the adults in the homes where our children have been invited to play? It is said that it takes a village to raise a child, but for the most part, at least in our so-called civilized societies, the villages are long gone.

Happily I continued to grow and learn. My friend Pamela was a good year older and so started school. Now, the great thing was that everyday when she finished school, Pamela would run to find me and I would be waiting eagerly to learn from her everything she had been taught that day. Given this advantage, I could read and write before I started school.

Did I mention I was the youngest in the family? My mother and father were forty years old when I was born, and my three older brothers were well spread apart in age. At the time I was born Robert was 16, Sam was 10 and Donald was 4. Robert did not figure much into my preschool years as he was already considered to be a man and was out working. Donald was more in tune with his little sister, but Sam—now that was a different story! Sam was something of a bully from the word go, or perhaps a typical brash teenager. He would take my much-loved monkey and throw it back and forth to Donald over my head until I cried. The monkey was old and his fur was almost gone, but I loved him passionately and Sam knew this. I don't know where my mother was, but when he got the chance, Sam would hold me down and tickle my feet until I screamed. There is no doubt as to the lasting effect of these traumatic experiences, as to this day I cannot bear to see a child have its feet tickled, even in play. But in my mind they appeared to be instances that just came and went, although I did learn to fight my aggressor.

Then there were the times he tied boxing gloves to my hands in an effort to make me his sparring partner. I can still recall the smell of the canvas from which they were made. It would not be until years later that Donald confided to me that Sam bullied him miserably every time they walked to and from school. This old lady now recognizes that these actions were perhaps an indicator of future dark clouds gathering. So I suppose all days were not quite so sunny, but until we start to delve into old memories, we tend to only remember the good times. I presume this forgetting is a protection mechanism, but finally there comes a time when our demons must be faced if we are to have peace in our old age.

But just for a moment let us think of my happier memories. Every so often the rag and bone man would come up the road pushing his cart and calling out, "Rags and bones, rags and bones." My mother would always have something for him, and in return I would get a beautiful, gleaming goldfish—such treasure! Talking about treasures has revived a most wonderful memory. All the little girls in the neighbourhood had little, flat, rectangular tins in which they kept beads from old necklaces. They would sit on the front doorstep totally engrossed in swapping these treasures with their friends. However, the biggest treasure of all was just down the road and around the corner. It was *the diamond dump*! Such was the name given to it by all the children in the neighbourhood. It was the best place ever to find all kinds of jewels, and we children would dig through the rubble with the enthusiasm of a little horde of archaeologists. What a wonderful place—and what a sad place, for what we children perceived as a treasure trove was in fact a bombed jewellery shop, the remains sparkling with scattered beads and diamantes, all that was left of the owner's future and his dreams.

Soon my time for running free drew to a close. As the summer turned to autumn and the autumn turned to winter it was time to start school. The day was December third, my fifth birthday. I remember it well because it was the day the chimney sweep came, along with his poles and brushes, to sweep the soot out of the chimney. Also, from who knows where my mother had managed to obtain a pack of jelly. In those days of food rationing, with no sugar, powdered egg and only what we could produce on our own island this was unheard of. With the Germans blockading Britain, nothing could get in from overseas. Well, I don't know how far a jelly can be stretched but I do believe every child on our street had at least a spoonful that day. It was red! Very soon I passed from kindergarten to Class one A where I had a wonderfully unconventional teacher named Miss Foden. In this class I honed my reading and writing skills and soon learned my times tables. At home my mother would entrust me with the job of counting how many sacks of coal the coalman dumped into the coalhouse. It was easy to have a dispute over the quantity once the coal was dumped.

The year 1945 was one of changes. The war was over, and all over the country people were celebrating and holding victory parties in the streets. I remember in our street we had tables put together down the middle of the road, with children sitting on either side. It was during this time that my eldest brother, Bob, married his sweetheart, Gladys. What a lovely, lovely person she was. They moved into two rooms in the house next door, where they had the downstairs front room and the upstairs front bedroom. Being only five, I did not know why, but by the end of the year, Bob and Gladys moved into my home and I and my family moved to a big house on the next street.

2.

Friendship Found (the Girl)

*D*ecember 3, 1946, was moving day and my sixth birthday. At the time I was not to realize what an incredibly important day this was to be in my life. The events that unfolded would have effects that would last a lifetime. To facilitate our move, we used the big maroon moving vans that belonged to Uncle Jack, mother's youngest brother. (Wait—it has just this minute struck me! Father worked for Uncle Jack as a mechanic, and the maroon colour of the trucks was *exactly* the same colour as my tricycle. Huh, after all these years, suddenly I see the connection.)

Anyway, back to our moving day. The only thing that stands out clearly in this old lady's mind is that I must not have been at all happy about this change in my living quarters. I have no memory of ever having seen the house ahead of time in order to prepare me for the move, and even at that age I did not like change. Had I been born in this current era, I think—no, I know—I would have been diagnosed as having a little obsessive compulsive disorder (my how we like to hand out labels in this current day and age). One clue to this occurred at Christmas when I was three years old. I had a grey and white knitted penguin with a yellow beak, and for Christmas my mother had made the penguin a dress out of my old nightgown. However, mother noticed after giving it to me that the opening at the back below the button was a little too large. So she stitched the back seam a little higher. Well, I was so upset that I undid all those new stitches because that was not how it was supposed to be. It was supposed to be the way it was when it was given to me. Definitely a little OCD! Oh my, here I am digressing again. Back to the moving day.

My one clear memory is of standing on the edge of the now almost empty moving van. I was holding a mop and crying, and standing a few feet away was a boy about my own age, watching me. What caught my eye was that he was wearing a kilt, complete with sporran. How strange; I had never seen anything like this before, but somehow there was an instant connection between us. This event is so clear in my mind, although what followed is just an ordinary part of the whole. We chatted as children do, without the constrictions of etiquette that would govern adults meeting for the first time. The boy told me his name was John, and I told him my name was Cynthia. This was the pivotal moment that started a friendship that has thus far lasted 64 years. At that moment no one could foresee how much I would need the stability of this friendship to see me through the trials to come.

The new house was palatial in comparison to the house we had just left behind, and instead of a small garden there were several acres where I could roam with my friends. Instead of a tiny front yard with a gate and a path leading to the house, there was a wide, sweeping driveway leading up to a front porch framed with huge jasmine bushes. After stepping onto the front porch, one was faced with a beautiful, arched wooden door into which was set a patterned leaded window, and the windows on either side of the door patterned this same design. Once having stepped through the front door the hall was wide, with oak flooring and a sweeping mahogany banister curving up to the next floor. The house had the same number of rooms as the previous dwelling, but they were all so much bigger and fancier. On the doors leading from the hallway into the front room and living room were small brass door knockers in the shape of an old galleon. Each of these rooms had bay windows and beautiful fireplaces, with the one in the living room having a highly polished bevelled surround and an extravagant mantelpiece. My mother must have found the kitchen a total joy. Instead of the small, postage stamp-sized one we left (it was crowded if two people stood there at the same time), this one was large and had real red brick tiles on the floor. The kitchen also had a fireplace! Attached to one side was an oven that baked the most wonderful bread and cakes. We also had room for a kitchen table and chairs, and leading off the kitchen was a pantry with a window of its own. But mother's big delight was its size and the fact that it had a thick, marble cold slab (no refrigerators in those days) and a wire mesh "meat safe."

Exiting the back door, one stepped into a glass veranda that ran half the width of the house. It had slatted shelves all around for potted plants, and wonder of wonders, through another door inside the veranda was an outside toilet! I had never seen such a thing except at my grandpa's house. Upstairs was a huge bathroom, big enough to hold an old, marble-topped washstand, besides it having all the modern conveniences. Plus there was a substantial airing cupboard for holding all the towels and bedding.

Sam and Donald shared the back bedroom and my parents

had the front bedroom with the bay window, and both of these rooms had gas fireplaces with artificial coke to make them look real. Back at the old house before Bob was married, he and Sam shared a bedroom and Don and I slept together in a single bed in the little box room. That was all the room would hold, just that one single bed.

Well, when I went to look in my room, I could not believe my eyes. It was built out over the garage and had so much room—room for a bed, a dressing table, and (when I became older) a bureau and chair. But for the present there was room for the doll's cot my father had built for me. Then, wonder of wonders, I realized there was another door off my bedroom. I opened it and found a "secret room" that was actually a big box room tucked under the sloping roof of the house. In it I found a most wondrous thing: a shepherd's crook. Oh what fun!

My bedroom windows overlooked an expansive front lawn, and in the middle of that was an ornamental blossom tree surrounded by a circular garden containing forget-me-nots and London pride. Bordering the lawn was yet another garden with globe-shaped privet bushes of alternating green and gold foliage. All down the other side of the front driveway were tall laurel bushes looking very grand and leading up to a huge double gate with twisted, circular iron handles. At the side of these was a single gate just for a person to walk through. Beyond the double gates the driveway carried on all the way down past the back garden.

But I am getting ahead of myself. First we must finish the tour of the house, a house in which I would be living for almost the next 20 years. But was this house to be a home? There were seasons to my living here, but that will come later. Under the long sloping roof of the house and partially beneath my bedroom was a garage. It had double doors opening out onto the driveway and a regular door at the back. There were also windows, under which my father had his work bench. It was always piled high with the most fascinating things, including an antique instrument for pouring molten lead to make the ball shots for old guns, and tools for just about everything. My father never said much, or perhaps I was too young to realize at the time, but he must have loved his garage. As an adult, John confided in me that he loved following my father around when he was working in his garage on some project or another. My father was a patient man and would have enjoyed explaining things to him.

The next part of our little tour is the back garden. Whoever lived here before us must have had great pride in and love for his garden (I later found out the previous owner was Mr. Slater, the milkman). Bordering the large square lawn on three sides were flower gardens, and what a wonderful assortment of perennials there were. Oh how I loved that garden. On the side bordering the driveway were all kinds of apple trees. Some were very sweet and others were what my mother called "cookers," which were too sour to eat but she put to good use by making all kinds of scrumptious desserts.

In the centre of the lawn was a circular rose garden. Over the years I came to realize that it contained one rose bush with blooms that were almost black, and these roses were always in bloom on Christmas Day. At the far end of the lawn the garden was raised up and much larger than the borders. Now this was a garden that was dedicated solely to roses and it was magnificent. From the lawn there was a little pathway that circled around the back of the rose garden and emerged on the other side. The pathway was trellised and formed an arbour with many varieties of climbing roses. As a child it was like walking through a secret wonderland, hidden from the eyes of the world. It was at the end of this pathway and right next to the pretty pink tea roses that my father built my swing. I shall never forget those tea roses; they were so tiny and beautiful, and when I was on my swing I smelled their perfume. Perhaps it was this early influence, but roses have always been my favourite flower.

My, this little tour is becoming quite extensive, so my apologies. Perhaps this chapter heading should have read "House and Garden Tour. Two shillings and sixpence per adult. Children under ten, free." Hmm, I had better state my case. You see, in order to understand me (I was a complex little character), you will need to understand the environment that helped shape who I have become. So please bear with me as I indulge myself in my happier memories of my home—a home that would too soon become just a house that held darkness, fear and eventually anger. So for now (if you wish to continue this tour—no refunds—tea and scones served at its conclusion) we will travel back to the girl who is exploring her new home.

The wall at the back of the rose arbour was old, red brick; rough, warm and comforting to the touch. Perhaps it subconsciously represented strength and stability to the girl. Now if we go back onto the driveway and walk beyond the boundaries of the garden, we will find that the driveway in fact swings 'round in front of the red brick building, which turns out to be a stable and coach house. Whereas the coach house was just a big empty room, the stable was so interesting. It had a big window and a typical two-part stable door. The floor was made of deep ridged patterned tiles of a dark purplish grey hue, slanting slightly toward a gutter made of the same tile. On the back wall was an iron manger with a trap door above it for throwing down the hay from the loft. One could access the hay loft by climbing a vertical ladder attached to the wall of the stable and then going through a square hole in the ceiling. Alternately there was a door at the other end of the loft with wooden stairs leading down to the ground and to a little milk house.

Having been born and raised at Cole Hall Farm, where generations of his family had been tenant farmers, my father spent many happy hours in the greenhouse attached to the barn and in the big kitchen garden at the side of the greenhouse. This garden included red currant and black currant bushes that yielded vast quantities of fruit. Now for our last item on the tour—one huge hay field! It did not take my father long to put together a hen house and a large area surrounded by high wire netting. We had big Rhode Island red hens and a rooster, but my favourites were the little bantams. They were tiny and colourful and more like pets. John loved these bantams and has never forgotten them. In fact, three years ago he bought an original painting of a bantam rooster that now hangs in his cabin. Oops, I believe we just traversed a few decades and had a little glimpse into the future of these two childhood friends, John and Cynthia.

3.

Grandpa (the Girl)

I do not recall much about my grandpa prior to moving to our new house, although I must have visited him fairly frequently. My focus was probably more on my Aunty Lil, who was one of my mother's sisters and also my godmother. Being a "spinster," it was she who looked after the house and the cooking for Grandpa and Uncle Tom, my mother's bachelor brother. Looking back I just get little images—like snapshots—of that time. I can visualize my little, lacy, crocheted socks that Aunty Lil made for me; that she was a large woman who I somehow associate with lavender colours; and that Grandpa's dog Judy had puppies, which delighted me (I can still recall that distinct smell of warm puppy breath). Aunty Lil died in February 1944 while I was just 3, and her Bible was passed on to me. The inscriptions inside read, "To Lily Mary R. Caudle, from her father and mother, Christmas

1915." Underneath this is another inscription: "From Auntie Lil M. R. Caudle to Cynthia, February 18, 1944."

It was only in January 2011 while I was talking to my older sister-in-law in England that she told me what really happened. Apparently Aunty Lil was found dancing half naked in the street and was taken to Ladywood Hospital. In later years I recall hearing how much my father (a gentle and compassionate man) had hated Aunty Lil, and I could never understand this aspect of his character, which was so out of keeping with the person I knew him to be. I think perhaps there are some family secrets here I know nothing about, and of course there is no one left to ask. But perhaps now I have the answer to why I do not remember much about my grandpa before I moved. He was 80 years old when I was born, and walking to our house would have been a challenge for him, but our new house was much closer.

From our new house one only had to walk down the street past ten houses, turn the corner, and then Grandpa's house was about five houses up on the opposite side of the road. So now I could run 'round on my own to visit him, apart from which, each morning he came to our house for a cup of tea and a piece of my mother's delicious homemade cake. Between his house and ours, the tops of the walls in front of the gardens were built in a turret style, so Grandpa (who used a walking stick) would come with a small piece of plank and his old dog Judy, and periodically he would place the plank across the tops of the turrets so he could rest along the way.

From the time of our move I spent much of my time with my grandpa, and I loved him dearly. He had all the patience in the world for me and taught me so many things. Like us, he also had a red brick horse stable with a hay loft. Before my time he had a horse named Kitty, and he would hitch her up and ride around with his pony and trap. He also had a big garden, and halfway down was a sty with a couple of pigs. I was allowed near the pigs, but farther down was a huge pen filled with black and white speckled turkeys, and I was never allowed to go in there as they were quite aggressive.

Then there was the orchard. How I loved running around in there. It had so many different kinds of fruit trees, but my favourite was the one with the big, yellow Victoria plums. My mouth waters at the thought of how sweet and juicy they were!

Oh, I have to stop writing and go make a cup of tea. Whew, such strong memories! So here I am, back again (you can take the English out of their country, but you can *never* take away their cup of tea).

Now where was I—oh, yes, in the wonderful old orchard. Apart from running around and picking fruit, I spent many happy hours on the big old swing Grandpa suspended from the bough of one of the trees. Another favourite activity was sitting on the grass under the trees and having picnics with my friends. Sometimes, when I was alone, I would watch a spider's web with the dew drops shimmering like crystals as they were caught in the sun's rays, and lying on the grass I would watch as a ladybird with its pretty spotted wings climbed up a blade of grass. Even as a child I loved natural things, and now, as an old lady, I can still appreciate these small wonders of nature.

Grandpa's house was old and full of wonderful things. Each area had acquired its own unique smell that gave a comforting feeling of stability. I remember the smell of the glass-fronted kitchen cupboards where the dishes were kept, but I cannot put a name to it. Perhaps the smell was from the type of wood from which they were built; it was a little bit spicy and somewhat pungent; but whatever, I loved that smell. Actually, there were two kitchens, the back kitchen where the cooking and the dishes were done and then the kitchen where everyone ate.

Two things I remember distinctly were the old coal-fired range (Grandpa used to put his feet up on this to warm them and ended up burning his boots), and an old one-armed couch. It was made of velvet and rather dusty. It had a hand-knitted blanket presumably made of odd bits of leftover wool, as it was comprised of little squares and triangles of different colours. Now I am thinking that, as I remember lying and studying this blanket, perhaps this is where I was put down for a nap when I was quite young and my mother was visiting. It seems to me the process of writing this book has become the catalyst for all kinds of memories that have been long buried, either intentionally or just through the passage of time. Whether or not this writing of my life's memories will prove cathartic in easing and helping me understand some of the emotional pains of my life remains to be seen, but at least I will have found a release for all that has been held inside my mental wall for these many decades. Because of the age of my parents when I was born, my two grandmothers and my paternal grandfather had passed away before I was born, and by the time I was old enough to ask questions, there was no one left to give answers. Therefore, I am hoping my grandchildren will choose to read this book and know exactly who I am and perhaps ask questions while they still can.

Although he was already well advanced in years when I was a youngster, my grandfather was still an imposing figure. He was a little stooped, but it was evident he'd been a very tall man. The top of his head was bald and he wore a cap most of the time, but his hair on the back and sides was white, as was his moustache. In his bedroom, with its big, old brass bed was a picture of Grandpa as a small child. He'd had blond, curly hair and his eyes were a sparkling blue. Now my mother's numerous brothers and sisters all looked identical, and obviously there was a strong gene on my grandmother's side. They all had jet-black straight hair, dark-brown, almond-shaped eyes and a dark complexion. How I wish I had known my grandmother!

There was a beautiful old German piano in the living room, with candle holders attached to the front to give light when playing after dark. I wonder if this was my grandmother's piano. It was still beautifully in tune, and as a child I spent hours trying to play the ivory keys. Perhaps this was the reason why, when I was only 7 years old, Grandpa bought me a piano of my very own. I took lessons for years, and playing my piano was my escape. How lucky I was, especially as Grandpa had already bought me my first two-wheeler bike. It was pale blue and gave me a wonderful sense of freedom, as now I could explore farther afield.

So what about the boy I met on my sixth birthday? Well, he and I had become the best of friends and were always in each other's company. His home was halfway between mine and Grandpa's, so John would visit with him almost as often as I did. He still has fond memories of visiting Grandpa, and in his cultured way expresses, "He was a really delightful man." When I ask him what it was that he remembered about our times at Grandpa's, his memories are much the same as mine, with just a few exceptions. When he envisions Grandpa, he sees him sitting in the old, glass summerhouse, whereas I picture him in his wooden swivel chair in the kitchen. John remembers the animals (the cats, dogs, turkeys) but for some reason does not recollect the pigs, and I had not thought about the cats! We both had a laugh when we recalled the piece of seaweed that always hung on the wall outside by the back door, as neither of us has seen this elsewhere either before or since. It was what you might call an ecologically acceptable barometer. In other words, when it was dried up it indicated good weather, but if it started to become limp and slimy we knew rain was on the way—that of course was rather the norm in England.

So this was my grandpa: my friend, my teacher, my soul mate and an ever-loving, patient presence in my life, with never a cross word or word of discouragement. I think he was a wise man who was aware of what was lacking in my life from other sources.

4.

Loss of Innocence (the Girl)

For the past two days, the events that are pivotal to this chapter have been going around and around in my head, but I have not been able to put pen to paper. Neither have I been able to think of anything but these episodes, and they have just become a swirling mass of memories, increasingly needing to be put into words as they have become all-consuming. These days have been completely lost to my past, and if I am to move on with my life, these emotions demand to be written down and organized into some sort of perspective. Throughout my life I have been pulled in all different directions with little time to think about my past. Of course there have been times I have dwelt on what effects the experiences of my younger years have had on me as an adult, but then there was always something needing my attention to draw me out of my reverie. But for these past two or three years, I don't know why but the memories are always there, maybe sometimes just below the surface, and along with the memories comes anger. I have never felt so angry at the injustices done to me as I do now, and this is something I cannot, will not, live with. Hence my cathartic ramblings, and I thank you, dear reader, for being the ear to my unburdening.

As I have mentioned before, I had three older brothers. Bob and his wife, Gladys, were nicely settled into my old house, and in the August of my sixth year, they had a baby boy. So I was an aunt at 6 and found this very strange. Gladys would sometimes babysit me when my mother went out, and yet she was my sister-in-law. I loved Gladys, and she was very kind to me.

My youngest brother, Donald, spent much of his time making model airplanes out of balsa wood and tissue paper—he was actually very good at this. Some of them had little engines, and we would bike to Sutton Park so he could fly them. Of course he also got into the usual mischief common to twelve-plus aged boys. Let me give you some examples. He was playing cowboys and Indians, and I somehow ended up being tied to one of the roof beams in the hay loft. At that point, Donald's friend came to ask him if he would like to go to the Saturday afternoon matinee at the picture house. Well, off he went with me still tied up and completely forgotten! Come tea time and mother asking where I was, it was a case of, "Oh yes, my sister is still in the hay loft"! One time he decided to bury me in the middle of a haystack down the field and then disappeared. I remember not being able to breathe, but I struggled until my head emerged halfway up the side of the haystack. From there I managed to wriggle about and drop to the ground. Strange as it may seem, Donald was never intentionally mean to me, and, in fact, we got along well. He just ... well, he didn't think.

Now for the pièce de résistance! Donald and his friends found some corrugated iron in an old shed at the bottom of the field. So they dug a deep, square hole and lined the four sides with this metal. They then put wood across the top, complete with a little trap door, and covered it with the sod they had removed. Upon raising the trap door, a ladder went down inside, and for light an oil lantern was hung from the ceiling. This must have been quite a feat of engineering, and I still don't know what they did with the earth they removed. Oh, and Don's friend Billy Jones had a periscope that he contributed so they could see what was going on outside.

One day the boys invited my girlfriends and me to go inside and have a look—it was fantastic—until the boys pulled up the ladder and closed the hatch. All the yelling in the world did not attract anyone's attention, and it took the collective efforts of all the parents involved to search for and find us. I'm not sure what happened to the underground house after that, but I have no further recollection of it being there. This was a situation that was horrendously dangerous, but of course we children did not realize that. Donald was actually very smart and was the youngest child in Birmingham to pass the eleven-plus exam and get into grammar school. Did I tell you he grew up to be an engineer? Surprise, surprise!

Outside the family we would stick up for each other through thick and thin. I remember when an older boy and his friends picked on Donald and tried to stuff grass in his ears. Regardless of any consequences I ploughed into them with fists flying. Who would have ever guessed that 14 years later this older boy would be the handsome guy to whom I surrendered my virginity—very willingly I might add! Life is strange out there.

Now what about Sam? As I mentioned previously, he was 10 years older than me. As he turned 17 at the beginning of

September, so I turned 7 at the beginning of December 1947. He was not overly tall (I would say about five foot nine inches or so) but big and athletically built. He was the one with the brawn in the family but intellectually had less going on for him than the rest of us. This does not mean that he was mentally delayed by any means—just not academically inclined. However, he was an excellent and intuitive driver and worked for Uncle Jack driving the big low-loader lorries. He also had a big AJS motorbike and would sit me in front of him on the fuel tank and take me for a ride.

This is ridiculous; why am I procrastinating getting to the crux of this chapter? Perhaps because of my vulnerability, or the fact that I am revealing secrets I have kept for so long. Only two people—and then only in the past couple of years—have heard my story. The first person was John and the other was my son, Toby. Looking back to so long ago, it's a little difficult to get the timeline just right, but Sam was called up to do his national service in the air force when he was 17 and served for 18 months. During this time he came home quite frequently, except for a stint in Egypt connected to the Suez Crisis. His job was to ride a motorbike as an armed escort guarding convoys through the desert. The Suez Crisis started on July 26, 1956, and ended in March 1957, so I assume Sam was there in the aftermath for a short while. (It is so difficult not having anyone left who can confirm details.)

Sam had a buddy from the forces who was welcomed into our home when Sam returned. This friend seemed like an amiable person—to everyone but me. His first act of perversion against me was when I was 7. No one else was home and he was supposed to be "looking after me." My 7-year-old mind could not understand what he was doing, but I can visualize every moment as if it happened only yesterday. He took me up to the bathroom and made me stand right next to him and watch as he masturbated into the bathroom sink. I cannot remember anything immediately before or after that event, but what I saw will be forever imprinted on my mind. These are the deep scars that will always be part of who we are: invisible, untouchable and unknown to anyone except the person who bears these emotional and psychological injuries. They insidiously work on our unconscious, forming our view of the world and the people in it.

Back in those days there was no such thing as sex education, and such things were never, ever discussed. One day I was in the veranda, and my dog Patsy was lying in her box. All of a sudden there was a gush of water and lying there was a baby puppy. I did not know what I was seeing but ran excitedly to my parents to tell them what had occurred. I was told it was just my imagination and the conversation was quickly hushed. Of course this did not explain the fact that we now had puppies, but one did not question one's parents.

After the first incident, Sam's friend's depravities sank even lower, with it being obvious even to me that this was just one big power trip for him, and he thoroughly enjoyed the fear and pain he was inflicting. My mother started leaving me with my tormentor more and more often. She must have been so happy to have a chance to visit with her friends without having to take me along and to have someone so willing to look after me. When I went out with my mother visiting, there were no other children present, but then, as I said, my mother was 40 when I was born. This meant her friends' children were all grown up, and they were free to socialize without the encumbrance of a child.

Sam was working for Uncle Jack driving lorries, so his friend was sometimes alone at our house. His next step was a very dangerous one. My friend was at my house to play—she was a year and a half older than me, but her mother had gone to school with my mother and the friendship had naturally spread to the next generation. She was an only child, and her mother had been widowed, remarried and then divorced, so she and her mother were very close, as there were just the two of them at home.

Sam's friend must have thought this was a perfect opportunity. He took us both upstairs and had us stand outside my bedroom door. First he took my friend inside. She emerged after a short while looking very unsettled and just gave me a furtive glance. I had heard no exchange of conversation inside my bedroom while she was in there. Next it was my turn to be taken inside and have the door closed. I honestly do not recall what happened. Perhaps I just wanted to shut the memory from my mind, or perhaps his perversion had been satisfied with whatever he had done with my friend. Then again, just maybe he realized that once my friend was gone he could not control what she would say or to whom. She and I never, ever talked about that day, but when we played it was usually at her house.

So far it had been "show but don't tell" time, but that did not satisfy this loathsome creature for long. He was getting away with what he was doing, so the sky was the limit. He was always careful not to leave any evidence that could be connected to his actions. I do remember "kicking up a fuss" when my mother was going out and I knew I was being left with him, but she left anyway. Did she not ever wonder why he was so obliging? What 17-to-20-year-old man wants to be saddled with a 7-to-10-year-old little girl when he could be off enjoying himself with his friends? Oh yes, his next set of actions lasted three years! As soon as my mother was gone he grabbed my hand and took me upstairs, but this time was different and we went into his bedroom. Once inside he laid me on the bed, removed my underwear, and proceeded to lie on top of me and commit a sexual act. This was no spur-of-the-moment thing; he had thought out all the details. Spreading a large handkerchief under me on the bed, he commenced sexual interference but never actually penetrated. This was the reason for the handkerchief—he ejaculated onto that.

For the next three years, he took advantage of me at every opportunity, and in every instance I fought and screamed and kicked as he physically dragged me up the stairs. In my mind's eye I can still see him grinning and leering at me as he dragged my little body up the steps one by one for the inevitable indignity. Being a child I could not know that this was probably a big turn on for him. Oh, how I hated him! So why did I not tell anyone? Well, he told me that if I did he would be sent to prison, and his ruse worked because I was too scared to open my mouth.

By the time I was 10 my breasts were starting to develop and I had started to menstruate. What a blessing! After this he left me alone, at least physically. Instead I had leering looks and crude comments when he was around—"Oh my, what a smasher, two fried eggs and a gammon rasher." Anything he could do to upset me in any way he did. The strange thing was that my parents saw the way he taunted me and did nothing. My father was probably unaware of anything being amiss, but not my mother. It was obvious she was scared to challenge him but she started to refer to him as "Town saint and home devil." Just what had she realized? I wonder. Her health was not good. She had a bad heart and had suffered with ulcerated legs since before I was born, and we were not a family who discussed things together or found it easy to confront one another. That would never do! After all, my mother had been born a Caudle, one of the oldest and most well-known families in the district. We could not have scandals. As for my father, he worked six-and-a-half days a week, leaving for work before I woke and coming home late. So he was not much of a presence in the home. My childhood memories of him are of a quiet, gentle man who loved tinkering around in his garage and working in the garden. While he dug he would place a flat rock close to him, upon which he would put worms. These were for the little robin who always kept him company while he dug.

Outside of the "incidents," my life played itself out in much the same way as any other child's. When I was not in school I continued to spend most of my play time with John, although I did have other friends (all girls) who lived close by. But it was John and me who had that once-in-a-lifetime rapport and so spent much of our time together. We loved to go off on our bikes and explore Chelmsley Woods, where the bluebells grew. When we were 7 he kissed me 100 times and said that he was going to marry me. As quickly as we could we ran to tell his mother. I remember to this day what she said: "John, you can't marry Cynthia until you earn at least 100 pounds a year." At this we went off quite satisfied, probably to play with his black rabbit that lived in a hutch at the bottom of their garden.

Now John was the eldest of three children. Next came his brother Robert and then Rosemary. His father, Mr. McCaw, was the assistant director of education for the city of Birmingham. John's mother was both an artist and an author, and when she stood painting at her easel I watched her with absolute fascination. She also had a beautiful glass paperweight with carved flowers and tiny, tiny, white rabbits set inside the glass, and I would study this magical object for hours. She was probably about the same age as most of my cousins and always had lots of time for John's little friend. Being older and in poor health, my mother did not really have the energy to do very much with me, and with my father being at work I was pretty much left to my own devices.

Mr. McCaw looked a little bit stern, but his looks belied what I knew of his nature. Knowing our love for nature and the countryside, I remember him taking John and me outside the city on the Midland Red bus. This was a big adventure. We explored to our hearts' content and were delighted when we found a little snake. This little creature was held carefully on our laps as we sat in the front seat of the bus coming home. We held it so gently and examined it intently. Mr. McCaw never did spoil our enthusiasm by telling us it was actually dead! Actually, I am not sure when, how or even if we came to know this. And so my young childhood passed with my days seesawing between the happiness of being free with my friends and the dark secrets behind the walls of the house where I lived, a house that should have been a home and a haven of safety.

5.

Kate Elizabeth Caudle (my Mother)

So who was Kate Elizabeth Caudle? Perhaps I should start at the beginning and tell you what I remember. Unfortunately, what she was before I was born is, for the most part, lost to me. But there is one thing I am certain of: she had spirit, and I thank heaven that this is something I inherited from her. I admired my father's peace-loving, passive nature. But I believe my mother and I needed that spirit of survival.

Kate was born on January 27, 1901, to Thomas and Jane Caudle. She was one of the younger of their many sons and daughters, and, like me, was born when her parents were 40 years old. She was consequently brought up to be everything a proper young Victorian lady should be. I have heard that her upbringing was strict (Grandpa was a sergeant in the local constabulary), and it was rumoured that when the children misbehaved, he put his handcuffs on them. But strictness was the norm for that era. One thing I can tell you is that as a teenager, she worked as a packer and had the reputation of making sure every box and parcel was wrapped perfectly. In my childhood I remember people saying, "Katy Caudle's house is like a palace," so she was also a particular housekeeper. There is a photograph on my mantelpiece of my mother as a young woman—possibly about twenty years old. Without bias I can testify that she was stunningly beautiful. She was short (perhaps about four foot eleven inches) and very petite, with a long neck, black hair and almost black, almond-shaped eyes. Her cheekbones were high and she was fine-boned. In fact, she does not look very English at all! My eldest brother, Robert, was born in1926, so she must have met and married my father sometime in the early 1920s.

Due to my lack of knowledge, I now need to skip forward to when my mother was 40 and I was a baby. After living through World War 1 she was now two years into World War 2. Sometime between the birth of Robert in 1926 and my birth in 1940 she had lost six babies but was nevertheless determined to have a little girl. Hence, here I am writing this book for you. Phew! I am so glad she was *so* determined; that was too close for comfort!

At the time of Sam's birth in 1930, Kate developed what was known as "white leg." Subsequently I have learned that this was a general term used for painful thrombosis of the femoral vein in the leg following childbirth. Consequently she spent a great deal of time in the Queen Elizabeth Hospital in Birmingham following Sam's birth. The condition obviously never went away and must have been a terrible ordeal for her. In writing this I have come to realize just how much I was wanted, as the risks in having me were very high. As far back as I can remember she wore elastic stockings, underneath which her legs were badly ulcerated and in need of daily dressings, and as if this was not enough she also had angina.

As I mentioned previously, the Caudles were an old, well-established family in the community, and my mother, having grown up here was still referred to as Katy Caudle by the local people even after she married and became Mrs. Whitehouse. Along with this she had inherited something of a sense of entitlement, and although the era was one in which wives were expected to follow the wishes of their husbands, my mother's dark eyes could flash fire, hinting at the spirit that (for the most part) she kept in check. After moving to our new home she walked proudly, with her head held high. She now had the status that was her due.

So how did I fit into this scenario? Well, amongst other things my mother was a talented seamstress who made use of her talents to ensure I was always beautifully dressed. I had smocked dresses, Viyella dresses, skirts with matching jackets and beautifully knitted sweaters. Despite their age difference my mother became friends with Mrs. McCaw, John's mother, and this may have been what inspired her to make me two kilts. One was the Buchanan tartan and the other the Stuart, with the finishing touch being a furry bird claw pin set in a silver base to hold the front flap closed. This, of course, was given to mother by Mrs. McCaw. Mother's skills also extended to making my costumes for our school plays. The most beautiful one was a large crinoline dress (very Scarlett O'Hara) complete with a wide-brimmed straw hat decorated around the crown with bunches of violets. When the play was over, this one dress was turned into several dresses for my little niece Carole, Robert and Gladys's daughter. Nothing was ever wasted.

Not being able to be active with me, my mother spoiled me in other ways. I suppose that now she had her girl she was indulging

herself by buying me lovely things. My shoes were the best, and
my soap was made by Cussons and was shaped and coloured like
a baby deer. In the city was a store that sold Chad Valley dolls
(how I loved my dolls), and my mother somehow managed to buy
me the store samples. During the summer holidays she always
managed to arrange a week's vacation at the seaside. Donald
would initially come with us and we would go to Colwyn Bay
in Wales. The thing I remember most is the park's big pool for
sailing toy boats.

Later it was just Mother and me, and we would go to Mrs.
Gubb's Guest House in Combe Martin in Devonshire. I loved
it there. There were fishing boats coming in with their catch,
rocks to climb, an ice cream store on the beach and a stable for
horse riding—one of my passions. Mother could pretty much sit
on the beach and keep her eye on me, so this worked out well
for both of us. Also, there were coach trips to see historic places,
such as Lorna Doone's cottage and the tiny church where she was
married. This became our traditional vacation. It did not require
too much exertion for my mother, and there were interests galore
for me. I absolutely loved the rock pools with their sea anemones
and the little crabs.

In return for all of this there were, of course, my mother's
expectations of me. If there is one thing I have learned, it is that
nothing comes without a price. The price for me was to be the
perfect daughter—and to be a Caudle, the latter being something
I was known to rebel against. I was to be a lady, with everything
that that implied. No ifs, ands or buts about it. Let me give you
a few examples. Gloves. Yes, you read that right, gloves! Whether
it was winter or summer, if I was going out other than to play or
just visit Grandpa, I had to wear gloves. In the summer they were
pretty, white gloves that looked very (dare I say it?) classy. Then

there was the etiquette thing. When my mother would meet one of her friends on the street and stop to chat, I was expected to quietly move far enough away so I could not hear their conversation. And there I stood, and stood, and stood. Not even I wanted the wrath of my mother's sharp tongue.

Sometimes when we had my mother's friends visit our home for afternoon tea I was expected to play the piano for them. Even today I can clearly remember the disapproving glances that passed between the ladies on the day I played with decidedly ill grace! After the ladies left and my mother approached me about this in the kitchen, I lost my temper, slammed my hand hard against a clothes horse full of freshly ironed clothing and sent it flying all over the kitchen floor. To my great surprise and puzzlement my mother burst out laughing. Looking back, I can only guess that perhaps she saw something of her own spirit and complexity in me.

Another facet of my mother was that, like me, she loved classical poetry, and we both enjoyed the quiet times when she would sit and have me read to her. Our favourite was *The Rubaiyat of Omar Khayyam,* and I still love this as much today. For some strange reason I had not inherited the Birmingham accent my brothers had and instead had an Oxford accent. Perhaps I picked this up from spending so much time with John, whose family was very cultured. The other thing I would willingly do for my mother was dance. Dancing was one of my greatest joys.

Did I mention that sometime during my early years (perhaps six or seven), my uncle Tom got married? He was not that young—older than my mother—but he and Grandpa must have needed a housekeeper, and one could not live unmarried with two men. Her name was Jess, my lovely aunty Jess. She was an older spinster, but I am sure she and Uncle Tom loved each other.

Her hair was long enough to sit on and she wore it in two braids coiled on either side of her head. When she sat on the old couch in Grandpa's kitchen I would sneak up behind her and pull out all the hair pins holding her braids in place. She would always pretend not to notice until her hair fell down and I was rolling around laughing! Perhaps I was the child she never had; she was so kind to me and I never, ever heard her say a cross word. My mother visited her often and they were very close.

Talking about hair, my mother always kept mine long. When I was 10 I started asking if I could have it cut, only to be met with a definite no. No discussion, no pleading, just *no*. Well … that sort of worked … for a while (I did tell you I had my mother's spirit, didn't I?). All that was needed was a catalyst, which of course came from the Caudle side of the family. My father's family was practically unknown to me. His parents had died before I was born, with his mother passing away when he was 4. His eldest sister, Aunty Nell, had been the one who raised the younger children. Now Aunty Nell and Aunty Mary were spinsters and lived together, and mother took me to visit them quite frequently. Aunty Mary would knit all kinds of outfits for my fashion doll, which was somewhat akin to today's fashion dolls except that it was made of plaster.

Their home was small but it was a treasure trove to me. The contents were very old and probably antique, but to my curious mind they were just fascinating. I especially liked the big stuffed owl that sat imperiously under a glass dome. On the wall was an old copper warming pan and some of Aunty Mary's incredible paintings. Then there were the cats and kittens, and I was just over the moon when I was given a very fluffy, pure white kitten for my very own. Having just seen the movie *Peter Pan* I called my kitten Tinkerbelle. Other than these two aunts, I did not even know the names of any of my other aunts and uncles on my father's side. Yet I was a Whitehouse. That was my father's name and that was my name—and I was proud of it (so why do I feel like sticking out my tongue and saying "so there"?). Now I must point out that my grandpa did not have any of the delusions of grandeur that emanated from the other members of his family. That sense of entitlement was not part of who he was.

But you must be wondering about this mysterious catalyst, and here I am just rambling on like an old lady. Oops, does being nearly 70 qualify as being an old lady? Anyway, there was several of my mother's family gathered together chatting about this and that when the conversation turned to me. "Oh, you can tell she is a Caudle by her looks." Here one may substitute words of their choice for "looks" (e.g., spirit, intelligence, manners, talent and on and on ad nauseum). Now I was not a child who lost her temper easily, but I'd had quite enough of being constantly validated by my kinship to my mother's side of the family. Wanting to put an end to these comments I took some scissors, went up to my room and cut off my long hair. There, it was done, that would show them! So I went downstairs again, flaunting my new short bob, only to be met with one of my uncles saying proudly, "There, you see? I told you she was a real Caudle—just look at her spirit!" I seem to remember feeling dumbstruck, mad and frustrated all at the same time. *I was a Whitehouse!* And I wanted to shout this from the rooftops! The next day my mother took me to the hairdressers to get my hair tidied up professionally and that was that.

By this time, John and I were approaching age eleven and the end of junior school. We were both in Mr. Chant's class, our last class before our exams for grammar school. Some time before, his family had moved from their house on the corner to a big, beautiful home on Manor House Lane. Fortunately this was still close to my home and we continued to hang out. I was becoming quite attracted to John, and this was not being helped by our being in the choir together and having to learn "A Highland Lad My Love Was Born." A childhood crush? Perhaps, but we shall see. This story has yet to unfold.

At the end of our time in Mr. Chant's class we were expected to take the eleven-plus exam and go to grammar school. As it happened, John and my paths took a different turn, and we were both sent to private schools. My mother had a wonderful time checking out the various schools, although I am sure her choice was based more on the attractiveness of the uniforms than the school's academic qualifications. The school she chose was Lawrence's College, which was situated in the middle of the city of Birmingham. The uniforms were carried by Dunn's, a prestigious clothing store, and I remember feeling quite awestruck when I went in with mother to buy my first uniform. Mother was completely in her element! Her standing in the community was now even more strongly established.

At the time I was starting Lawrence's College, which was co-ed, John was starting a private school for boys called Hallfield. His experiences there were not good, and just a couple of nights ago he told me that he entered the school a happy, well-adjusted child and was withdrawn from it a couple of years later very unhappy and depressed. One of the teachers there was the vicar from our Parish church who was a snob and a tyrant. When John started there, the boys in the class were asked to stand up and tell something about themselves. John's "something" was that he had a friend named Cynthia. Although this was perfectly natural to John, it unfortunately singled him out as the boy whose friend was a girl. What a sad situation this was, being judged on what was a strong, good friendship between two children who had common interests and a strong bond. I now have to wonder about the unconscious impact this had on my friend through the years. One thing it did not do was spoil our close bond. After being taken out of Hallfield, John was sent to a school in Solihull.

Before leaving junior school I had also become friends with a girl named Brenda. She and I had a lot in common, and like John's parents, hers were also young and welcomed me unconditionally. As it happened Brenda went from junior to grammar school, so academically all three of us went our separate ways. Being in grammar school, we did not have much free time to do things together as now we had homework every evening, and heaven help us if it was not completed! This was the old English school system and education was a serious matter. In my school the teachers even wore their black university gowns (without the colours—this was reserved for special occasions) to class.

During the six weeks of summer holidays, Brenda would visit her mother's family in Wales and John went to the family farm up in Scotland. John would send me postcards, and by the time I was 12 I found my heart racing when the mail arrived and I saw his distinctive handwriting. By this time, although it remained unspoken, I was in the throes of my first real love, and he meant the world to me. Our friendship, however, remained on the same level as it always had. By this time I had a beautiful, big red bike that Grandpa had bought me to replace the blue one that was now too small, so when we had the chance, John and I still took off to our favourite haunts. Meanwhile, Brenda and I had become good friends as well, and while she spent the summer in Wales we wrote back and forth all the time. Like me she played the piano and we shared a great love of books. Sometimes we would make up plays and act them out.

Sam continued to be his usual annoying self, although now he hung out with two other guys of the same age, along with a bevy of glamorous girls, who came and went at a steady pace, I might add! One girl in particular sticks in my mind. Her name was Betty and she was blonde and very pretty. Betty always made a point of coming to find me and talk with me. Sometimes she would bring me little surprises; she had a gentle voice and a kind face that I can picture even now.

Since I was now a little more grown up, my parents papered my room with pretty, pink flowered wallpaper, and Mom bought me a dressing table and a new eiderdown for my bed. My room looked lovely but needed a chair. During my childhood, my father had always made me little upholstered armchairs according to my size. However, now I needed a chair that would look nice in my grown-up bedroom. I had a little money saved and my mom took me to look at furniture. The chair that caught my eye was so beautiful. It was a dainty chair with highly polished wood. The framework of the back was filled with flat cane, and there was a thick upholstered seat, the fabric of which was cream with deep pink roses and green leaves. Oh how proud I was of my purchase.

In the evenings we would all sit around the fire in the living room and talk (yes, people actually did that in those days!). If everyone was home there were not always enough comfortable chairs to sit on, so I would bring my new chair down from my bedroom for myself. Enter Sam, stage right! Before I had chance to sit down he would lift his feet up from where he was lounging and put them, dirty shoes included, on the beautiful seat of my new chair. My father, I am convinced, was oblivious to what was going on, but not my mother. I could tell from her face that she recognized Sam for the tormentor he was. As for me, what could

I do? He was a grown man and I a child, but he could not have missed my look of seething anger. In return he just leered, as if to say, "I can do anything I want and no one can stop me." What a hateful creature! He may have been my brother but I really did not like him all that well.

My father had always been good to my mother and I had never once heard them argue. Every Sunday he would go over to Mr. Singleton the newsagent and buy her a box of chocolates. He would say, "Here you are, duck." "Duck" was a term of endearment my dad always used when addressing my mom. On Christmas Day, Dad would never let Mom into the kitchen and took it upon himself to cook the breakfast and our Christmas dinner. Since Mother had done the Christmas cake, the Christmas puddings and mincemeat pies in the days leading up to Christmas, this must have been a real treat for her.

By the time I was 12 and Sam 22, he was courting a girl called Lynette. She was two years his junior and nothing could have been further from his usual type. Lynette did not have the showy looks of his previous girlfriends and her dress was much more conservative. She also wore glasses. Fortunately we are now in an age where this is no longer a stigma, but back then it was a case of "boy's don't make passes at girls who wear glasses." Lynette was an orphan and had been brought up in the Church of England orphanage. Perhaps it was an advantage to Sam to not have to pass the parent test. Or perhaps it was a case of "if you want me, you had better marry me first"! Another impression I had was that my mother definitely did not like Lynette, although she never made any adverse comments to that effect. All I know is that my mother was shrewd and not easily taken in by anyone. Besides this, my mother was the only person to whom Lynette seemed to realize that she could not make any barbed comments.

Well, Lynette and Sam became engaged and were married in February 1954, not long after my thirteenth birthday. They were having a house built in Solihull but were staying with us until its completion. You know, I can't for the life of me figure out where Donald slept during this time. Huh, isn't that strange? He would have been 17 when Sam was 23. One's mind can certainly play funny tricks. How is it that so many memories are being triggered by my writing this book, yet little details such as where my brother slept once Cecil was married totally escape me? I suppose this is where the "what ifs" and the "could have beens" come into play.

So life carried on at our home on Garretts Green Lane. Sam continued to drive lorries for Uncle Jack's ever-growing transportation business, and my father continued his work as a mechanic, keeping all the vehicles in running order. Here I should have said "a very skilled mechanic." During and after World War I, while he was in the Royal Flying Corp, he worked on some of the very first aircraft engines. Lynette worked for the Birmingham Public Health Department as a day nursery teacher.

Spring arrived and the weather was beautiful. Birds were singing, the hens were laying and the flowers were displaying their varied hues, making a patchwork of colour in the garden. In the bushes under the front bay window was a nest of tiny blue tits, and a couple of times they were brave enough to fly in through our open window. It was on such a day that I saw my mother riding my big red bicycle down the front driveway. She was smiling with pleasure and she held her head high. At the ripe old age of 13 I wondered what someone as old as my mother was doing riding a bike! Now, looking back at this from the youthful age of 70, I realize she was still young and just wanted some pleasure on this beautiful day—and why not? It must have been a spur-of-the-moment thing as she did not say what she was planning to do and left without saying goodbye. I never saw her again.

At about five o'clock a policeman came to the front door. I can remember clearly that as soon as I opened the door and saw him standing there I knew. He spoke with my father and they left. The evening passed as it usually did and when it was time I went to bed. The next morning I was up and dressed when my father knocked on my bedroom door. When I opened it he just said, "Your mommy's not coming back, so you're going to have to be a big girl now." He said this gently and then turned and walked away, leaving me standing there to digest this information. I did not cry—until this day I have not cried, but I find that as I am writing this there are finally some tears welling in my eyes. Are these tears for me, or for the child I was who had just been told her mother was dead? Perhaps I can finally grieve and let go of this scar, a scar I have carried, without acknowledging it, all my life.

That morning I was sent to spend time with my sister-in-law Gladys, presumably so the family could discuss the situation and what arrangement needed to be made. Apart from the funeral arrangements there was the fact that my father was now a widower, working six-and-a-half days a week and with a daughter who was just 13 to take care of. By now Donald was 17 and more independent. I found out later that a learning driver ran into my mother while she was riding my bike, and instead of putting her foot on the brake, the woman put it on the accelerator by mistake. My mother suffered a ruptured spleen and a fractured skull and did not make it through the night.

Gladys and Bob now had three children. Robert was 7, Carole 5 and Alan 3. That morning Robert really put Gladys to the test by repeatedly asking me, "Do you know your mommy's dead?"

Gladys tried to make him hush, but he was just asking with the innocence of the young. He did not upset me.

While I was with Gladys it was decided that I would spend a week at Uncle Jack and Aunty Dorothy's. They had a huge house out in the country with lots of room for me. They did not have any children of their own so this was probably quite a challenge for Aunt Dorothy. So I packed my suitcase and off I went. This would have been a Sunday. A little way down the country lane from their house was the train station, so as of Monday morning I caught the train into central Birmingham to go to school. After school I was to take the bus to uncle's transportation company, and he would then drive me to his house. During this entire time no one mentioned my mother or informed me about her funeral. All I know is that she was buried in the Caudle family grave at Yardley Cemetery. I have as yet never been to her grave.

At the end of the week I came home to a house where everything appeared to be carrying on as normal, except my mother was not there. The only inkling I had of the week's events there was when I went into the front room. There I saw the imprint of my mother's coffin in the deep pile of the carpet. So this was her farewell to her lovely home. Katy Caudle was gone.

6.

Strange Happenings (the Young Teen)

*B*efore I start this chapter let me just state, unequivocally, *I do not believe in ghosts*! There, I said it. Now as you, dear reader, get into this chapter, you are perhaps going to question my sanity in making such a statement. Well, I've questioned it myself at times, and I am sure that if you asked my children they would *all* agree that their mother is (let's put this nicely) a bit of a free spirit at times—no pun intended! Now you see what I have done? We just had another little time warp into the future, right there.

While I was staying with Uncle Jack and Aunty Dorothy, the family was busy making decisions as to what to do about this new situation. Well, Sam and Lynette decided that instead of moving to Solihull and having a house built there, they would stay and live with us, presumably so Lynette could be the female presence in the home with regard to organizing meals and being there for me. The way it would work was that I would get home from school by about five o'clock and Lynette would be home just a little while later. At this point I will interject the fact that my mother had not liked Lynette. Lynette was bossy and pushy, and every comment ended with a barb. However, my mother was the one person with whom Lynette was not strong enough to get her own way. If she had chosen, Mother could have dropped her with one look. She chose not to, but this was one person Lynette did not try to take on.

So I would come home from school, play with my cat Tinkerbelle and find joy in playing my piano. It was summertime and the flowers were blooming and the sun shining. I had not seen much of John after my mother died, and he recently confided that he felt guilty about that, but he stayed away because he did not know what to say to me. I can understand how that was difficult for him. After all, we were both young.

The first strange thing that happened was rather innocuous, and if it had not been so definite I would have put it down to my imagination. I had arrived home from school and was playing the piano. The front room windows were open as it was a lovely day. Then I heard the strangest thing: sheep—the sounds of sheep "baaing" on the front lawn. When I got up to look there was of course nothing there, but the sounds had not been imagined. Next I heard a woman's voice calling "Lynette, Lynette," over and over very softly. These events did not scare me; I just found them rather curious. When the family came home I told them what had happened, and they likewise just looked upon this as a curiosity.

When the next event occurred, it was far more intense. Once again I was playing the piano with my docile little Tinkerbelle close by. All of a sudden she turned toward the open door of the front room and started hissing and snarling. There was a deep growl coming from her throat and her ears were flattened right back. Next she tore into the front hall and halfway up the stairs, snarling, spitting and striking at the air with her front claws. She was very intent on something that I could not see. Now this was scary. I told the family and they rationalized my cat's behaviour away for me, although I was not quite so convinced by their explanations. So life went on, except now I kept the doors locked when I was home alone.

Just a few days later came the next event. Once again I was sitting at the piano and my cat became quite snarly. This time I heard the front door (which was locked) close. Footsteps came along the hall, and then there was the distinctive sound of shoes walking across the kitchen tiles. Next, the backdoor (also locked) gave the sound of being opened and closed. Once again I told the family, and I'm sure they could see that by now I was really scared. However, I was reassured, and that was that. Being very sure of what had occurred I was more than a little concerned that the adults did not believe me, and when I went to bed (with my head firmly under the blankets), I tossed and turned and could not sleep.

Eventually I got up and went downstairs. Well, this was strange: everyone was in the kitchen talking and the door was shut. So I did what anyone in my position would have done—I listened! Oh what a surprise I had. Apparently, strange things were happening to the adults as well, and Sam was half scared out of his wits. It turned out he was about to get into the bathtub when the water started swirling about and there was an indentation in the water of another body in the tub. Bob was here as well and had had quite a shock a few days earlier. He was walking up the front driveway to visit us. As he reached for the old, round iron handle on the back gate, it turned by itself and the gate opened. Well, Bob turned and left pretty quickly, but not before seeing the gate close by itself and the handle turn once more. My father was a quiet, kind, down-to-earth person, but even he had had issues. In the living room we had replaced the open fireplace with an insert that had doors on the front. This meant the fire could be banked up at night with the doors closed so the fire would be just right for the morning. Every night my dad banked up the coal and closed the fireplace doors, and every morning there was the unbanked, unburned coal, placed in a straight line in the hearth.

After hearing this I ran and hid under my bedclothes as fast as I could. No one told me about these happenings and I did not let on that I had overheard the discussion in the kitchen, but from there on I was not ever left in the house alone. After school I was to take the bus to where Lynette worked and come home with her. In the summer holidays I went to work with her and helped out in the nursery. Actually, I really loved doing this. Now my father was a non-practicing member of the Church of England, but I found out he had a Roman Catholic priest come to the house. Whatever he did must have worked because there were no more strange disturbances. So do I believe in ghosts? Not in the accepted sense, but I do believe, that for whatever reason, my mother's spirit was not at rest.

7.

The Rocky Road (the Teenager)

*L*ife was not always easy living with Lynette. She had ebullient highs and some rather nasty lows, during which she made everyone's life miserable. Looking back I can give some perspective to things I did not have the maturity to understand at the time. She was an orphan, and from what I can gather must have been raised in a somewhat institutionalized setting, and so was applying her norm to our household. Apart from this she was 22, which was young to be taking on an established household. This is strange, but in writing this I am getting a new view of things in a way that I have previously never been able to acknowledge.

Apart from learning to live with Lynette's idiosyncrasies, I also had to get to know my father. He had always been a presence in my life but never actually took part in it. I must give him credit for stepping into this new role. One day he took me shopping at Lewis's, a big department store in the city, and bought me the

most beautiful dress I had ever seen. In my mind's eye I can still
see every little detail. It was dark emerald-green nylon with little
white flocked flowers all over it. The full skirt was gathered at the
waist, and there were short puff sleeves and a small white collar.
At the neck was pinned a little bunch of tiny flowers in orange,
white and green. The assistant must have realized this was all
new to my father and was really helpful. Because the fabric was
so light she suggested I would need a slip to wear with it. My
father bought me the prettiest underwear set I could have ever
imagined! The petticoat was silky and white, but at the front the
bottom was looped up slightly on either side with the fabric being
held up by dainty flowers. That summer my father carried on my
mother's tradition of taking me to Mrs. Gubb's Guest House in
Combe Martin, Devonshire. He did this every year until I was
old enough to start holidaying on my own with my friend Brenda.
Even so, once I was independent he still carried on going there
by himself, and would bring me back a lovely Hummel figurine.
All told I have seven.

   Whereas my mother and I always went down by train, Dad
and I would be driven down in a very elegant car! Let me explain
this. The car belonged to Mr. Singleton across the road, but he
was a newsagent, not a mechanic. On the other hand, my father
was a very skilled mechanic. So once a year Dad would bring Mr.
Singleton's car over to our garage and give it a complete overhaul,
and in return we were driven to and picked up from Mrs. Gubb's.
Before he took me there, my dad had not had a holiday for as
long as I can remember and it really did him good to get away.
Mrs. Gubb's daughter, Marcia, was a year or two older than me
but we would go horseback riding together and have lots of fun.
On the other hand, Dad intermingled and chatted with the other
people staying at the guest house and enjoyed the company. Being

a very fit man he was able to take me climbing up Hangman's Hill, something my mother had been unable to do. These holidays were good times and made me very happy.

In August 1954, a few months after my mother's death, I suffered another loss. John's family moved to Crawley in Sussex so I would no longer have his comfortable friendship to buoy me up during my trials at home. We did exchange addresses and continued our friendship via mail. By now I was very much in love with John, and his moving deeply affected me. When the postman put the mail through our letter box and I saw an envelope with his handwriting, my heart jumped with joy. Our letters were platonic, but that was okay with me; it was still a connection.

My friendship with Brenda had become well established, so I spent much of my spare time with her. Now we were in grammar school, our evenings in the week were taken up with mounds of homework—about five hours a night. This left mainly the weekends. Mr. and Mrs. Williams were really nice to me and I quite often slept over at their house on a Saturday night. Brenda was an only child and received lots of love and support from her parents, and lots of help with her homework.

Unfortunately, my situation was exactly the opposite. When Donald was home he would help me, but once he left I was on my own. No one even asked if I had homework, let alone gave any input. So once again, in this regard, I was left to my own devices. In spite of this I always did well at school. There were three of us girls—Anne, Betty and me—who always had the top three aggregate marks in the end-of-year exams. I always came either first or second. Naturally I was proud of this, but when my report card came home all I would get was, "Well, what happened to your geography?" It was perhaps an 84 percent while all my other marks were in the high 90s. Brenda's parents always bought her a present for doing well, whereas my achievements were totally ignored by my family. By the time I left school at 17, every one of my English certificates was First Class Honours. I was the school captain, the school sports captain and also my house captain. My dance teacher sent a letter to my father stating that I was a natural dancer with exceptional talent and should try out for the Sadler's Wells Ballet Company. He just said no and that I would "get into bad company." So that was that for my dreams. But let us get back to 1954.

Home life was rather erratic. Lynette loved having company over for parties and went all out with the fancy hors d'oeuvres and desserts. These could be fun times, although I somehow ended up with having to do a good amount of the preparation. She also liked to have her girlfriends sleep over, so guess who had to share her single bed with them? That's right, me!

Special occasions such as Easter and Christmas were always fun. Lynette loved celebrations and hence (with everyone's help, and why not) these were really fun times. In between these times not so much so, as she would ration everything, even the butter. Donald could not stand Lynette (or Sam, for that matter) and was very put out about the food situation. A year after Lynette moved in, and when Donald was 18, he married his girlfriend, Margaret, and declared that from now on he would eat as much butter as he liked! Although this early marriage was a form of escape, at 74 Donald and Margaret are as much in love as they ever were.

Lynette was always neat in her dress but was untidy and disorganized in all things domestic. She managed to burn the bottoms out of all my mother's saucepans, ones she'd had for as long as I could remember. Now who puts a saucepan of milk on the stove to boil and then goes next door to chat?—top marks, dear reader, if you have guessed Lynette. Doing this once is a mistake, but all the time? Roasts of meat must have quivered in fear when Lynette put them in the oven, knowing they would end up cremated—along with the roasting pan! Fairly quickly the "jobs" started to become my responsibility. On Friday nights I had to do all the baking for the weekend, as well as scrub and clean the kitchen. Saturday morning was laundry and hosing down the floor of the veranda. One Friday evening I was magnanimously told I could bake whatever I chose, only to be scolded by Lynette because my choices did not suit her.

Once Donald moved out of the house, Sam became even more pompous and overbearing. The fact remained, though, that other than being good at driving he was totally inept at anything else. Lynette bossed him around like a child, and when he was doing a job with Dad in the garage he had to be shown everything. Consequently, at 14 years of age I was someone he thought he could pick on, but I was now capable of showing him how despicable I thought he was, just with my looks of contempt. One night he really overstepped his bounds, and I think it was probably at this point that this house, in my mind, was no longer my home. Gradually, over the next few years, I grew to hate that house and everything it stood for. How that one fateful day, when my mother just wanted to enjoy herself and have a little fun, changed my life forever. This scar runs very deep within me.

Well, it was already dark and I was about to get ready for bed. Then out of the blue Sam just marched up to me and shouted, "Get out!" So I opened the front door and left, heading straight to my friend Brenda's house. She lived a few streets away so it took me about 15 minutes to get there. When I knocked on the front door, Mr. And Mrs. Williams answered; Brenda had just gone to bed. I told them Sam had thrown me out and they took me in without question. They said I was to stay there that night and I went to bed with Brenda (who was now wide awake). Some time later there was another knock at the door. Brenda and I looked through the upstairs window and saw my dad and Sam outside, with Dad talking to Mr. and Mrs. Williams. By now they were in their housecoats, ready for bed. Sam just stood behind my dad like a naughty schoolboy and didn't say a word. Mrs. Williams said there was no way I was going home that night and she was not going to disturb me as I had gone to bed. The next day I returned home, but from then on I was frequently invited to stay with Brenda's family for the weekend, and when she would visit her aunty Anne and uncle Joe in Gloucester for a week during the school holidays, I was invited to go as well. It was a great adventure to go on the train all by ourselves. Aunty Anne and Uncle Joe did not have any children of their own, so they gave all their love to Brenda and me. It was so nice to be tucked in at night and given a hug and a kiss.

This kind of affection made me feel special, and most of all wanted. Here I was allowed to be a child and have fun with no price attached and no worries or insecurity. The love I received was unconditional. Aunt and uncle lived in a maisonette right on the edge of the country and right next to Robins Hill. This was quite a big hill and comparatively steep, but it was covered in grass and wildflowers—such a pretty place. Brenda and I would go there and play for hours, climbing up to the top of the hill and sitting to take in the view from all around (and of course teenage girls *never* run out of things to talk about). One day Aunty Anne took us on a long boat ride up the river, stopping at Gloucester Cathedral, where we left the boat to explore this magnificent old church. It was built as a Norman abbey church in the eleventh century, old even by English standards, and has the added distinction of being the place from which William I ordered the Domesday Book to be written. Brenda and I were game for climbing the 269 steps up the old gothic tower while Aunty Anne wisely rested her feet on terra firma!

Back at home things carried on pretty much as they had before, with Sam as bossy as ever and Lynette either bubbling with excitement and silliness or alternatively mean and miserable. My dad had decided to carry on his tradition of buying a box of chocolates every Sunday, except now they were bought for me instead of my mother. He also gave me my mother's beautiful gold jewellery. There was an antique gold cross, an old, rose gold bracelet and a very old silver and mother-of-pearl handcrafted broach. Now don't get me wrong. When Lynette was happy we had some really fun times. One just didn't know when the tide would turn. By the time I was 15 I had developed a way of dealing with mean comments—I just stopped talking for as long as it took for Lynette to break the silence. At this point I would carry on as if nothing had happened. Also, I spent quite a bit of time visiting with Bob and Gladys, who always welcomed me.

One day Bob decided he and I should take the train to Stratford on Avon for the day and see the historic buildings. Unfortunately, at the last minute something came up and he was unable to go. So at the ripe old age of 15, I went by myself. The reason I remember this is because of the very old lady with whom I shared a compartment on the train. She engaged me in conversation and we talked about my going to visit Anne Hathaway's cottage and Shakespeare's birthplace. After a while she looked at me quietly, and I will always remember her words to me. She said, "You are very self contained, aren't you, my dear?" Why do I remember this so well? I think perhaps it made me see that I had a certain strength of will and that I was a survivor. I felt validated.

Before long Lynette decided it would be a good idea to turn the old coach house into a private day nursery and work from home. Actually I think this was a brilliant idea. She had all the necessary qualifications and was very good at what she did. Also, we had a coach house sitting empty. Anyway, my dad liked the idea and worked hard to make the needed changes. He knocked out the bricks to make a window in the back wall and the front was all widows from halfway up the wall, plus the door in the middle. The milk house was turned into a bathroom, complete with a miniature toilet (for little bottoms) and a low sink (for little hands and faces). It turned out very well, and with her connections Lynette soon had a nursery full of children. She then hired a cook, a daily housekeeper and a gardener. These children had a cooked lunch every day, and to give credit where it is due this nursery was tops in every way. Somehow, though, having a daily housekeeper did not seem to lessen any of the chores I was expected to do.

By the time I was 16 Lynette and Sam had a baby boy, Adrian, whom I and my dad adored. Sometime back Lynette had had her wish to have the kitchen extended and made twice its original size and had installed a sink in the veranda. Now I am not quite sure of the rationale, but for some reason it became my responsibility to use this sink for all of Adrian's clothes that needed hand-washing. Of course this was just about everything. There was no use arguing. Add to this the fact that I was doing my General Certificate of Education and had masses of homework and studying, this did not seem very fair. Especially when, in terms of household input, Lynette did nothing but the shopping, making sure she had full control over the food. Actually, there was one day when she decided to do some decorating. She painted the beautiful mahogany banister with cream-coloured paint! It is to my father's credit that he did not complain. Later on I found out just how kind and generous a heart he had. After my mother's death there was an inquest. My father refused to press any charges against the young woman responsible for the loss of his Kate, stating that the lady had suffered enough already. The judge then stood up in court and commended my father for his compassion.

As I mentioned before I was considered a dancer with exceptional talent for a person of my age. At my school, dance was part of the curriculum, and for the end-of-term production we were putting on a performance of *The Pied Piper* at one of the smaller venues in Birmingham. Not only did I contribute to the choreography of this ballet, I took the lead role of the Pied Piper. This was quite an achievement and I felt really good about myself. Come showtime, none of my family cared to come and see me perform, and although Mrs. Williams and Brenda came to support me, I felt very deeply hurt by my family. It seemed nothing I achieved really counted for anything.

Then came the time I was going away for a few days on a school trip. About five days before I was due to leave I once again had problems with Lynette and Sam regarding food. Now I was not a big eater. I was five feet tall, about 94 pounds and had a 17-inch waist—not exactly what you would call a glutton. Well, I talked to Gladys about this and she gave me everything I needed to eat in my room. I had bread, butter and jam and the means to make a cup of tea. So for five days I ate by myself in my room and spoke to no one, leaving for my school trip without saying goodbye. By the time I came back from the trip, about 10 days had passed since I had spoken to the family and I was prepared to keep that as the status quo. Now I don't know if they were feeling guilty or if my father had straightened them out, because when I returned they were so friendly I had to check to see if I was in the right house! I followed my policy of putting everything behind me as long as I was being treated fairly as part of the family.

During my 17th year my beloved grandpa died. He was 96. I was considered too young to go to the funeral despite our being so close. This was another event that just seemed to come and go in our family. Does something tell you we were not very close-knit? Perhaps one might even (dare I say it) call us dysfunctional?

At 16 John and I were still writing to one another, although not quite so frequently. He was taking his Advanced General Certificate of Education and had a heavy study load. At this time, Brenda and I undertook an activity that lasted a long time, sparked by a comment made by our vicar during Sunday Service. He suggested we teenagers of the congregation could help young couples with babies and toddlers by offering to babysit once a week for free. Brenda and I followed through with this and continued to babysit for the same family every Thursday evening until we were 24. The couple lived across the street from Brenda's house, and although we babysat for free they always left us a box of chocolates or some other fancy treat. Afterward the husband would always walk me safely home. Eventually Brenda and I were approaching seventeen and it was time to finish school, as we had both done our exams and received our certificates. Brenda wanted to become a teacher and was accepted to teacher's college. Not being able to follow my dream I was not sure what I wanted to do. Back then there were not many options for girls. You could basically be a nurse, a teacher or a secretary. Until I could decide on a path Lynette suggested I become a nursery nurse and pulled clout to obtain an interview for me with Miss Malley, the head of the Birmingham Public Health Department. Through Lynette I had acquired plenty of experience in this area so I was hired without any problem. My schooldays ended in December 1957, and as of January 1958 I began my working career.

8.

Welcome to the Real World (the Young Lady)

It was the middle of January when I had my very first day at work. The nursery I was assigned to was in an extremely poor slum area where a great deal of clearance from the aftermath of the war was ongoing. The war had ended in 1945 with the Japanese surrendering in August of that year, but rebuilding a city takes time and money. Because of the area, the children (age 6 weeks to 5 years) were suffering from various deprivations. There was rampant poverty, malnutrition, head lice and many fractured families. I worked with the toddler group of 3 to 5 year olds, and I really loved what I did. At my current age of 70, I am still passionate about children and an advocate for their rights.

The nursery was open from six in the morning until six at night Monday to Friday, so we would either work six to three or nine to six p.m. Very often there were shortages of staff at the different locations, and due to the fact that I could work with all age groups I would quite often be sent to fill in at the nursery with the most desperate need. My experience working in nurseries extended back to when I was 13, so I had dealt with most situations. I clearly remember one place I was sent to help was a converted house with three floors, with the babies being on the top floor. Well, I worked with the babies—all 12 of them— entirely on my own. May I point out that it was required that all of them went to the back garden to spend time outside in their pram? So by the time the last one was fed, changed and put in its pram, it was time to bring the first one in and start all over again. Remember, there were no disposable diapers or wipes back in those days, and the diaper rash on some of these babies (through neglect at home) was horrific. I had to apply gentian violet to their little bottoms to help them heal. There were very few staff at this location so I worked long hours, and then after the babies had gone home, the days' diapers had to be sluiced and boiled before the next day. It was hard and tiring but I was young and strong, and for this I was paid 2 pounds and 5 shillings a week, which would be about $4.25 Canadian.

Of course, once I started earning I had to pay Lynette for my keep—in itself fair enough. Except this was just for my basic meals. If I wanted fresh fruit (of which she always had an abundance), I had to buy my own, and the same applied to other things that were not part of a meal. Boy, she really knew how to work things! For all this she seemed to keep the peace and get along with my dad, whom she called "Pops" or "Poppsie." Perhaps he was the father she never had? Perhaps this was the scar she was carrying. Whatever, she desperately wanted to play up to the Caudles. Big mistake! Uncle Jack was smarter and more ruthless than she was, and she and Sam would eventually come to learn this the hard way. Uncle Jack told me he and my mother had arranged for me to get into the "family" business after I had finished school, and that I was to have a high profile position and eventually take over the business. Well, everyone kept saying I was a proper Caudle, but I was smart enough (or maybe Caudle enough) to beat them at their own game. I just said no. I was not going to be beholden to anyone, and I knew that would be the outcome if I gave in. I would have been bought. Maybe this was a glimmer of how my personality would develop as I grew older. I would be fair with everyone, but I would be my own person. In other words: "Don't mess with me!"

On a lighter note, during the summer of our 17th year, Brenda and I went on holiday together, our very first time without our parents. We decided to rent a caravan for a week at a campground by the sea at Great Yarmouth. It was a small caravan by today's standards but it was warm and cozy and had everything we needed. It was such a thrilling moment when we were handed the key and opened the door for the first time. What a delight! Being on a bit of a rise we had a view of the ocean that we loved. Once settled in we went grocery shopping, and I must say we ate well that week. In the mornings we would cook bacon, eggs and toast, along with a pot of tea—a good start to the day. Then we would tidy up and go off to explore. Parts of the town were quite old and I was particularly fascinated by the name of a little arched alleyway between some old cottages. It was called "Kittywitches Row." Doesn't that just grab hold of one's imagination? I am sure there must have been quite a story behind that name.

Now dear readers, hit the fast forward button: destination, the twenty-first century. Here I was, indulging in all kinds of fantasies about little kittens and witches with tall, pointy hats, so I decided to use all of the modern technology at my fingertips to see if I could find any information regarding this provocative name. Perhaps (or perhaps not, depending on one's perspective) the cold, hard facts detract somewhat from more fanciful thoughts. Anyway, this is what I found out.

In Great Yarmouth there were numerous narrow alleys, most of which had been bombed during the war. Several still remain, the narrowest of which is Kittywitches Row, which ran from Middlegate to King Street. In "The Folklore of East Anglia," Enid Porter reports that "women dressed in men's clothes and with their faces smeared with blood rushed from house to house demanding money, which they spent on drink." It has been suggested that the word "kittywitch" derives from the Dutch word "kitwijk," meaning a house of ill repute, and that Dutch visitors to the old Yarmouth Free Fair of herring may have given this name to a public house.

So, no sweet kitties perched on the shoulders of benevolent witches with traditional pointy hats. Perhaps I should have just held on to my illusions. Unfortunately, fact always seems to get in the way of fantasy, and that seems to be the path that my life has been destined to take.

Memo to readers: *Please hit rewind here.*

After all these years I can only guess at how Brenda and I must have spent our days. We got on very well together and never, ever quarrelled. I am sure we must have gone to the beach and gone swimming. There was also quite a majestic pavilion where we may have gone dancing. As well, there were a few amusement rides and the usual ice cream stands, but we were just happy in each other's company and enjoyed looking around. We were also quite domesticated and enjoyed cooking our meals in our cozy little caravan. Both of us liked reading and had taken some books with us, so if there was a rainy day we relaxed, had tea and biscuits and read.

One day when we were out strolling we met two young sailors who were in port for a couple of days. Like us, they were about seventeen and the four of us had great fun. Unlike our present day, there was no fear we could come to any harm. It just didn't work that way. These boys were young and full of fun, and of course we thought they looked very handsome in their white naval uniforms. We walked and talked and then sat on a bench on the sea front and talked some more, finally arranging to meet them again the next day. Brenda and I had so much to talk about that night!

As arranged we all met again, but on this day we actually held hands with our sailors, although we remained as a foursome. It was a bittersweet day as we said goodbye to them, but their two days were up and they were off to sea again. We each hugged our chosen companion goodbye and that was that. We did not exchange addresses so as to keep in contact but took it for what it was—two lovely days in the company of two nice, well-mannered young men—*in uniform*!

Our wonderful holiday ended all too soon and we returned to Birmingham and our regular routine. Brenda still had a few more weeks of holiday as she was attending teachers' college in Coventry. She had finished her first year and had one more year to go. Fortunately Coventry was just a hop, skip and a jump from Birmingham, so she was home just about every weekend. During her time away I continued our babysitting by myself.

By now John had finished his first year at University in London, where he was studying to be a doctor of medicine. Before leaving school he had passed his GCE in eight subjects and his AGCE in four subjects—brilliant! It must have been some time in

October or November of that year when I received a letter inviting me to London to visit him. Since I had last seen him when I was 13, I was beside myself with joy at the prospect of reconnecting in person. So it was arranged. I was to take the train up to London on a Saturday morning and meet him underneath Big Ben at noon (very dramatic).

The big day arrived and off I went. When I reached Big Ben there was no John to be found anywhere! There had been some delays with the train and I was a little late arriving, so all kinds of thoughts were going through my head. Just when I was becoming really worried, a very nice young man came up to me and asked if I was Cynthia. Apparently John was in the rowing team (in fact, he rows to this day) and had waited as long as he could for me at our appointed spot and then had to leave. However, he had arranged for one of his friends to pick me up, take me back to their digs and look after me for a short while until he returned. I was so spoiled. Here were all these delightful young men making me tea with biscuits and thoroughly entertaining me. (Who was to know I would meet for a second time the young man who stepped in for John? Only then it was about 47 years later at a party in a condo in Victoria, British Columbia.)

Then John arrived. I could not believe my eyes; he had grown from a 13-year-old lad into a very handsome young man. Wow! I must admit that I was flattered at all the young men wanting to know where he had been hiding me. He thanked his friends for looking after me and we set out to find some lunch. It was as if no time had passed at all, and we just picked up our conversation where we had left off all those years before. This was just heaven and I was so happy!

Lunch was on the outside patio of a little restaurant close to all the tourist sites. We had sandwiches, cakes and tea before I was given the grand tour of the Tower of London and Westminster Abbey. While we were walking we had our photograph taken by a street photographer—I still have this. After dinner John had tickets for us to go to the theatre—a real London theatre—*could this be happening to me?* It was a well known and well received play by Ibsen, but for the life of me I cannot remember its name. What I do remember is that John had arranged to have tea and biscuits brought to our seats during the intermission. Yes, you're right, we English do rather indulge ourselves on tea and biscuits. Just call it a cultural thing.

What happened after the intermission has stayed with me all these years. I felt someone's hand tentatively reach out and hold mine. In that second our childhood friendship stepped up to a whole new level. If one can be shyly ecstatic, that was how I felt: sheer happiness and joy. Too soon I was back on the train on my way back to Birmingham, but the person going back was not the person who had arrived in London some hours earlier. After all, I believe a person is the sum total of her experiences. By now John was 18 and I nearly so.

Once home, life carried on as usual, and John and I continued to write as we always had, but on my birthday I received a gift from him. It was a powder compact and some lipstick and I remember that the powder was by Coty in a fragrance called *L'aimant*.

Soon it was Christmas, and I must admit that Lynette put her all into Christmas festivities, although Dad still insisted on taking over the kitchen on Christmas Day. We would go to church on Christmas Eve for the midnight Mass, leaving Christmas morning free to visit Uncle Tom and Aunty Jess. She always had homemade mincemeat pies for us and a bottle of advocaat. Every Christmas she would give me a pretty little bottle of her homemade cherry brandy. It was so good of Aunty Jess and so kind to make me feel special. The tradition of the little bottle of brandy started when I was 16, and now I had recently turned 18. Goodness I was getting old!

Just after Christmas I saw an advertisement in the newspaper. The general post office (always referred to as the GPO) was looking for young ladies to train as telephonists to work in the huge telephone exchange on New Street in the middle of Birmingham. Before being hired and trained one had to take a test, which was then assessed and one was notified by mail of their acceptance or non-acceptance. Once I had completed and handed in the test I was called aside from the rest of the group and hired on the spot. Wow. Then commenced the three weeks of training on the dummy switchboards before we were let loose on the poor, unsuspecting public. The pay was way more than I was earning as a nursery nurse and I really loved the job. We worked shifts, but only men worked the night shift. The biggest drawback was getting to work. Although the corporation buses ran every few minutes, by the time they reached my bus stop they were already full. So I had to allow a great deal of extra time to allow for this and still get to work on time. The compensation for this was a good job, the bunch of girls and ladies with whom I worked were cheerful and friendly and I got on well with the supervisors. Because it was a twenty-four-hour service, the shifts sometimes included working weekends, and once I even worked on Christmas Day. I must be fair and add that as there were no buses running on holidays, Sam was more than willing to give me a ride to work and back. Such is the nature of essential services. Before too long I was promoted to handling the 999 fire, police and ambulance calls, along with the ship-to-shore calls. How antiquated this all seems by today's standards. After that I worked on the initial testing for self-dialled overseas calls.

On the home front, life went on as usual. Each year starting in January, Brenda and I would collect travel brochures and start to plan our annual summer vacation. Throughout the ensuing years we travelled to Belgium, Holland, Spain, Majorca and Italy. From England it was cheap, quick and easy to fly to Europe and we took full advantage of this. Having decided where to go we would save for six months to pay for the holiday and have spending money, and also shop for pretty summer dresses. I was fortunate enough to know how to use my mother's sewing machine and was able to make most of my summer wardrobe. But half the fun for us was looking through the catalogues at all the exotic locations, and later going into town to browse the dress stores and dream of what we would like to buy. We also took care when choosing so we would not clash with each other colour-wise. Getting along together was easy.

There were many memorable occasions during our various holidays, and a few stand out in my mind. For instance, the year we travelled to Majorca, it was not the thriving tourist Mecca it is today. Some of the hotels were still under construction, although a few (such as the Amazonas, where we stayed) were already catering to tourists. Of course we had the usual teenage holiday crush on a couple of the waiters (Jose and Antonio—how original) and went dancing with them after they had finished work, but mostly I remember the camel. Yes, camel! Not that I went dancing with him or anything like that, but he (and his owner) certainly rescued us damsels in distress. We were hurrying for the bus to take us shopping in the main city of Palma. Unfortunately, the bus was leaving just as we arrived at the pickup stop, so our gallant knight on his charger (the camel) chased after the bus and stopped it for us. Now this bus, if you could call it that, was incapable of going very fast, and as we mounted the steps we were greeted by many locals, along with their chickens, goats, children and other assorted livestock. It was crowded and rather smelly but oh so continental. We loved it!

Italy was the setting for my other most memorable holiday event. We were staying in a little town on the Adriatic Coast but went on day trips to places of interest, including Venice. We visited one large city (isn't it funny that I can't remember the name?) that was bustling with people. At one busy intersection there was a rather young and handsome policeman standing on a white box directing traffic. He blew his whistle and directed the pedestrians to cross, and then it happened! I was halfway across the street when he pointed at me and indicated that I was to go over to him. I complied, all the while wondering what rule I had broken. Then he asked me to go out with him! Oh boy, now what? Of course I said no, but he would not settle for anything but a yes. I continued to refuse, so he said he would not let any traffic move until I said yes. By now people were honking their horns, standing on their cars yelling and being what I assumed was very Italian. What was a girl to do? So I said yes—and gave him the wrong name of the hotel. Phew! I got away—the traffic started moving—and I never saw him again. Brenda and I had an unspoken rule: never, ever split up. Although we were young we were not foolish.

During the summer of 1958 John came to Birmingham for the day to visit me. We had a wonderful time. We just slipped right back into the rhythm of our younger years, exploring our favourite places. On top of this, John wanted to show me his old school in Solihull, just a short bus ride away. The day was idyllic and full of warmth and sunshine. I wore my prettiest pink dress with a big, frilly crinoline petticoat, as was the style then, which only served to enhance my tiny 17-inch waist, and I felt very good about myself. Too soon it was time for John to catch the train back to university. However, in the autumn I was invited to visit his home in Sussex for the weekend. How happy I was. All the issues at home paled at the prospect of spending a whole weekend with John and his family. By now he had another brother and sister, Charles and Jane, who were still quite young and whom I had never met.

This was to be my first experience of going away in this context, both town and country, so I carefully chose what I packed, including a really nice pleated skirt in a milk-chocolate brown (some might have called it taupe, but my mind is usually on chocolate, my greatest addiction). I teamed this with a pretty white knit top for the evening in London and a classic, raglan-sleeve pink sweater for the next day in the country. Then I crossed my fingers and prayed this would be appropriate.

Saturday came and with something of a mixture of excitement and apprehension I set off with my little suitcase and boarded the train. John was there to meet me—no missed connections this time—and when I saw him I knew everything was going to be fine. For that evening he had bought theatre tickets for us to see the musical *Salad Days*. It was light, breezy and so much fun, and John and I had not missed a beat picking up from where we had left off the last time I saw him. He always was (and still is) the perfect gentleman, but at this time we were both inexperienced in this new role of boyfriend and girlfriend. However, we had our years of friendship to fall back on and were never uncomfortable with each other.

After the play we caught the train to Crawley and arrived at John's home somewhere close to midnight. His sister, Rosemary, had stayed up to greet us and show me where my room was and such, and then she was off to bed, leaving John and me sitting on the settee in the living room. It was a beautiful room with classic, regency-striped wallpaper, which I was admiring when I felt an arm slip around my shoulder. Oh my, this was my dream come true—and I blew it! I was so nervous of being a bad guest and disturbing the household at that hour that I suggested that perhaps it was time to go to bed. Missed chances; paths not taken when they could have been. How these small moments in time can have such a huge impact on the rest of one's life.

The next morning there was a knock on my bedroom door, and I saw the friendly faces of Mrs. McCaw and Rosemary peeking in at me. I sat up in bed, complete with rollers in my hair, and they came and sat with me while we talked and talked. It was so good to see them. After breakfast John showed me around their lovely garden. There were no awkward feelings from the night before, and this was the start of a beautiful day. After a while Mr. McCaw took us in the car, along with the children, Charles and Jane. They brought a bag of bread to feed the ducks. Now wasn't this just the kind of thing Mr. McCaw took John and me to do when we were young? Some things never change.

Later we all went for a walk over the downs and down to the seashore, where we skipped stones into the waves. How can a day be so simple but so pleasurable? I guess deep down we were still those two youngsters who loved nature. Too soon the day was over and we had to catch the train back to London, John to University and me to Birmingham. I was sad to leave the McCaw family. Who could have known that seeing them smiling and waving to me from the Crawley train platform would be the last time I would ever see them?

All too quickly my train arrived at London station and it was time to say goodbye. This was a bittersweet moment. John took my suitcase and stowed it in a compartment for me and there were still a few minutes before the train was due to depart, so he took my hand, leading me behind some lockers. Here he kissed me goodbye—not as a friend—our relationship was now on a whole different level and I thought I was in heaven. That was when I blew it again! I suddenly had visions and worries of the train leaving along with my suitcase and leaving me behind—and I panicked at the thought. If I had not cut short our goodbye, I believe it would have become really intense. *Why do I do these things to myself?* I have always had a habit of letting my worries get in the way of my pleasures. That is, up until the past few years. But I know John understood. That December he sent me two books for my birthday, *The Essays of Elia* by Charles Lamb and the *Rubaiyat of Omar Khayyam*. Inside was a simple "love from John." These books are still among my dearest treasures.

So time went by and we stayed in touch by letter, but John had his life in London and I mine in Birmingham. Brenda and I still babysat each Thursday and went on vacation together in the summer, but we were also old enough to go out dancing and have the odd date with boys we met. This was fun but never serious and the boys went as quickly as they came, especially if they started to get serious. If they actually proposed to me (and this happened from time to time) all you would see of me was a puff of dust on the horizon. No thank you; I had other plans.

When I was 20 I saw an advertisement in the newspaper for a telephonist/receptionist at a car dealership that was quite close to where I lived. At the GPO they were planning to make me a supervisor, which would be very good money. I had been chosen as one of five telephonists representing our telephone exchange in a verbal competition against an outside team. Every question that was being asked I answered before they were hardly finished asking, to the point where the male executive who was conducting the competition asked laughingly, "Should I ask the question or would you like to answer it first?" We won on every question—all of which were answered by me. This boded well for me in terms of a career move within the company, but there was still the transportation problem and having to work shifts plus weekends. So I thought, *What could it hurt to just enquire about this other position?*

They phoned me back immediately—at work—to offer me an interview. To say I was surprised is an understatement. My interview ended with my being hired on the spot. My work hours would be nine thirty to six p.m. except for Tuesdays, when I would finish at noon. This was to compensate for working Saturday mornings. Later I was told that as soon as they heard my voice on their answering machine enquiring about the position, I was already hired. Wow!

Before I knew it another year had passed and I was celebrating my 21st birthday. In England this is cause for a big celebration, and Lynette made sure my party lacked for nothing. She put her all into organizing it and I will always be grateful for that effort. The party was held in the nursery (formerly the coach house) and was well attended. Lynette and Sam bought me a silver charm bracelet with one charm on it, and every guest brought me a different charm, which I could then add to the bracelet. What a great idea! Dad bought me a very dainty, pure gold Girard-Perregaux watch with a thin calfskin strap and a delicate gold buckle. And so began my adulthood.

9.

Heartbreak and Anger
(the Young Woman)

*H*ow can we pinpoint the exact time our relationships start to drift? Or how would one recognize that a particular action, or inaction, could be the tip of the wedge that would eventually lead to a deeper divide? In our young adulthood we struggle with so many different facets of our lives—our job, our friendships, romantic diversions, family dynamics and the struggle to establish exactly who and what we are. What are our personal boundaries and will we allow those boundaries to be compromised?

As I grew into adulthood I had a strong sense of style and always dressed well. Once again I was fortunate enough to be able to sew and made nearly all of my own summer clothes. Although I was petite (five foot nothing), my figure was proportionate (thirty/seventeen/thirty-two) and if I may be allowed to brag a little, I looked good and attracted a great deal of attention from the young men. Brenda and I were still the best of friends but our work and the fact that we both dated usually meant we did not see each other so much. We still babysat on a Thursday evening and this was our time to catch up on each other's activities, as well as plan our vacation.

John was now in his fourth year of medical school and so was deeply entrenched in his studies. We still wrote to each other, but as time progressed the letters became less frequent. From my current perspective I can appreciate just how overwhelming his workload must have been. But at the time I began to feel as if I was a little less important. The one thing I realized both then and to this day is that the love I felt for him when I was 12 was no crush. It was real love and love hurts.

My job was going well and I loved it. The company had even collected for a gift for my 21st birthday. I still have it: a beautiful silver bracelet and a gossamer stole. The stole has long since become the acquisition of one of my granddaughters (another little peek ahead?). But the bracelet is safely tucked away. My small office was in the main showroom of the company and right outside the managing director's office. From here I handled all the incoming and outgoing calls as well as being the company receptionist, and the busier it was the more I liked it. Now the only problem was that the showroom was inundated with salesmen, most of them married and willing to be unfaithful at the drop of a hat, or anything else for that matter! However, I made it quite clear (in a friendly way) that I was not available to married men. Anyway, I was still a virgin and planned to keep it that way. (Deep down I still felt John and I would come together and get married, but time passed with very little contact between the two of us. There were the Christmas cards containing a brief letter but little else.)

At 22 I was beginning to question my circumstances. Lynette had another baby boy (Adrian was now 6) but was as erratic as ever. She had many friends with whom she was the life of the party. They didn't have to live with her! Adrian was sent to a private school in Stechford that was two bus rides away. Have you guessed whose job it became to take him? Full marks if you guessed me. This meant my catching a total of four different buses in order to get to work. Now, I loved my nephew very much. He was an extremely bright boy, and when I was at home I spent a great deal of time showing him things in books, and I would buy him Beatrix Potter stories. There was a mutual bond between him and Dad, and Dad even made him his own little overalls, just like Grandad's, out of an old pair of his own. I'm not sure Dad really thought about my circumstances.

Do you remember my telling you, on our first little house tour, that my bedroom was over the garage? This meant that in the winter it was extremely cold. The other rooms all had gas fireplaces but mine did not. During the past couple of winters ice had started to form on the inside of my one bedroom wall and I had to pull my bed out to keep the bedding from getting wet. The solution was that in order to heat the room I had to buy myself a Valor Stove, which burned kerosene. On top of this I had to walk about four miles with a container to buy my own fuel and then four miles back again. It was really heavy, and although Sam had a car he would not dream of picking it up for me or even taking me to buy it. Now I considered that this should have been a household expense, but of course it did not matter. I think that this was when I started to become really hurt and angry. I was on my own—deal with it! But when Lynette and Sam decided to buy a new rug just because they wanted it, all of a sudden it became a shared expense and I had to put in a third of the cost.

It was no use arguing—what was the point? So in my eyes I had been abandoned by my family and had lost John. Therefore, why should I care about anything?

One day during the summer of my 22nd year I was on my way home from town. The bus stop was by John's old house, so I just had to walk a little way to my house. Between the bus stop and my house I came across one of my neighbours working on his car outside his home. He was someone I had known since I was 6, but as he was about eight or nine years older than me we had not really had anything in common. His mother had died a few years back and so he was living with his sister and his father. As I was walking by, he looked up and said hello. At that point his big Alsatian dog jumped over the privet hedge and landed in front of me. At first I was taken aback, but he was a very friendly dog. Bruce apologized and held on to his dog, but this gave us a starting point for a conversation, and after that I went on my way.

Now, whether it was coincidence or not I don't know, but the next two or three times I walked past his house Bruce was out at his car. Well, of course this ended up with him asking me out on a date, to which I willingly agreed. He was good looking in a rugged kind of way and had sparkling blue eyes and black curly hair. I found him very attractive. He had been a marksman in the army and was one of the 62,000 men whom England had sent to fight in the Korean War, which took place from June 25, 1950, to July 27, 1953. He was physically fit and well muscled. In retrospect I think he made me feel secure. Being only 94 pounds and very petite, he could pick me up with ease. His special name for me was "Elfie," as he said I reminded him of a little elf.

Bruce kissed me gently on our first date and it was wonderful. Our relationship progressed in intimacy, but I was still a virgin.

One night we were sitting on the couch—it was dark outside, the house was quiet and we were cuddling by the glow from the firelight. This was the night; I was ready and did not want to hold back on a thing. Bruce was courteous, kind, loving and gentle and I was in absolute heaven. He had never pressured me into making love, but once it happened there was no going back for either of us. He was an experienced and sensitive lover and I gave him my all. Even so, I cannot say I was in love with him, but we definitely had fun together and were never at a lack for conversation. Add to that the fact that our lovemaking was incredible and we were very compatible. Our relationship lasted a long time but I think we both knew, great as it was, this was as far as it was going to go. Gradually we saw less and less of each other and finally parted, still very good friends. I shall always be grateful for the way in which he gently led me into womanhood, and for how protected he made me feel.

By now I was 24 and summer was approaching again. I was really questioning what to do with my life. Although I was not interested in marriage, I didn't wish to continue living in that awful house, never knowing if I was coming home to happiness or some other weird kind of mood. Lynette had a way of rationalizing that whatever was going wrong was my fault. One particular day I came home and Lynette, Sam and my dad were all in the kitchen. As soon as I came through the door Lynette started going off about something or other and Sam just stood there smoking his pipe, looking so smug and superior. That was it! It takes a lot for me to lose my temper but I just let them have it. Out came every secret I had kept since I was a child. My emotions were in overdrive and I was shaking and crying as I accused Sam of everything his friend had done to me. My father just stood there looking blank, but I was aghast when Lynette turned on me and said (as if it was my fault) that Sam had told her everything and to stop making a fuss. This was totally beyond my comprehension. How could anyone condone what had been done? He had just totally gotten away with his depravities and I was a victim all over again.

I stormed out of the kitchen and that was that. It was as if nothing had happened. That was when I saw a posting in the newspaper advertising positions onboard a ship with P and O Orient Shipping Lines. Here was a way to leave everyone behind and start a new life as a ship's telephone operator. To hell with them. I needed no one.

10.

David (the Young Woman)

It is strange how life has a way of throwing one a curve when it is least expected, and that is what happened to me. My 8-year-old nephew, Adrian, was enrolled with the Cubs, and the group scout master had arranged for a parents' camping weekend along with the boys. Lynette and Sam were going and asked if I wanted to go with them. They were going to camp from Friday night until Sunday, in a beautiful little valley in Wales. Partly because I worked Saturday mornings and partly because I was not interested, I declined. The evening before they were due to leave I was alone in the house when there was a knock on the door. I opened it to find a tall, young man in Scout uniform who wished to speak with Lynette and Sam. They were going to be home in about 15 minutes, so I asked if he would like to come in and wait. I invited him into the living room so I could entertain him until Lynette and Sam arrived home. To say I was bowled over was an understatement. All I can say is from the moment we started talking I was determined that I was going to that camp. He was tall (taller than six feet), with curly blond hair and blue eyes and had the most refreshingly genuine attitude I had seen in a long while.

We chatted easily, with him introducing himself as David while I explained I was Adrian's Aunty Cynthia. In no time at all Lynette and Sam were home and I excused myself to go and analyze what had just happened. From the second I saw David, I was in love with him. Is it possible to love two men at the same time? As my life unfolds we will find the answer to this, but that is part of my future. I was still in love with John, but it was apparent I was out of his personal picture. It had been such a long time since I had heard from him and I assumed this to mean that his life had taken him in a different direction. Oh, the tricks life plays on us!

In no time at all I sorted out my arrangements for getting to camp. On Saturday morning I would work as usual and then go straight to catch the train that would take me to the local station near the camp. From here Sam would pick me up and drive me to the campsite.

What an idyllic setting. There before me were all the tents nestled in a little valley in the Welsh hills. Folks were sitting around campfires outside their tents, having tea and chatting with their friends. Everything was so peaceful. I had pulled a camp chair up to the fire and was having a cup of tea when David strolled over and sat down to join us. We all talked for a while, but as he was running the camp and in charge of the other leaders, his duties soon pulled him away. By now I was so glad I had come. Although David was talking to all of us, he frequently looked my way.

We passed a peaceful afternoon visiting and getting to know the people in the various tents and I think everyone was enjoying themselves. After the evening meal we all sang songs around the campfire before David announce a hike up the hills in the dark for anyone who wanted to go and see the sheep. Of course I grabbed a flashlight and was definitely ready for whatever lay ahead.

What did lie ahead was magical. A group of about 15 or more of us set out for the hike, moving as a group as we wended our way up the hill. Within a short while I found David walking beside me, and pretty soon we were chatting away. Upon reaching the top of the hill we discovered the flock of sheep. The group was quiet and respectful of these woolly critters but they seemed very tame and used to human company. Their eyes shined a beautiful green in the light of our torches. David held back a bit out of the light and that was when I felt his hand reach out for mine and hold on to it. How was it that I just knew this was going to happen? Next thing he bent down and kissed me. Wow! We then continued to walk hand in hand. I was to quickly learn that once David made up his mind about something he did not see any point in waiting. He was, I found out, just six weeks older than me. As we descended the hill he once more assumed the role of leader and I integrated back into the group. He was a private person and I respected him for this discretion. After our hike we all enjoyed a mug of hot chocolate around the last glowing embers of the campfire, and then it was off to our respective tents for a good night's sleep.

When I woke, the various families were stirring and starting breakfast preparations—English style—that is, eggs and bacon with sausages, mushrooms and fried bread. I elected to walk to the water pump to fill our container so we could have tea. Who should be there but David. In the presence of the other folks he was friendly in a way that he would be to anyone. We were later to find that we did not fool anyone! The camp finished about noon after the Cubs finished their activities and had their closing ceremonies. Then it was off home, with my mind trying to make sense of what had passed between David and me. Was it just an opportunistic kiss in the dark? Somehow I did not think so.

Back home we set about putting the camping stuff away, and I needed to make sure my things were ready for work the next day. This had been a good weekend, with both Lynette and Sam in a happy, friendly mood.

I had been somewhat concerned about Dad lately; he had been contentious (not like him at all) and had been acting strangely. Up until now it was nothing I could put my finger on; it was more intuitive. This evening was different. When I went into the living room he was trying to change the television channel by turning an imaginary knob on the arm of the chair. I offered to help and he said he wanted to watch boxing, which was something he enjoyed. Back when he was in the Royal Flying Corps he represented the force by boxing. Unfortunately there was no boxing on any of the channels but he did not seem to comprehend this, insisting I turn the channel to boxing. Oh dear. There was definitely something amiss here, but I did not know what. Throughout my life I have noticed that the closer one is to a problem the less likely one is to notice it. Also, if the person is dear to you, you tend to try to find some rational explanation for the unusual behaviours. After all, how could it be happening to someone you know so well? Everything must be okay really, right?

While I was at work the next day I did not have much time to think about the weekend. As usual, I was very busy. There were six incoming lines on the switchboard and at least ten extensions in the building, not counting the salesmen's "other office," which was the Bull's Head pub across the road. I also handled customers coming in to pay their bills and any visitors for the Managing Director. I must admit I was in my element handling all the different tasks. These days I believe it would be called multitasking, but back then it was just in a day's work.

By the time I arrived home it was usually about six thirty p.m., so I ate my supper. By about seven there was a phone call for me. It was from David calling to ask if I would like to go out for a while. How quickly can one say yes without sounding totally over the moon? I must have pretty nearly broken the record. As for David, he arrived in record time. He had a blue Bedford van that he used for carrying around the Scouts—I think it must have seated at least eight people. Anyway, it was big enough that I could stand upright in it. This was a beautiful summer evening so we drove to the quaint old village of Coleshill, where we wandered around looking at the old stores and ancient cottages, all the while talking and getting to know each other. He was so interesting to talk to and our personalities just seemed to click. Now I am sure we must have stopped somewhere for a coffee and a snack but all I can remember is how wonderful it felt just holding his hand and talking. We had so many things in common regarding our likes and dislikes.

All too soon it was time to go home. By now it was dark and we both had to go to work the next day. David stopped the van in our driveway and turned off the engine and the lights. That was when we kissed and held each other close—I was ecstatic. He was so different from anyone I had dated. There was a brief moment of panic when he took my hand and placed it where I could feel his arousal. I remember thinking very clearly, *Oh no, not you as well! Please don't be just like everyone else.* At that point I was expecting him to want what most dates wanted and what

I was not prepared to give, but this was not the case. It was just a brief gesture to, I think, let me know what he could not put into words about his feelings for me. What a relief. I desperately wanted him to be different. Then it was time to say goodnight. He walked me to my front door, but he was so tall that I had to stand on the doorstep to reach up and kiss him goodnight. Then he was gone, leaving me with my feelings in overdrive. All this had happened so quickly. What did it mean?

Tuesday passed in a daze thinking about David and wondering if I would see him again. I told no one about him. What there was to tell was too personal and special and it would only serve to cheapen the whole experience if I were to discuss it. This was private. On Tuesday evening I had barely had time to eat my supper when the phone rang. It was David, wondering if I would like to go and see a movie. With my heart pounding I said yes, and within a short while he was knocking at my front door. We went to the Sheldon Picture House, but I have no clue what the movie was about. Partway through David took off the signet ring he wore on his right hand, and reaching for my left hand he placed it on my third finger, turning it so that it looked like a wedding band. He did not say anything but just looked at it for a while, smiling, and then slipped it off again. By now I was completely befuddled—what was he thinking? Here was a person I had just met who obviously must like me.

After the movie we walked for a little while looking in the window of the antique store next to the cinema. In the window was a bronze head and shoulders of Lord Baden Powell, the founder of the Boy Scout movement with the words "The Great B. P." inscribed in the bronze. This was a memento of his returning from the Boer War a hero.

David, I had discovered, devoted his whole time to running

the various groups at his local church where he was the Group Scout master. This made seeing this bronze of B. P. rather special. Finally the evening was over and it was time to drive home. Again he parked the van in the driveway with the lights and the engine off. This time was different. Right out of the blue he turned to me and said, "Let's get married and go to Canada."

Rockets went off in my head, and like an idiot I said, "Pardon?"

He repeated, "Let's get married and go to Canada," and to that I very quickly replied, "Okay."

Then came the hugging and the kissing. How could this wonderful man here beside me want me? But he did. We decided not to tell anyone right away. Heavens, this was only the fourth time I had set eyes on him and only our second time being alone together. But it felt right, one of those moments when there is spontaneous and reciprocated attraction. We were not going to be able to see each other again until the following Saturday because of prior commitments we both had. He was deeply involved with the Scouts and Brenda and I were still doing babysitting.

By now little Jenny was eight but she had a brother now who was about two years old. Sometimes Brenda and I would spell each other if one of us had a date, but we usually kept Thursdays clear, although we no longer saw much of each other in between times. On Thursday I told Brenda about David and that we really liked each other, although I did not mention his proposal. She was also dating but more casually at the moment. Thursday was our "catch-up" night and we both enjoyed it. Plus it gave the couple we babysat for a chance to get out once a week. By now we must have been doing this for eight years. My goodness how the time flies!

Saturday was an eternity coming—would we both still feel the same? Was this for real? Had I really found my future husband?

As soon as we saw each other we knew everything was all right. David confided that he had been a wreck all week wondering if I would have changed my mind. Not a chance. Ours was one of those instant, magical connections that was to last a lifetime. In fact we had 40 happy years before David passed away, but that story has yet to unfold, so pretend you didn't read that. A deal? Right on!

This Saturday afternoon David was taking me to meet his parents. They lived in a council house on what was locally known as "the New Estate." This was a subdivision of houses that had been built to provide modern, affordable rental housing to those who needed it.

As soon as I entered David's house I knew it was a home filled with love and caring. His mother was sitting by the fire knitting and his dad was standing looking at one of his many fish tanks. I was later to learn that he was a brilliant man who was a perfectionist and excelled at everything he did. Unfortunately he was pretty crippled with arthritis, but he still managed to work until he was 65. The front garden was filled with rose bushes of every kind, each unique and each one perfect. Now these were Harry Redfern's show roses and no one was allowed to touch them. These were not for cutting and putting in a vase in the house, they were a work of art.

David introduced me to his parents, who made me feel right at home. We had a cup of tea and chatted, and I could see this house was filled with things David's mother had made. From the curtains to the placemats to the handmade sweaters everyone was wearing, her touch was everywhere. After a while David's dad disappeared, only to reappear carrying a bunch containing one perfect rose from each of his rose bushes, which he then presented to me. There was a stunned silence and everyone's jaw dropped as he casually explained to me the variety name of each one of these wonderful blooms. At the time I memorized all the names, but I am afraid the passing of too many years has taken that from me. Well, I had definitely been accepted by the Redfern household! Since then I have wondered what David's dad perceived that inspired him to welcome me in such a special way.

David was the second youngest of four boys in the family, with there being three-and-a-half years between them all. Bob was the eldest and was married to Pat, and they had a baby named Andrew. Next came Don (yes, two of David's brothers had the same names as two of my brothers), then David and the youngest was Mike. He and his girlfriend, Mary, had been dating since they were in school together and it was a given that they would marry. This was to be a summer of changes.

Toward the end of August I was taking my nephew, Adrian, on a weeklong trip to Ostend in Belgium, and David had two Scout camps booked. One was in Wales and one was a two-week camp in Cornwall, so we would not be seeing each other very much. We worked it out that we could see each other one day in the week and on Saturday and Sunday. On Thursdays David stayed home with his dad so his mother could go out with her friend from next door. Because of his poor health, his dad was not left alone.

One Thursday David asked me if I would like to go over to his place and spend time with him and his dad. First I went over to where Brenda and I babysat and asked if she would mind if I went to see David that evening. We had been best friends for many years and had always respected the fact that sometimes one of us may have plans for a Thursday, and this was fine. Her response totally shocked me and I shall never forget that moment. She did not meet my gaze but said, "You can either be friends with David or with me."

I turned and walked out the door and went to David, and that was the last time I ever saw her. This saddened me greatly, but I will not be given ultimatums about my friendships.

Shortly after this David took the scouts camping for a week in Wales. He wrote me the most tender, loving letter (I have his letters to this day), but it was during this time that it became apparent Dad was very ill. He was admitted to hospital and they even brought in a specialist from Harley Street in London. We were told his body was riddled with cancer, that they dared not open him up and that by all standards he should have been dead at least a year ago. Yet he was working just the week before. What an incredibly strong man he was! Unfortunately, he had been a chain smoker since I was a baby, but back in the early 1900s, when he started smoking, there was no information or knowledge about how harmful cigarettes were.

As there was nothing that could be done we brought him home and the family doctor came in every day to keep an eye on things and give him morphine shots. Fortunately, David was soon home, and he came in and organized things for the better. He had a bed set up in the front room downstairs so Dad was with us and there was no running up and down the stairs all the while. He also got a reclining lounge chair for the back garden so Dad could be out on the lawn among his flowers. It was while he was out there enjoying the sun that we told him we were going to be married. This gave him the comfort he needed, knowing I would be all right. We did not tell anyone else at this time. Lynette did her best to cope with the situation but she was emotionally unstable—fine one minute and neurotic the next. I remember her waking me up in the morning screaming, "Your father is dying and you are lying in bed sleeping!"

Within three weeks—and just three weeks before he was due to retire—Dad passed away. It was a Thursday close to midnight, and at seven the next morning I was supposed to be taking Adrian to Belgium. The last thing Dad said was that he wanted me to still go, so I respected his wishes and went. I believe there was some harsh criticism from some of my relatives about my not being there, but I followed my father's last request. Believe me, it was not easy for me to just leave, but it was probably better for Adrian. He and his granddad were very close.

Once again David came to the fore. He drove Adrian and me to catch the coach and then, as the local funeral director was a friend of his through scouting, he arranged all of that as well. Sam seemed to just hang around in the background and not really do anything. David went to the funeral and told me in a letter about the flowers he sent from us. He wrote, "My own dearest Cynthia, it's been an awfully long week away from you … no doubt Lynette will be telling you all about the funeral. I went feeling you were there standing by the side of me all the while, thinking the same thoughts, saying the same prayers. I sent a spray of flowers from both of us; they were mainly large yellow and white chrysanthemums with some pink and white carnations and just a single gladiolus at the back. I'm sure you would have chosen them with me and Dad would have liked them." He also went on to say how hard Lynette had worked that week and that she had been just wonderful. One has to give credit where it is due; when Lynette tried, she really put her all into whatever she was doing. He also said he tried to thank her for everything, but it was difficult to talk seriously to her, but he thought she got the message.

By the time Adrian and I arrived home David had just left for two weeks in Cornwall with the Scouts. The house was lonely and I was not told anything about the funeral. Adrian and Julian now had single beds in what had been my father's room, and Lynette and Sam had taken over the house lock, stock and barrel. They gave me my father's suitcase and a photo album, which I had bought him, as a memento. So now I had lost my father, my best friend, Brenda, and was a lodger in what had been my home. Thank God I had David because I had nothing else.

11.

Marriage (the Wife)

*E*arly the next week I received a letter from David asking if I could go down to Cornwall to spend the second week of Scout Camp with him. Originally he had thought that his friend Ray was driving down and that I could get a ride with him. Unfortunately, Ray's plans fell through so I made plans to go down by train and David would pick me up from the station. Susan, the girlfriend of another Scouter was going to be there and I was able to share a tent with her. This was going to be a really nice break. The previous week had been rainy, but when I arrived the sun came out and the weather was simply beautiful. I had never been to Cornwall before but it was quaint and picturesque.

As planned David picked me up at the station in his blue Bedford van and we set off for the camp. Partway there he pulled over to the side of the road and stopped the vehicle. It was time to catch up on some kissing and cuddling. Since I had met him we had actually spent very little time together, and until we were married it looked as if it would remain that way. Well, we were so happy to be together again and I felt so secure in his arms. At that point I would have done anything, but kissing and cuddling was as far as it went. In David's words, "We have the rest of our lives to be together, why spoil it now?," and that is the way it remained throughout our courtship.

The camping experience was great. I had never met Susan before but we got on really well. In the mornings the older scouts would cook bacon and eggs and bring us our breakfast in bed. Talk about being spoiled! The days passed exploring and doing activities with the boys. We would go into the village and buy supplies for the evening meal and do some tourist things. David and I had our photo taken by a street photographer. I was holding a monkey and David had a parrot sitting on his shoulder. It was fun. He also bought me a little furry, stuffed cat that we called Corny William. Corny William travelled all the way to Canada with us and could quite possibly still be in one of my storage boxes. I will have to look someday. Oh, and the Cornish cream teas! Tea and scones with homemade jam and clotted cream—absolute heaven! In the evening we had time for just the two of us to go on walks down the country lanes. One evening a black cat crossed our path (this is considered very good luck in England) and following that we saw a shooting star. What better omens could there be?

Too soon the week was over and we were back to work and our normal routine. By the end of September we decided we had better let our families know we were planning to get married. We chose a time when Lynette was away and took Sam out for supper at a country pub in Coleshill, and during our meal David told him of our plans and that we hoped Sam would give me away. (Right up until the time he died I never did tell David about Sam's friend's aberrations toward me. This is something I have kept locked inside for many, many years.) Well, that was that. Afterward David told his parents and his mom immediately began planning what she could do to help. She was a wonderful woman who had always worked hard yet had managed to do an incredible job raising her four boys. Each one of them was brilliant and successful. Mind you, she had a knack of getting herself into the most awkward pickles. One time she decided to paint the bedroom floor. That was fine except she started at the door, painted herself into a corner and was blocked in by the bed that she had stood against the wall. But she always saw the funny side of these situations and would have a good laugh at what she had done.

When Lynette found out about David and me it was a bit of a different story. Lynette liked to collect people, particularly people who had some standing in the community, such as the Group Scout master. So when she realized that "her" David was more interested in me she decided that she really didn't like him so much after all. Go figure!

David worked as an engineer at the Alpha Television Studios in Birmingham and loved his job. On Tuesdays when I finished work at noon I would catch the bus into town and meet David for lunch. We had a favourite Chinese restaurant in the Bull Ring and would eat lunch there. It was on one of these Tuesdays, after we had eaten lunch and were looking at a few stores that David stopped at a jewellery shop. There in the window was the most exquisitely dainty ring—a solitary, beautiful diamond in a platinum setting, mounted on a gold ring. He said nothing but just looked at me, and then took my hand and went into the shop. It was the first and only ring I tried on and it was a perfect fit. He bought it right there and then. Once outside he stopped, took the ring from his pocket and put it on my finger. He wanted me to have it right away and I was thrilled. I felt like the luckiest, most beautiful person in the world. Then I realized, wow, I'm engaged!

Our plan was to have a party in a couple of weeks and hold it in what was the old coach house. We would send out invitations to a "Down the Garden Party" that would be a party to celebrate the fact we were engaged. Well, Lynette was hopping mad because I was already wearing my ring. She said we should have waited for the party and have a proposal and the whole nine yards. She missed the point that it was a party to share our happiness with our friends and let them know of our future plans. As always she was mad at me but nevertheless put on a fabulous party for us, complete with a cake made to look like a ring. And yes, in front of everyone she was the life of the party. It did turn out to be a great time, but one never knew with her when the next storm would blow in.

It was now October and time to do some serious planning. Our wedding date would depend upon the first sailing of the New Year as the ships had to wait for the ice to break up on the St. Lawrence River. We went through the immigration process quickly and without a hitch, and David booked us a first class cabin on the Empress of England, sailing from Bristol on Tuesday April 5, 1966. Our wedding was planned for Saturday April 2. For our engagement, Lynette and Sam bought us a huge, expensive cabin trunk so we would be able to pack all our things in it. The things Lynette did were so thoughtful, and she put a lot of effort into things, but there was just this other side of her that unfortunately kept popping up and getting in the way.

I would have liked to have been married in my own parish church, St. Edburgha's, that was more than a thousand years old, but David was very involved in the activities at his parish church, St. Thomas's, so that was the obvious choice. This was a new and very modern church, but David and the vicar were good friends. Next we had to sort out our passports. Because mine needed to be in my married name it had to be sent to Vicar Hayward, who could only give it to us at our wedding once we had signed the register. Doesn't life get complicated sometimes? October 18, 1965, was David's 25th birthday. To surprise him I went back to the little antique store we had looked in on the evening he proposed to me. The bronze bust of Lord Baden Powell was still there, so I bought it for his birthday. To this day it still hangs on the wall in my hallway.

David and I had no one to help with the costs of the wedding, so it was up to us. No one came with me when I shopped for my wedding dress and veil, but I managed to get just what I wanted at a very reasonable price. There were going to be two bridesmaids, and my niece, Carole, was maid of honour. Adrian and Julian were to be pageboys to carry my traditionally long wedding veil. I made their outfits other than the shirts, so this was a savings. My dress was only ten pound (I am sure this was a mistake but they were just putting the dresses out when I saw it). I made Carole's outfit and got the two bridesmaids dresses on sale. There were to be just family (30 people) to the sit-down reception right after the wedding, and then in the evening a big buffet for everyone. David's mom made the three-tier wedding cake and it was fantastic. She got one of her friends, who was a professional, to decorate it. Also, David's mom and the ladies of the church pulled together to put on the buffet. There were about 500 people who came to this. Shopping for my trousseau was a bit of a challenge as I was so tiny, and I ended up buying a lovely green skirt and white, lacy knit top in the children's department. The only other new things I bought were a coat and a lacy nightgown for our honeymoon. For my birthday in December David had bought me a string of real, graduated pearls that I wore on my wedding day. Sam offered to buy the flowers for me and my bridesmaids, but the corsages were all courtesy of David's dad's greenhouse, and his family put them together. Bill, a family friend, had a taxi service and he offered to drive Sam and me to the church.

Our wedding day finally arrived, and guess what? When I woke, it was snowing. I will remind you that this was April and we were in England. This was not at all how April was supposed to be! That morning I rose early to go to church for a private communion service, and Lynette came with me. Then it was home for breakfast and trying not to continually look at the clock to see if it was time to put on my wedding dress. My hair was long and I wore it up in a French pleat, doing it myself, so there was no hairdresser's appointment to go to. All in all I think weddings were just much simpler back then. David and I received beautiful gifts but people did not go to the extremes that are the norm today. Our gift from Lynette and Sam was a fabulous canteen of cutlery. It was stainless steel made by Old Hall of Sheffield and came in an elegant, redlined box made of oak. They had asked if this is what we would like and we were given the choice of stainless steel or silver. Remembering the many hours I spent polishing my mother's silver, I did not hesitate to choose stainless steel. It was (and still is) simple and elegant.

Dear reader, at this point I feel I must stop and explain to you how confused I was at this point in my life. Not about marrying David, but just my day-to-day life. Lynette could be so kind and caring and really put a great amount of effort into things on my behalf (e.g., our engagement party), but I just never knew when her mood would change. By now Sam pretty much stayed in the background and did as he was told. One day she suddenly announced in front of everyone, including guests, that her two boys were the main love of her life and that she would choose them over Sam. Also, I must explain that when I am writing about these different seasons in my life, it is as if I am reliving them, and I find myself being pulled into the feelings and emotions I had at that time. I despise some of the bitterness and anger I have felt and hope that by writing this account of my life I can shed some of my demons and view the actions of Lynette and Sam in a more forgiving way. Anyway, enough of this introspection—I have a wedding to attend!

Finally it was time for me to change into my wedding dress and fix my hair and makeup. My veil was attached to a pillbox headdress made of French lace, which gave me a bit of height. The flowers in my bouquet were delicate and beautiful. All were spring flowers, but it was predominantly made up of fragrant freesias. My shoes were made of white leather, with an insert of lace at the toe, and a small heel. They were stamped as having been made by the queen's shoemaker, and there is no way I could have afforded to buy them. One day when I was at work, one of our very wealthy customers came in. She knew I was getting married and asked if I would like to have the shoes she had brought in for me. They were brand new and fit like a glove. Such generosity was overwhelming, but that's just the kind of person she was—kind and thoughtful. How could I be so lucky?

Next the taxi arrived bedecked with white satin ribbon, and for the last time as a single woman I left the house where I had lived for the last 19 years. I was not sorry to leave; I just wondered at the circumstances that had turned the happy home I had moved into on my 6th birthday into such a place of pain, anger and sadness. Life has many twists and turns as we progress through the seasons of our souls, and I was hoping my new life would bring me the happiness, love and stability I so badly craved.

I arrived at the church ten minutes late and apparently (as I was told later) David was beginning to become rather anxious. But I arrived, although what I saw when I walked through the door took my breath away. The church was packed so full that extra chairs had needed to be placed in any niche that could accommodate them, as well as down the aisle—and this was not a small church! Another surprise was that the choir had been replaced by David's Cubs and Scouts, all in their uniforms. It was visibly obvious how much the community cared about him. These people were here for him and I was in awe of him for the respect he commanded.

The organ started to play and I walked down the aisle between the throngs of smiling faces to stand next to the man who, within a few minutes, would become my husband. The ring David placed on my finger was another surprise. He had had it made in the goldsmith's quarter in Birmingham and it was a work of art. The 22 carat gold had been fashioned in such a way that it sparkled as if covered in diamonds. It was the work of a craftsman.

After the traditional Church of England ceremony we had to sign the register, and it was at this time that the vicar gave David my passport, in the name of Cynthia Redfern. Walking back down the aisle we were surrounded by a sea of smiling faces. I was so very happy.

We emerged from the church to yet another surprise. David's scouts were all in their uniforms and forming an honour guard as we walked out beneath an archway of flags. By this time it was pouring rain so we were not able to have our pictures taken outside, but instead they were done in the church hall where the caterers were going to be serving our meal. Somehow I managed to get covered in confetti even before the photos were taken, but why not? Everyone was enjoying the happiness of our day and that mattered. The cake my mother-in-law (I could say it now) had made was just a perfect picture, with delicate trellised icing on the corners.

The meal and the merriment over, we went straight to see David's dad. His health and nerves had prevented him from attending the ceremony so we needed to go and show him my dress and such and tell him all about our wedding. On a more mundane note, how does one use the toilet in a big, lace crinoline dress and long, trailing veil? My answer to you is "very carefully." My dress barley fit into the washroom! David's dad was a wonderful man, quiet, gentle, patient and incredibly intelligent. I wish I could have spent more time hearing him explain such things as the intricacies of breeding neon tetras (he was the first person to accomplish this) or telling about all of the butterflies he had studied and were in his copious collection.

For the afternoon we went back to what was now Sam and Lynette's house, where I changed into something more comfortable so we could sit and drink tea while we chatted with my relatives and other guests. It was during this time that Lynette suddenly announced that at the evening buffet she was going to gather all of my family and guests into a big circle with their chairs facing inward. This would effectively separate them from all of the other guests. Why she would do this was totally beyond my comprehension. There was no rationalizing her actions other than to suppose that she just wanted to create tension and bad feeling, and of course she followed through with her plan. The people in the circle all looked a little bewildered and uncomfortable at her actions but went along with it anyway. David and I chose to ignore the strange formation of this group of guests and treat them just like everyone else. As there were about 500 people at the evening buffet, this little circle looked silly and insignificant anyway.

Before going to the evening reception I had changed into my travel clothes, and David and I both had our overnight bags. He had booked a room at a brand new hotel in Birmingham for our wedding night. If I recall correctly it was The Albany. At the reception we spent the evening mingling with everyone there. After all, this was probably the last time we were going to see them as we were moving 3,000 miles away to Ontario, Canada. It was a good evening, though I don't recall David and my finding time to stop and eat any of the buffet. Our plan had been to call a taxi and say all our farewells, but instead of having a big emotional scene we slipped out quietly to the bus stop outside and took the corporation bus to the city. Once in our hotel room we ordered room service—soup and sandwiches—as we were both starving, and after that … well, it was our wedding night. We made love together for the very first time and it was wonderful.

Promptly at nine o'clock the next morning the phone beside our bed rang. Of course it just had to be Sam and Lynette. They rang to let us know they were going away for the day and would not see us. Why oh why did they need to call us on our first morning together? We had not told anyone where we were staying, so they must have guessed or phoned the hotels systematically until they found us (3,000 miles was not going to be far enough away). They probably thought they were getting at me by saying they would be away, but quite frankly I couldn't have cared less. It actually turned out to be an advantage for me.

Once we were up and ready we went back to David's mom's house. She was sitting knitting and it was such a calm and relaxed atmosphere. We sat and talked and had tea—it was so nice to be part of this family. Eventually it would turn out that David's mom would be my mother-in-law for longer than I had my own mother. After lunch we took the Bedford and went back to Lynette and Sam's house to collect the things I wanted to take with me to Canada. It did not take me long to do this. Of course my piano and my few bits of furniture had to stay behind, but at this point I didn't care. I took a last look at the room that had been mine for the last 19 years and then turned and walked away, never to see it again.

Back at David's house my wedding dress proved useful. Taking into consideration the fact that we were going overseas, most of our wedding gifts had been Irish linen (what could be more beautiful?) or other unbreakables. However, David's brother Don, who had been best man at the wedding, gave us a set of smoky glass dessert dishes and large dessert bowl, all patterned in gold leaf. Now this is where my dress came in handy. I put it in the travel trunk and anything breakable was nestled into the layers of silk and lace to be cushioned against impact. In fact this set has withstood the test of time totally intact and as elegant as ever. Just a few weeks ago I passed it on to my middle son Toby and his wife, Tara, as a present for the new home they had just had built. This house is big and elegant, and the dishes will be just right for entertaining some of Toby's high profile contacts (I had better quit this while I am still not ahead)! As a gesture of how I felt, I gave my wedding bouquet to David's mom. She worked so hard, with never an unkind word or grumble, and this was the least I could do.

We were to spend the next two nights at the home of a couple of our friends. They worked with David and we had been out together as a foursome quite a few times. On Monday morning we went into town, as David had a mysterious errand to run at Lewis's Department Store. Once inside he asked me to wait for just a while. I clearly remember a salesperson coming and asking if I needed help and answering that no, I was waiting for my husband. Waiting for my husband! You have no idea how saying those simple words made me feel. I was a married woman and on top of the world. The day passed and David suggested that on the way to Jim and Gil's house that evening we should probably stop in quickly to see Lynette and Sam. They were very sociable but we did not stay too long. Lynette made some off-colour joke about married couples that quite frankly I did not understand. So that was that. Her only parting shot was, "Oh, I thought you would take your bouquet to your dad's grave."

The next morning was Tuesday, April 5, and we went to David's house to put our things into the Bedford and say goodbye to his dad. It was something of an emotional goodbye, but that was understandable. The rest of the family piled into the Bedford and we headed for Bristol, where we were boarding the *Empress of England* of the Cunard Line. At the docks we said our goodbyes and David gave his younger brother Mike the keys to the Bedford. Boarding this huge ship was exciting, and we eagerly went on deck to wave to everyone as the ship pulled out of the dock. We were amazed at how many people had made the journey to Bristol just to see us off. Obviously my husband was very well loved by all who knew him.

Once we pulled away from the dock and headed for open water I discovered what David had been doing at Lewis's the previous day. He turned and fastened something around my neck, which turned out to be a little round St. Christopher, the patron saint of travellers. The medallion was gold and suspended on a dainty gold chain. On the back he'd had it engraved, and it said "Chris R." A new husband, a new life and a new identity. From this point on this was how I was known to everyone. Dear readers, may I introduce you to Chris Redfern? Cynthia Whitehouse no longer existed.

12.

A New Beginning (the Wife and Mother)

*O*ur new life had begun, and what better way than with our honeymoon on the ship en route to Canada. The voyage would take a week, and although we were passenger class for everything else, David had booked us a first-class cabin. What luxury—we had our own porthole window, a lovely bathroom along with a wardrobe, a chest of drawers and a dressing table with a triple mirror for me ... and *two single beds*! Thank goodness we were both slim! Being on this huge vessel was like being in the fanciest hotel. There was a movie theatre, swimming pool, sports facilities and a gym. In the evening there were dances and live entertainment of all kinds, and we made the most of it. We even played Bingo a couple of times. Dinner was a dress-up affair and the food was just out of this world. I have actually saved all the menus from each night as they had interesting designs by Leonardo da Vinci on the cover. They are also a wonderful memento.

In the mornings we would go for breakfast (casual dress) and explore the ship. We loved being up on deck with the wind blowing briskly in our faces. David's mom had knitted us identical cozy sweaters for the trip. David's was beige and mine a pretty salmon pink and we felt very special. His mom was fantastic in that between all of the wedding preparations she found time to do this for us, and what a thoughtful gesture it was. After lunch we would go to our cabin, relax and make love. Later we would have the steward bring us tea and biscuits while we chatted about our plans. I loved getting dressed up for dinner. I had some very pretty dresses, and as they were all handmade they fitted me perfectly. There is one in particular I remember as it turned heads on the evening I wore it. Remember, my waist was only 17 inches. The dress was made of forget-me-not blue raw silk. There was a full skirt and it was fitted at the waist. Then the bodice was fitted and came right up to my neck—very modest—and there were no sleeves. At the back the neckband extended 'round my neck and fastened at the back, but other than this my back was totally bare down to the waist and the full skirt! I can still visualize the scene as I walked between the tables and all heads turned to look at me. I looked good and I knew it.

Partway through the voyage the weather turned. One day folks were sunbathing by the pool and the next day it was snowing. Apparently there was a hurricane, so we had to divert north in order to miss its impact. Nevertheless, we still caught the edge and everyone on board was seasick, including me. Even the doctor had to inject himself before making his rounds to the passengers. He gave me an injection of Gravol. Only six people made it to the dining room that night and David was one of them! The next day I was fine but it was considerably colder on deck. We were now a day behind schedule and the immigration officers came on board the ship at Quebec instead of clearing us at Montreal where we docked.

Our first sight of Canada was from the deck as we sailed up the St. Lawrence Seaway. There were tiny little white-painted churches dotted here and there and the air smelled so different. I must admit that along with my excitement there was a little apprehension about how things would be in this new country of ours. But David and I had decided that no matter what, we would not leave before having been in Canada for two years. One has to get to know a place in order to make an informed decision. As it happened, there was no decision to make as we loved Canada. There were such opportunities here that we would never have had in England.

Now David's Aunt Beryl lived in Canada and had for many years. She was his mother's youngest sister and the youngest in the family (his mother being the eldest), and as their mother had died when Beryl was 8, she was then brought up much like a sister to David. He was very fond of her, but as the years progressed I realized just how much she had used him. In fact, she used everyone she could and left England under a cloud because of the way she cheated her brothers and sisters. But right now she had driven all the way to Montreal to pick us up.

Along for the ride was her husband, Ken, and her tagalong cheering section, Dolores. I quickly learned that Dolores was, and had for many years, been having an affair with Ken. The only thing I remember about the ride home was that I was in the middle of the backseat of the car with the heater turned up full blast. I just about managed to stand it without passing out! I had to remind myself that these folks had driven all the way from

Galt, Ontario, to Montreal in Quebec (a distance of some 500 miles) just to pick us up. For that I should be very grateful.

In her strange way, Beryl was also very attached to David and she was putting us up at her home while we found an apartment and David found work. We were so happy when we finally arrived at the house and had time to relax for a while. David had three cousins: Philip and Tony were late teenagers and had been born in England, and then Beryl Anne, who was about eight or nine. This turned out to be a weirdly dysfunctional family, but it was only over the course of getting to know them that I came to realize this. Beryl was the centre of her own universe and the only way she connected with anything or anyone was in the context of how it affected her or how it was to her benefit.

We quickly found a lovely little apartment we would be able to move into in two weeks. This was just as well because at the end of the first week at her home she turned 'round and asked us for rent money for staying there, and believe me she was definitely wealthy. She owned a big nursing home and was doing very well. We arrived in Canada with very little money, and after demanding a second week's rent, we had just enough to pay for our apartment and buy an old 1957 Ford Fairlane for $200.00. It was a good car with low mileage but typical of the big American cars of that era. It was white and apple green and had huge fins and was built like a tank. David was fortunate enough to get a job right away. The job he had in England did not exist here, but he was also bringing technology that did not exist here. Consequently he had three engineering firms in a kind of bidding war to hire him. Marsland Engineering in Waterloo won out, and he started working for them at $100 per week, which was nothing short of a fortune back then. The company was just half an hour drive away and he started there just as we moved into our own place.

I was so happy in our little apartment. It had a bedroom, small bathroom, living room and a small kitchen and there were laundry facilities in the basement. We furnished it with old furniture from the basement of the nursing home. This was on loan until we could gradually replace items with our own things. David did not want me to go to work right away. He thought that with all the adjustments it would be nice for me to have time at home for myself. This is the kind of thoughtfulness that was typical of David, and this was a very happy time for me. I loved the domesticity and routine of looking after our place, doing the laundry (I even ironed his socks!), and fixing lovely suppers for when he came home. Our apartment was one of four in a big old stone house.

Two of the apartments were occupied by elderly retired ladies, and underneath us were the older couple who were the superintendents. They had never had children and treated David and me like their own. What lovely people they were, and the elderly ladies got quite a kick out of having a tall (six foot two and a half), good-looking young man in the building. In those days I sang all the time and really think it cheered up the old ladies by bringing a bit of youth into the place, because one day I heard them listening to me outside my door. Sadly, my singing was one of the things I would no longer do as our life changed. First I stopped dancing, then I stopped singing and ultimately I stopped laughing. But I am getting a little ahead of myself. These things are a little further into the future and happened under trying circumstances. For now we must get back to the joy of the young married couple.

Although our apartment was small we entertained quite a bit. Beryl would drop in quite frequently for a coffee, plus David had made friends at work who would sometimes come to our home for supper. One gentleman in particular sticks out in my mind. His name was George Cox and he wrote the manuals for the electronic products produced by the company. He was a middle-aged bachelor with impeccable English. When I made wiener schnitzel, he would say, "Madam, Vienna is proud of you," and David was proud of me.

This first year was our time to be playful and have fun. Once I was teasing David and he threatened to pick me up and put me in the shower. Of course I did not believe for one minute that he would. How wrong I was, for in I went giggling and screaming, clothes and all! But it was fun and we laughed and laughed. Another time he walked in the door from work and without a word scooped me up and carried me to the bedroom. Supper was late that night! Then there was the night we had a terrific downpour, but it was summer and very warm, so at ten o'clock at night we were running and jumping in the puddles under the streetlamps as the warm, refreshing rain poured down on us. On the weekends we would lie in bed a little longer and watch the birds and squirrels on the branches of the tree outside our bedroom window—and we would make love. So far I have omitted telling you of the one thing that happened that I had to lock away in my heart, only to be remembered and thought about when I could no longer keep the memory from creeping into my consciousness.

Just four weeks after our wedding, a letter that had been sent to my address in England arrived at our new apartment, having been forwarded to me by Lynette. The letter was addressed to Miss Cynthia Whitehouse and was written in a hand that I instantly recognized and that made my heart pound. It was from John. He must have written the letter at just about the time I was getting married to David. One of the hardest things I have ever had to do was write to tell him that I had just married. I truly, truly loved David, but I also loved John. However, there could be no question as to where my path lay. It had to be with David. Fate had really thrown me a curve ball, although in later years I came to recognize why this had to be. David would need me, and my childhood trials had helped me develop the strength of character that I would need to be all that I needed to be for him. John and I continued to stay in touch by letter maybe three or four times a year, plus a Christmas card, and after about two years he told me of his engagement and impending marriage. Eventually he and his new wife moved to Canada also, but they were in British Columbia on the west coast while we were in Ontario in the east, a difference of 3,000 miles—the same distance from Ontario to Britain.

But let us return to the time when, as a new bride, I received John's letter. Naturally I showed it to David and as there was nothing overt he saw it for what it appeared to be, two old friends staying in touch; and that was that. David and I were very happy and in love and we had a most wonderful summer exploring different places in our old Ford Fairlane. It was a great car with a big, wide front seat where I could tuck my legs up beside me (no seat belts in those days).

Summer turned into fall and fall to winter, our first taste of cold and snow. We spent Christmas with Beryl and her family so we were not without festivities. On Christmas night we stayed over and it must have been the night I became pregnant for the first time (and I thought the Boy Scouts motto was "Be Prepared")! Our joy was short lived as I had a miscarriage in early March, but within a very short time I was pregnant again. This time I recognized the signs of a problem and contacted my doctor in time to avoid a second disappointment.

By now we had moved into a brand new two-bedroom duplex that we were renting, but I had to stay flat on my back for two months in order to keep the baby. Each day before work David would put a cooler beside my bed with my lunch, snacks and drinks. Then he would turn on the television to my favourite channel (no remotes back then) as I was not allowed out of bed. This early intervention worked and on the tenth of January, 1968, we had a healthy baby boy, Richard Martin Redfern, eight-and–a-half pounds and twenty-three inches long. After a long and difficult labour I ended up with a caesarean section as I was so tiny and Richard was, well, rather a big boy. David and I were in heaven and I was able to come home when Richard was two weeks old. What a big help David was. He would change diapers (cloth back then), bathe the baby, fix a meal, just whatever was needed.

However, by the time Richard was 4 weeks old a small, dark cloud appeared on the horizon of our happiness. David had started to experience some rather severe pain in his joints. He was definitely not the kind of person to complain, but this had come on very fast. Although I was extremely concerned I had no way of knowing just how great an effect this would have on the rest of our lives together, or to what extent it would test my love and commitment to David.

After seeing our family doctor he was given an immediate appointment with a rheumatologist at London University Hospital. Here it was confirmed that David had a rapid and severe onset of rheumatoid arthritis. He was started on the drug prednisone and it was predicted that he would be in a wheelchair within 10 years. I was quite shattered by this news, but David just took it in his stride. What an incredible man! His outlook was, "If worrying will do any good, then worry, but if it will not, then why are you worrying?" And that was that.

One more early miscarriage, and by the next January I was pregnant again. The same problems ensued but this time I was only laid up for two to three weeks. My doctor informed me that I would need another caesarean section and that this would have to be my last child. Knowing the date of the next birth, David's mom came a week ahead so she could take care of Richard. She was so good to come all the way from England just to help. On October 8, 1969, we had Catherine Louise Redfern, three weeks early and already seven pounds seven-and-a-half ounces and twenty-one inches long. My doctor had expected her to need a complete blood transfusion but she was healthy and strong. It was me who needed the transfusion and then I had an allergic reaction to it—go figure. Nan (David's mom) stayed for three months and I don't know what I would have done without her. She had already seen Richard when he was eighteen months old.

At that time we took Richard to England, where he was christened by our vicar in the church where we were married. This also gave David's dad a chance to meet his grandson. As it happened, this was just in time, as he passed away shortly after we returned to Canada. Nan took this particularly hard, as in the same year we married, his two other single brothers married. Bob and Pat were already married and had a little boy, Andrew, but were planning to move to New Zealand. Now she was going to be alone. In subsequent years David and I brought her over to Canada to visit with us. She was fantastic with the children and never interfered with what we said to them. She would stay anywhere from three to six months at a time and sometimes even longer. But once again I am getting ahead of myself. When will I ever learn?

David and I were happy in our home with our two adorable children (and whose children are not adorable?). After they were in bed in the evening we would go to the basement and do upholstery for people while listening to plays on the BBC radio station. For my birthday, David had saved up the money to buy me a beautiful coat. However, I was listening to "swap shop" on the local radio station and there was an industrial sewing machine for sale. This was far more practical than the coat, and with it we were able to upholster furniture, make boat covers and sew all kinds of things. Pretty soon word spread around the neighbourhood and everyone wanted their furniture done. This turned out to be quite profitable.

Cathy turned 2 and David and I started thinking about having another child. Even before we were married we had decided we would like to adopt a child. Well, now fate had dictated that this was our only option. To us, it honestly did not make any difference whatsoever, a child is a child. Richard and Cathy were both turning out to be exceptionally bright children (Richard had taught himself to read by the time he was 3, and by the time he was 4 could add and subtract in his head and understood the concept of binary computation), so we decided to adopt a child with a disability. We considered that ours would be a stimulating environment for such a child and therefore to its advantage. Going through the formalities did not take long, and soon we were in the process of "choosing" a child. As we did not have any specific requirements, we were soon presented with the profiles of several baby boys. They did have what was considered a disability—their colour! To say we were shocked to discover that this was considered a problem is an understatement. We based our choice on the child who had been waiting the longest for a home. He was 13 months old. For some reason the agency did not have a picture of him to show us but this did not matter as to us, such things as looks or colour were not part of our priorities.

Soon we were heading up to Toronto to bring home our new baby boy, although it was a possibility he may "make strange," as the saying goes, which would require us going back two or three times. We arrived full of anticipation at the Children's Aid, where we were to meet him. First we were shown into a fairly large room and invited to sit down. After what seemed like an eternity a door at the back of the room opened, and in came a worker carrying Toby. He was the most beautiful looking baby, with soft, curly black hair and a medium-dark complexion. He was wearing a knit outfit in soft baby green that enhanced his big, dark eyes. I could not believe we could be so blessed. The worker brought him over to us, and he immediately held out his little arms to David to be cuddled. This was to be the beginning of a lifelong bond between the two of them that surpassed anything I have ever seen.

Well ,Toby definitely did not make strange, and things looked good for our being able to take him home. It was suggested that David and I go out for some lunch and then come back again. We did this, having so much to say to each other about this beautiful baby and praying we could take him home with us that day. Back at the Children's Aid we went through the same routine again, and once more when they brought him in, Toby came straight to us and sat on my lap. Well, that was that. There was no question of his not coming home with us, so we were given his little snowsuit to put on, along with his toys and his favourite blanket and a bottle. Soon we were on our way home with him cuddled up fast asleep in my arms. He was born on January 11, 1971, so was just three years plus a day younger than Richard.

Before we left that morning we had taken Richard and Cathy to Beryl's house. We knew we would be late getting back so she was going to put them to bed there and we would also sleep there once we arrived. It had been a long day, and by the time we arrived at Beryl's our two eldest were already asleep. Everyone else in the house was wide awake waiting to see the new baby and were taken aback by how beautiful he was. I felt humbled and oh-so-grateful to the mother who had given him up out of pure love, wanting him to have a stable home and the best possible chance in life. She wanted a family who would "help him reach his full potential." What had we done to deserve this incredible gift? All I know is that as soon as he was in our arms, we immediately felt all the love we did for our other two children, and I knew we were a true family.

The next morning Cathy and Richard were wide awake and ready to meet their new baby brother. I can honestly say there was no jealousy or acting out; he was accepted as one of us. The next thing on the agenda was to get him home and see about buying him some clothes. All he had was what he came in. The shopping was a fun thing to do, with Richard and Cathy helping choose things for "their Toby." I also made an appointment for him to be seen by our family doctor, for whom I had the greatest respect. Already David's health had been such that I needed to call Dr. Howson for problems with pneumonia and flare-ups of his arthritis, and he would come the same day and make a house call.

We were quick to realize that the foster home from which Toby came was far from ideal. He had physical, emotional and psychological scars from lack of care, but nothing we could not work on and diminish with caring and love. Until he was 5 years old there was not a single time he did not end up in bed between us in the middle of the night. Fortunately, he was very bright and soon caught up to where he should be with his sounds and walking.

The house we were renting only had two bedrooms, so the three children were sharing a room. I suggested to David that maybe we should buy a house (I should interject here that I had always taken care of our finances), and his first response was wondering how we could afford it, to which I proudly replied that we had enough money in the bank for a down payment. All that reupholstering had paid off! David naturally jumped at the idea and said I should go and look at some houses, narrow them down to three or four and then he would come and take a look at them with me.

I quickly found a brand new semidetached house being built by a private builder that was almost complete. It was perfect for us, and at this point we were able to choose the carpet and kitchen cupboards. It cost us $17,600 with $2,000 down. This was in 1972 when a week's groceries cost about $10. So by early spring we moved into our first home of our own. We had been married just six years and had arrived in Canada with no job, no home, no furniture and $200 in our pocket. Personally I think we had done pretty well as we had no help from anyone.

My family and my home were everything to me, and my time was totally consumed by them. Oh I had friends who, like me, had small children and we would get together during the day and have a coffee while our children played. But once the children were bathed and in bed I would set about putting the house in order and tidying up the toys in the backyard. Heavens, I even swept our drive and the sidewalk in front of our house! Everything had to be perfect. Do you remember my mentioning that as a child I had a tendency to be a little OCD? Well, at this point I think it was in full force. Now I never expected perfection from anyone else, but I certainly expected it of myself. David, on the other hand, lived in the moment and frequently told me I pushed myself too hard. Why was I like this? I have often wondered, but I just know I cannot live with disorder. In order to be happy I needed my small, personal universe to be orderly.

As if to wean me from being too organized I had my precious little boy, Toby, in my life. With him around I could never really take myself too seriously. He was a wonderful, inspiring challenge! We moved into our new home when he was about fifteen to sixteen months, and he progressed rapidly to become an intelligent, inquisitive and very inventive child. We learned quickly that we needed to keep the side of the crib down as he would find a way to get out no matter what we did. So if you can't fight it, join it! By eighteen months he was coming downstairs before anyone was awake and getting into things in the fridge. Now, the refrigerator had a strong, magnetic seal, but we discovered Toby would hold the handle, walk up the wall and then push with his feet and pull with his hands.

Our next step was to put strips of masking tape across the fridge door to stop it opening. Too easy—Toby just got a pair of children's scissors and cut the tape. I have no idea why I didn't think of it earlier, but at bedtime David and I would start leaving a snack and a drink on the kitchen table for him. This worked well with regard to keeping him out of the fridge, but it did not stop him from turning each carpeted step on the stairs into peanut butter sandwiches (with carpet as the bread). Thanks to a knowledgable and inventive husband we were able to remove all the peanut butter. Fortunately we had the foresight to scotch guard our new couch and armchair, as Toby opened one of my carefully bottled jars of red pickled cabbage and spilled the juice on the pale green and cream tweed of the chair. Life was definitely not dull, but please, dear reader, do not be lulled into a false sense of security by thinking his spontaneous nature was somehow miraculously quelled. Oh no, that would be too easy. Before he was 3, there were a few more highly memorable moments.

One morning I got up early as usual to get David off to work. It was absolutely teeming with rain, and as we watched the various cars driving past our house out of our dead end street we realized something was going on. All the drivers were slowing down, peering back down the street and chuckling. The children were all still sleeping, so we slipped on our raincoats to go and take a look. Well, down the road a huge puddle had formed and there, dancing with naked, gay abandon, was Toby. I quickly snatched up a big towel and ran down the street to retrieve my little water nymph. How can one be mad when she cannot keep from laughing?

Whatever would he do next? It did not take us long to find out. This little child had tremendous determination. McDonald's Restaurant had recently migrated to Canada, with one having opened just up on the highway near us. The children loved it and would ask to go to what Toby called "Donald's Land." One particular Saturday we had said we would take them when we had some unexpected company. Of course this delayed things a little. Sitting in the living room with our guests I saw our station wagon backing out of the driveway. My first thought was, *I wonder where David is going.* But just a minute—all the adults were present and accounted for—so who was in the car? Now we were on a busy bend and our driveway was on a slight incline. The next thing I saw was our car sail backward down the drive, across the road and up the opposite curb, miss a fire hydrant by two inches and stop just a foot from our neighbour's bay window. Everyone was running and when we got to the car, there was Toby in the driver's seat with Cathy sitting in the passenger seat crying her eyes out.

Toby just said, "Go Donald's Land." We don't know how he even managed to reach the door handle to get in, let alone put the car in neutral and back it down the driveway. I just thanked God that, being on a bend, they had not been hit. As our future unfolds, dear reader, you will learn just what a remarkable and resourceful man this child became. But for now he is still a little two- to three-year-old.

In 1973 David had to go to Japan for three months for work. He was working on developing the Automated Canadian Postal System, and Japan already had the technology he could adapt to Canada's need. This was an exciting time and I was so happy David was doing so well at his job and getting this opportunity. As far as my being left with the children, this did not bother me one bit. I loved children and enjoyed being with them and doing things with them. During the time we had been in our home we had planned and worked on the backyard to make it enjoyable for our children and all their friends. The garden was long and pie-shaped, and at the bottom it dropped off into a steep little hill. So David built a three-sided concrete wall jutting out from the hill and made it into a great sandbox. Above this was a swing set, and beyond this and closer to the house a good vegetable garden.

My friends and neighbours had told me all the children in the neighbourhood would ruin it, but I solved that problem. When I planted the seeds I got them all to come and help, explaining to them that these little seeds would grow into good things to eat, and that when they were ready we would pick some tomatoes and peas etc. for them to take home to their mommies. Well, these little preschoolers watched with interest as "their" seeds grew, and they helped water and nurture them. Between the vegetable garden and the house was the lawn where we had the toys and a small trampoline David had made. There was also a little colourful garbage bin. The rule was that I did not mind who came to play, but once finished he had to pick up his garbage and put it in the bin. Consequent to all this was the fact that my yard was the home base for all the neighbourhood children, and this suited me fine.

With David off to Tokyo I settled into my own rhythm with my days. However, I soon began to realize how much I had let my personality be submerged by David's, to the point where I could not even buy a box of cereal without asking him what I should get. This self-realization came as something of a shock to me and was perhaps the consequence of my having to fight for my existence before I met David. Now I had relaxed and let his strong personality totally take over. If he had not gone away, would I have ever realized? That was a rather scary thought. I remember sitting down one day, thinking about my lost identity and equating myself to a cabbage! Something had to be done. What I did not realize at the time was that throughout our marriage, for reasons beyond our control, I would have to submit to David's will and yet also be the solver of all problems and the family's backbone. I thank God I had the health and strength and tenacity to do this. The thing is I loved David with all my heart and was totally committed to being there for him, no matter what.

Getting back to my "cabbage" stage, I decided there and then to do something about it. I think perhaps I was just so happy to be with David and had slipped quite comfortably into this mindset. Well, no more! First, there was the drainage ditch. Did I not tell you about that? Ah well, you see, the downspout at the back of our house produced some flooding on the lawn when it rained, but my brilliant, inventive husband had a solution. He would dig a trench from the downspout out several yards, with it being on about a 45-degree incline away from the house. Under and around it he would lay a bed of gravel and then attach an extension to the downspout and run it down the trench. He had bought a pickaxe and had just started the project when he went away. *Aha,* thought I, *I will dig the trench.* Once the children were in bed and asleep I would go into the yard and start swinging the pickaxe. With my newfound determination I completed the project and felt really good about having done it. That was when one of Richard's little friends asked him, "Does your daddy allow your mommy to play with his pickaxe?" Talk about gender discrimination ... out of the mouths of babes!

David arrived home bringing us all kinds of unique gifts. Richard had a wooden Samurai sword, complete with sheath and Cathy was thrilled with a pair of red and gold kimono shoes. I can't for the life of me remember what Toby's gift was, but mine was a black, silk kimono lined with white silk, and the back was embroidered from top to bottom with a golden dragon. It is so beautiful, and yes, I still have it. Of course there were many other gifts, including a Japanese tea set for me and an ornate tin containing wafer thin, dried seaweed. Each time we opened the lid our big, orange cat would appear like magic to beg for some. Umm, yummy. As soon as there was an opportunity, I sat down with David to discuss my "cabbage" revelation, the result being that he came home with a book for me called *The Sky's the Limit* by Dr. Wayne Dyer. It discussed being controlled by external influences, and I gained a great deal of insight by reading it. Ever afterward David would joke with people, saying, "I never should have bought her that book." The cabbage was well and truly gone—banished, buried—and Chris had triumphantly re-emerged.

We lived in our first home until Richard was almost six-and-a-half years old. He had started kindergarten in September 1973 and the teachers quickly found out that he already knew how to read, do simple math and everything else that would normally not be taught until Grade One. We were told he needed to be constantly challenged. He would be shown something new, be able to do it without a problem and then be asking what was next. He was a bright boy, but like me a little OCD. Even at 3 years old his dresser drawers were perfectly in order and he never broke any of his toys. After he had played with them they were carefully put away.

In the spring of 1974 David and I decided to move to the country. The cornfield that had been across from us when we moved in was now a subdivision, and the neighbourhood was getting a little rough. Now, even in broad daylight, one ran the risk of the children's bikes getting stolen—not a good environment for young minds. Well, we started looking and finally settled on buying 20 acres and an old farmhouse south of Mount Forest, Ontario. We listed our house for sale and got $29,000 for it, a good return for the short time we had been there, and we bought the old farmhouse with the land for $28,000. That summer we moved back to the land.

13.

Back to the Land (the Would-Be Farmer)

*P*rior to moving to the farm, David and I bought a 19-foot travel trailer that we planned to live in while doing the basic renovations to the farmhouse. It had everything we needed, including a furnace and a bathroom with a toilet, sink and shower. I made some new, pretty curtains to freshen it up and cleaned it thoroughly.

The week before our big move it was taken out to the farm in readiness for our arrival and was positioned some 20 to 30 yards from the house. Now, the farmhouse had not been lived in for at least 50 years as far as anyone could remember, but the roof had been kept in good shape and the house was constructed of triple brick, with the brick being the hard, yellow kind that did not crumble and deteriorate like the red brick. Consequently the house was dry and structurally very sound. It had been built by an Irish immigrant named Johnson Shaw, who had pioneered and cleared the land, living and raising his family on this 100-acre concession. When he, died the house was left to his son, Robert Shaw, but he never took up residency there. Eventually the house and land were incorporated into the 100-acre farm next door, so now there was a 200-acre farm with two houses and barns. The one house (ours) was left empty until the farmer next door decided to separate the house and 20 acres and sell it. Later we found that our old house was marked on the map in the Wellington County Museum.

At the time we sold our brand new house in town and moved to the country, our friends were doing exactly the opposite. They were moving into bigger, fancier houses in new subdivisions that required both husband and wife to work in order to make ends meet. They all thought David and I were more than a little crazy (and perhaps we were) to be moving out into the country, let alone buying an old farmhouse and living in a trailer for three months with three young children, a cat and a golden retriever named Honey. But we were not concerned about luxuries—we had a dream for ourselves and our children, one that had the benefit of my being able to be a stay-at-home mom and exposed the children to nature and the simpler things in life. The subsequent years proved that we had definitely made the right decision. All the children had a strong set of core values and a respect for nature, and each benefited in different ways due to the fact that with the space and the freedom from consumerism they could develop their natural talents and grow in their own direction.

Moving day finally arrived, and with the help of friends we loaded up the truck with our belongings and said goodbye to city life. Our friends came along in their vehicles to help us unload at the other end. Truthfully, I think they just could not wait to see just where and how we were going to be living. David and

I were excited; no trepidation on our part. We were ready to overcome whatever challenges we might meet. We realized we had years of work ahead of us, but that did not bother us at all, and between the two of us we optimistically referred to our farm as "Camelot Acres." The journey north took about two hours. We eventually left the major highways behind and travelled north up Highway Six, a twisty, turny road that was rather on the narrow side. After passing through the farming town of Arthur we continued for another seven miles until we reached the tiny village of Kenilworth. Here we made a left turn down a gravel road to the first concession, where we made a right turn onto a lesser gravel road. Ours was the second farm on the left. We went through the gate and up the more than a quarter of a mile driveway and we were home. To me that boarded-up old farmhouse with our lovely little trailer beside it under the apple trees was the most beautiful sight in the world. I looked at that old house and saw what it could be, and then I looked at the fields and the little stream with its marsh marigolds golden in the sun, and I saw the beauty that was already there. How could we be so lucky!

Attached to the back of the house was the old, wooden summer kitchen, and this was where we stored all our belongings—perfect. But before we unloaded our things, I complied with the English tradition that we had brought with us from our homeland, by going into my pretty, neat trailer and making everyone a cup of tea. I was home. The children were ecstatic. They could run and play with no fear of danger and busily explored their new environment. Our wonderful friends helped us unload and stack our things and then we all sat down to eat and relax. Having lived in town with the noise of cars and buses there was a calming peace to the silence of the countryside. Certainly there were some noises. There was the trickling of the water in the little stream, the song of the birds, the mooing of the cows in the neighbours pasture and best of all, the laughter of the children. Somehow, our friends seemed as much at peace as we were and oddly reluctant to leave to go back to the city, and somehow I knew we would be seeing them frequently.

Evening descended and the children were showered and tucked into bed, with Honey and our big, old cat Sandy curled up near them. David and I sat at the table with some tea and toast and talked about the day. We were happy. The next day we would start our assessment of what we would need to do first, but for now this was our time and we sat and drank in the peace and tranquility of the rural twilight. Up in the back 40 we heard the bush wolves howling to welcome the night. They were shy creatures and no threat to anyone, preferring to stay away from people. Soon we were also tucked in and asleep. It had been a long day.

On our first morning as "country folk," we did not rise with the sun. After the busyness of the previous day we woke at our leisure and took our time to cook breakfast and chat. It was Sunday, but David was off work for the next two weeks as it was his summer holiday, so we did not have to rush to get things started right that minute. Of course the children could not wait to finish eating and go outside and were soon running around the apple trees with Honey romping after them. At this time Richard was 6, Cathy 4 and Toby 3. Even so, we did not have to worry about them as our laneway down to the road was more than a quarter mile long and the roadway rarely had any traffic, and most of that was the horse-and-buggy kind used by our many old order Mennonite neighbours.

Eventually we strolled over to the old farmhouse that our dreams were going to turn into our home. This dwelling had never had hydro, running water or a furnace, with the only heat being from the pipes that ran from the big old cook stove up through the bedrooms where they emanated warmth. Actually, the lack of facilities was an advantage to us as there was no old wiring or plumbing to remove before starting to install the new utilities, which would be up to code. We were also lucky in that before we moved we were able to purchase a really good, modern second-hand oil furnace from someone who was changing to gas. We decided we would take a photo of each room as it was when we first saw it and keep a photographic record of our progress over time. There was something about this old farmhouse, an indefinable feeling that I had come home. The atmosphere was warm and welcoming inside this old structure, and for some reason I felt very much at peace. When I placed my hands on the big, round, carved knobs at the top of the banisters I somehow felt a warmth and connection through the ages, but this had the feeling of being more a connection to the house rather than the people who had originally lived here. I kept these thoughts to myself as my dear husband, ever practical, would have thought I was romanticizing and imagining all of this. To sum it up, I felt safe here.

The layout of the house was simple. Half the downstairs was the big, old farmhouse kitchen, and the other half was a parlour and a smaller room. The backdoor was centred in the back wall and was opposite the door to the basement. Likewise, the front door was opposite the stairs going up to the bedrooms, these stairs being in the centre of the dwelling.

Upstairs were four bedrooms of equal size, but what I really loved was the old landing that went 'round all four sides of the stairwell with banisters on three sides. Also, the stairs reached the landing at the back of the house, but at the front was a gable underneath which was a beautiful, arched window. It was not large but it almost reached floor level. Eventually I was to place an old, wooden rocking chair on a rug by this window, and on this chair I place a handmade wool throw. This little space was my retreat when I wanted a quiet place to read or knit, and through the window I could see the fields and the whole length of the laneway.

Now to the basement. It was typical of an authentic Ontario farmhouse. The rocks forming the solid walls were large and rough; the beams were big and solid and 20 feet long. Half the floor was concrete and the rest was dirt. At each end of the room was a small window. Primitive was the only way to describe the hybrid ladder/stairs descending to the basement, so this was the first thing to be replaced by a nice new set of sturdy stairs that David built.

Soon we had a list of the things we needed to do before we could move into the house with the basic necessities, having a time frame so we could be in before winter. We needed new windows and had them custom-made in the same style as the original, except they had screens and were double glazed. We needed plumbing. This was easy to do with the new style plastic pipe that just had to be glued together. We also needed electricity. Once again, David was an electronics engineer, and with a code book was able to do all of this himself and have the inspector pass it without any problems. But before we could do any of this we all got to work together tearing out the old lathe and plaster walls. Halfway up the kitchen walls was one-inch thick red oak tongue and groove wainscoting. I would have liked to have kept this, but as David pointed out, we would never get rid of the old musty smell unless all the walls came down. So we completely gutted the interior. This turned out to be the right thing to do as once the plaster was removed, we found dead flies six inches deep inside the walls. Yuck! Now came the fun part—reconstructing our home the way we wanted it to be. Once David was back to work our time was more limited, so we completely closed off the upstairs for the winter and concentrated on the first floor. David installed all the new downstairs windows (we were never short of help as our friends loved to come up on the weekends and lend a hand), and then we put fibreglass insulation between the joists and covered this with a vapour barrier.

Soon we had everything ready for moving into the first floor of our home. We had turned the smaller room into a double bathroom and for now the erstwhile parlour became the bedroom, with all of the mattresses placed on the floor dormitory style. One end of the big kitchen became our living room and the other end fulfilled its legitimate function as a still sizeable kitchen.

The one thing we hired a contractor for was installing the furnace and the heating ducts. When he cut into the kitchen floor we had a huge surprise. The wooden floorboards were in need of a good cleaning and refinishing, but when we saw the pristine wood that had been exposed, we discovered the kitchen floor was made up of alternating boards of cherry wood and white maple. Such contrasting colours were quite dramatic and very beautiful.

You know, I must stop doing this! Once again I have become so caught up in describing our exodus from the city and the features of our new (or should I say old?—it was built in 1860) farmhouse that I have not told you about our life in the country, so please bear with me, dear reader, and forgive an old lady for getting lost in her reminiscences. Now I must get on with my story.

Summer had turned to fall, and in September (we were still in the trailer at this time) Richard and Cathy started school. Richard had already done kindergarten and was going on to

Grade One, whereas Cathy (not quite five) was going to school for the first time. She would be going every other day rather than half days because of the need to go by school bus. Kenilworth School proved to be excellent. It went from kindergarten to Grade Six and had only 150 students—what an advantage over the city schools. Another added bonus was that the teachers were, on the whole, more old-school in their teaching methods and the children definitely benefited from this. Unfortunately, the only exception was the kindergarten teacher. She was young but rather strange. Later we found that she had talked to the children about hellfire and brimstone. Her run-in with Cathy came very early on when she asked Cathy to come to the front of the class and count to ten. Cathy was very shy and just stood there, so her teacher told her, "Little girls who don't count to ten do not do well in my class." That was enough for Cathy's stubborn streak. She absolutely refused to speak to her teacher for the rest of the term. It was reported to the principal by her teacher that she considered her to be developmentally challenged, so the principal would make a point of doing yard duty and would casually engage Cathy in conversation. What he found was that she could count well into the hundreds, could read and write and was in fact way ahead of the other children. She just plain refused to communicate with her teacher. Incidentally, said teacher was institutionalized shortly afterward.

Richard, on the other hand, had a teacher who recognized his abilities and arranged for him to take math with the Grade Two class. At the end of the year he went straight from Grade One to Grade Three, skipping Grade Two altogether. After the Christmas break, it was back to a teacher who had been given new insight into her "retarded" student's abilities, Cathy actually decided to open up to her. From here on it was all smooth sailing with my offspring loving school and everything they were being taught. On the first day at this new school I had dressed Richard in neat, clean but ordinary clothes, only to have the other kids ask him, "Why are you all duded up"? From then on it was flannel-lined cords or jeans and a plaid flannel shirt! We were country folk, don't you know.

By the time the snows came in October we were snugly tucked into our farmhouse. With the upstairs sealed off until we could work on it in spring we were warm, happy and cozy. This was "snow belt" country, so I made sure our cupboards and freezer were well stocked against the times we would be snowed in. How was I to now that within six years our contentment, home and way of life would change within the space of one week? (More on that later.)

No one knows what twists and turns life's path holds for them, but I think I can pinpoint this as being the start of my roller-coaster ride through life—my merry-go-round going ever faster with no way off. I truly believe it was our heavenly Father's plan that I should marry David. The following years proved that I had the strength, love and commitment to get us through whatever trials came our way.

During all this time John and I stayed in touch through letters, maybe two or three a year, and Christmas cards. We were both proud parents telling about our lives and the achievements of our children. Then there were the photographs of our children that we would exchange. By now we had moved on to a whole different level of friendship. John had his life with his lovely wife, Jean, and their children and I had mine, and we each respected this. Our paths had been set. But they were very different paths. Jean and John were both doctors and had their own practice in an upscale area of Victoria, British Columbia. David was the chief engineer of his company, and I … well, I guess I was a farmer of sorts.

Once again I am getting ahead of myself here, so let's jump back to that first cozy winter on the farm. We had become friends with various neighbours. Apart from the two or three older, established farmers who had been born on their farms, our neighbours were mostly our age with children of similar ages to ours. These were people who had decided to make farming their living, but with a young family and only 100 acres it was almost impossible to make a viable living. Consequently, they were financially poor. Yet the positive thing about this was that, with this being the case, everyone needed the help and support of each other. Services were exchanged with no fee asked for or expected, and we had a good pool of resources. David dealt with anything electrical, Joe was a former mechanic, Ivan and Gary had both done drywalling, Garnet was a welder and Willard was our experienced farmer.

We had a great little community. Sunday afternoons were for visiting, and it was the norm that if a family was visiting, you did not ask if they were staying for supper, it was a given. No one took advantage of this and we all enjoyed meals at each other's homes. I can honestly say I do not recall quarrels of any kind between our neighbours. The attitude was to pull together for the good of everyone. Not only did we swap services but also garden produce, meat, eggs, baking and clothes our children had outgrown. My newly married young Mennonite neighbour could sometimes be seen bicycling up my driveway in her long dress with a delicious loaf of fresh, home-baked bread for me. If this all sounds idyllic, well it was, but along with this friendship went plenty of hardships and long hours of work. David and I were more fortunate in that he had a very well paying job, so we were not dependent on my future hobby farm for our livelihood.

During that first winter we took our initial step into what might be termed, politely, as being a little eccentric (here one may substitute their own adjective [crazy, soft-hearted, curious … take your pick]—this is where you are allowed to be as inventive as you wish!). David's drive to work took him about one-and-a-quarter hours each way, which could be a challenge in the winter. Thank goodness he was a good driver. When he arrived home I would make him some tea and the children would run to him to have a story while I put the finishing touches on our supper. At this point he was still seeing a rheumatologist at London's University Hospital every six months. This doctor was trying different drugs and/or combinations thereof, but so far nothing was helping other than the prednisone, which he had started taking when he was 27. David's strength of will was incredible and he did not let any of his health problems keep him from fulfilling our plans.

One very cold and snowy winter's evening David arrived home from work with a huge smile on his face. Then, from inside his coat he produced a chicken! No, not the kind you see in the store ready for the oven. This one had feathers and clucked (probably with a mixture of relief at being warm and alarm at the many humans clustering around it). So where did this chicken come from? Apparently David was almost home and driving up Highway Six behind a big truck when he saw this chicken fall out of the back of the truck. Of course, David being David, he was not going to leave it there to freeze, so he picked it up and brought it home. Actually, it was a pullet, larger than a chicken but not yet a fully grown hen. She was so pretty, with black and white feathers. Immediately the children wanted to give her a name and came up with the rather obvious choice of Henrietta.

Ah, I remembered that half the basement had a dirt floor, so the solution was clear. We would get some chicken wire and make her a home on that side of the basement. Easy, right?

The next day being Saturday we accomplished this, but she also needed feed. Of course the place for this was at the feed mill opposite the school in the village. Our whole family trooped rather proudly up the steps of the mill, feeling very countrified, and asked for chicken feed. Now this process became rather more complicated than we had envisioned. After stating our need for chicken feed the mill owner wanted to know how many sacks and when did we want it delivered. We tried to explain that it was just for one chicken, but his concept of an order of chicken feed seemed to block his understanding of the situation. With much gesticulating and explaining, one could see the understanding gradually dawn on his face. He laughed heartily, grabbed a bag and went 'round various sacks, putting in a handful of this and a handful of that. Then with a big grin he gave the bag to the children and said, "Here you go folks; no charge and good luck." It seems we made his day and I am sure the story quickly got around the community and that our reputation (in the nicest way) was sealed. Time would tell that this would be just one of our rather wacky adventures as we became immersed in country living.

Henrietta was apparently happy with her new situation, but when she wanted some company she would fly out of her pen, come up the basement stairs and peck on the door. Somehow it never occurred to us that it was a little bizarre to have a chicken come to visit us in our kitchen. In fact she was just a pet with a bit of an identity issue. So what—we were open-minded. It seemed apropos that she laid her very first egg on the top step of the basement stairs. This event was greeted with excitement by the whole family. We would-be farmers had a chicken and this chicken had produced our first egg. Wow!

In the country life moved with the rhythm of the seasons. Eventually the snows began to melt and the weather turned warmer. Attached to the old summer kitchen at the back of the house was a big shed, and backing on to the side of this there was a long, narrow room that made the perfect hen house. So Henrietta now took up residence there along with a few more fowl we acquired, and we no longer needed to make daily trips to the basement as there was nothing down there except the furnace.

That was, until we had a massive thaw that caused the creek to overflow and wash out part of the driveway. At this point we thought we had better check the basement for flooding. Sure enough, on the concrete was water about to reach the height of the furnace. This was easily remedied by installing a sump pump that took away the water and prevented any future problems. Now for the most amazing part of our little flood. On the dirt side where we had Henrietta's pen, there, in all its glory, was a field of grain about 18 inches high. I had grown a crop! The only problem was that it was almost pure white from lack of sunshine. Well, when our neighbour was getting ready to plant his grain I jokingly boasted that my little crop was already grown! At least this little faux pas gave us a laugh and our neighbours had a good chuckle. They were probably wondering what we were going to do next.

14.

Fulfilling Dreams
(the Farmer and the New Mother)

Spring eased into summer and we were able to unseal our upstairs and start the renovations. Despite his young age, Toby was able to lift a crowbar, which he swung with gusto, taking down the lathe and plaster on a half wall by himself. We decided to let him go to it, which kept him happy and involved. Actually, he accidentally achieved more than we could have imagined. For when he took down the lathe and plaster, plaster so old it was mixed with horse hair, there was another layer of plaster directly on the bricks. In this plaster was a rough drawing of a man's profile, along with some lovely garlands of ivy leaves. All this must have been drawn by the original builders when the plaster was still wet. It also contained the date, 1860. Before closing the wall up once more I added our own names and the date of the renovations. Who knows, sometime in the distant future maybe some person will renovate the house again and discover both Johnson Shaw's and our messages behind the wall.

Richard and Cathy were equally involved with the work as they had chosen their own rooms and were looking forward to them being completed. The work proceeded at the pace of our income. We did not borrow any money and based what supplies we could buy each week on how much money we had to spare. Although it was not unusual for David to come home and find that our neighbour Ivan had come over and put up some drywall if he had a little time to spare. This really helped move things along. Previously, David had completely rewired Ivan's barn as the old wiring was unsafe. People up and down the line just helped each other as a natural part of living. How refreshing this was from anything we had previously encountered in town (especially from David's aunt—any dealings with her always came at a price!). Although people here worked long, hard hours, especially in the summer, there was a natural flow to the work that went with the seasons. Toby had become a little shadow to the farmer next door and followed him everywhere. This man was like a grandfather to the children and assured us that he was happy to have our little fella tag along with him. He showed Toby so many things while ensuring he was safe.

So summer progressed into fall and fall into winter, and by that time our bedrooms were finished and drywalled. We had also installed the new upstairs windows, with the only surviving original window being the arched one on the landing. David and I had a dream that one day we would turn this into a stained-glass window that we would make ourselves. Unfortunately, life had other, crueller plans for us, and this was not to be. But for now our home was all insulated and cozy against the winter storms.

In our area the elevation was higher than the surrounding land so we were always about four or five degrees colder. The words "snow belt" were definitely an understatement as the snow level was almost to the top of the children's swing set and halfway up the apple trees. Sometimes the school buses were cancelled because of the amount of snow, and on those days we called an impromptu holiday in which we did only fun things. We made homemade doughnuts and potato chips, had a picnic on a cloth laid out on the living room floor and built a snow house where we took our single jet propane stand and heated a big saucepan full of soup for our lunch, which of course we ate in the snow house. Our environment presented the opportunity to do so many interesting things with the children, and now they are relating these stories to their own offspring. Oh yes, I am blessed with six wonderful grandchildren.

At the beginning of February, David and I decided we were ready to adopt another baby. Naturally we talked to Richard, Cathy and Toby about this. Toby was a bit young to really give input but nevertheless liked the idea. Cathy was thrilled and said she would like a baby sister. Richard liked the plan but said he would still like to be the oldest, so we assured him we would respect his sense of place as the eldest. The next step was to call the Children's Aid with our request, so they arranged to send a worker to do a home update study. This was because we had moved since adopting Toby. Perhaps this is a good time to mention the baby pig that had been given to us. You are probably wondering, "What has a baby pig got to do with adopting a baby?" All I can say is, "Don't forget Toby!"

Ivan and June, our neighbours across the road had a sow that gave birth to a litter of piglets, but she went berserk and killed all but one. Consequently, Ivan came walking up our laneway with a bucket filled with straw—and one tiny baby piglet he gave to us. It had never been fed by its mother so the chances of it surviving were not good. My maternal instincts kicked in and I fed the little thing every two hours, day and night, with ordinary evaporated milk halved with water. It slept in a box in the bathroom under a heat lamp, and wonder of wonders, it not only survived but thrived. Little pigs are very clean and smart and this one was paper-trained by the time it was three days old. We decided to call him Wellington after The Iron Duke. I was so thrilled—my little pig had survived while under my inexperienced care and now I had not only chickens but a pig to boot! I was well on my way to becoming a farmer. Wellington's only problem was that he thought I was his mother, so he followed me everywhere and always liked to have his nose touching the back of my leg.

Finally it was Tuesday, the big day when the social worker was coming to meet us and see our home. Wellington was relegated to the bathroom and everyone was warned not to mention him or let him out. Well, it did not seem to me the social worker would consider it particularly normal to have a pig the size of a kitten wandering around the house. Better safe than sorry. This lady was a young professional and *very* well dressed. Once settled on the couch, we all chatted about our family. She told us that there were no babies available for adoption and that the youngest we could get would be a 7-year-old, and there was a three-year waiting list. David and I agreed that was fine and said to put us on the list. During our conversation I had been watching Toby closely. He just had that look in his eye and was skirting around the edge of the room.

He was obviously impervious to my silent, maternal glares as the next moment he ran to the bathroom and threw open the door. Oh what a commotion! Out comes little Wellington going at full tilt with his little tippytoes skittering on the kitchen tile. Next he makes one big leap right onto the social worker's lap. David goes to grab the pig; the children are laughing hysterically and I just threw my arms up in despair. The poor worker was saying, "Oh, oh" as she grabbed Wellington's warm, writhing little body in her hands. Then the most amazing thing happened. She fell totally in love with my little piglet, and her "Ohs" turns to "Oohs" as she delightedly said, "How many children would you like?" And that was that. We were approved on the spot. After she left we breathed a sigh of relief and accepted the fact that we were going to have a very long wait for our next child.

Two days later it was a very normal Thursday (well, as normal as it got in our household) with Richard and Cathy in school and Toby helping me in the kitchen. The phone rang and a lady's voice asked if I was Mrs. Redfern. She told me she was an administrator with the Children's Aid and would I like a 3-month-old baby girl. To say I was taken aback is an understatement. All of a sudden, seven years had become two days and magically a baby had appeared. She explained that the baby was biracial but understood that I already had an adopted biracial son. Of course I was overjoyed and asked when she would be available, only to be told, "As soon as you can get here." I asked where "here" was and it turned out to be Halifax, Nova Scotia! Well, I said I would call her right back after calling my husband at work. David was thrilled but said the decision was mine because, "Well, love, you're the one who will be doing all the work." David booked our flight out for Saturday, two days hence, and the return flight for Sunday. He also booked a hotel. I called the administrator back with all the details and she arranged for the baby to be brought to the hotel when we arrived. I was in a total fog. But what was I going to do for baby stuff? I had already given away all I had. When I called our friends and neighbours to tell them the good news, they were really happy for us, and June and Ivan offered to watch the other children while we were gone.

Saturday arrived and off we went to bring home our baby daughter. The journey seemed to take forever, but at last we touched down in Halifax. It was grey and overcast, with a strong, cold wind blowing off the water. This made it icy underfoot. When we arrived at the hotel there were two ladies in the lobby, one of whom was holding a beautiful, tiny baby girl. Oh, she was so perfect and adorable. She had big, dark eyes and a little, round face. She had lots of wispy, curly hair, and more than anything she reminded me of a little bird. Apparently the ladies had travelled for two and a half hours to get to Halifax, so perhaps this was why things happened so quickly.

One asked, "Mr. And Mrs. Redfern?" When we said we were the baby was thrust into my arms. They did not ask for ID or for us to sign anything, which quite frankly amazed me as we were taking this little child out of Province. We chatted for a short while and were given her little suitcase, bottle and formula, and that was that. I asked them how I came to have a 3-month-old baby in just two days after being told there were none.

Her answer was, "My dear, there are hundreds of babies like her here, but the whites don't want them because they are half black and the blacks don't want them because they are half white."

What a strange world! With this we were left alone with our new baby. We had decided to call her Susan Leslie Redfern, Leslie after David's father (Harry Lesley Redfern). My maternal instincts immediately kicked in, and from the minute she was placed in my arms she was mine.

Susan was such a good baby. That night she slept peacefully

in a little fold-up carry cot a neighbour had given us for her. Her pretty little suitcase was packed with all her things, including new undershirts, sleepers, diapers and some spare soothers (her favourite kind). What a difference to how Toby came with just what he was wearing. This foster mother had obviously gone all out to make sure Susan had everything she could possibly need.

The next day we headed back home to Ontario with our precious little bundle. We could not believe how good she was. Even being on the plane did not bother her and she slept most of the time. Once back at the farm the other children could not wait to see their new baby sister, and Richard (who was now 8 years old) felt very much the big brother when he was able to hold her. David and I also had a big surprise when we returned home. In our short absence the neighbours had all gathered and provided us with everything we could possibly need. We had a high chair, stroller, a crib with all the bedding and several big bags full of clothing. In fact, the person who gave us the crib was a neighbour's relative who drove 50 miles to bring it for us, and this was someone we did not even know. How grateful we were. All this was organized in such a short time. Of course all of our neighbours could not wait to drop in and see our baby girl.

Susan was such a good little sleeper and rarely cried, and then it was just a soft little cry and she was quickly satisfied with her bottle and some cuddle time. After a couple of days I became a little suspicious of how well she slept, even when others were running around her carry cot whooping and hollering. I mentioned this to David and we tried attracting her attention with various sounds—no response! Finally I sat Susan on my knee facing one way while David slammed two saucepan lids together behind her head. Again no response—Susan could not hear a thing.

Immediately we contacted our family doctor and took Susan to see him. He slammed the metal doors of his examining table shut and she did not even blink. He confirmed what we already knew; Susan was deaf. Fortunately we were able to get an appointment with a specialist in Guelph within a couple of days. We also informed the Children's Aid, who immediately thought we would send her right back to them. Well, they were wrong! She was our daughter and we loved her no matter what. The specialist confirmed that she could not hear even at 90 decibels, the highest they tested, so we were sent to the hearing clinic at the Hospital for Sick Children in Toronto. They told us deafness was the most frustrating disability to deal with and suggested we would be better off not keeping her. David and I were astounded. This was our child and there was no question of "sending her back." She was not a commodity to be returned under warranty! It was then explained to us that she would have to start school at 3 years old and attend the School for the Deaf in Milton, not far from Toronto. So when the time came we would move. Meanwhile, the specialists wanted to see her every three months.

At the six-month and nine-month checkups the results were the same, even though at eight months she said her first word: "Mom." You see, whenever we talked to Susan we looked at her full in the face and mouthed the words to her. I believe she copied the shape of my mouth and the appropriate sound followed. I was overjoyed. Susan was tested again at 11 months and lo and behold, she had started to respond to sound. Pretty soon her hearing was above average—and they'd wanted us to "send her back." Apparently her ears had not finished developing at birth, and we were told this condition was more common than people realized. Inexperienced parents could have such a child who eventually hears, without ever knowing there had even been a problem. So life settled back to normal at the farm. At least it was normal by our standards. Susan had grown to be a beautiful little girl with big, dark eyes and a mass of very curly hair.

Life on the farm was never dull. The same year we had Susan, David drew up the blueprints for us to build a barn. Wellington (you remember my little piglet, Wellington?) was now too big for the house so temporarily slept in the old back shed. During the day he liked to just follow me around—after all, I was his mom. Oh dear, that does sound rather strange, doesn't it? That summer we also bought a Toggenberg goat named Gloria. She was an absolute sweetheart and her milk was very good for Richard, who had the odd bout of asthma. Nothing too serious, but the goat's milk helped. So now we had chickens, a pig, a goat, three rabbits (that David's aunt gave to Richard, Cathy and Toby at Easter) plus two dogs and assorted cats. After my success with Wellington I seemed to have a steady flow of piglets from various neighbours, and I must say I had a pretty good survival rate. We were able to finance the materials for building the barn by selling our trailer.

David and I did the building ourselves, and I must admit it was a good barn. Of course our neighbours all had a much-appreciated habit of showing up to help when they had some time, even if David was at work, so there was no shortage of labour. This was probably as well, because although he continued to keep busy with projects, David's health was rapidly getting worse. He was still seeing a rheumatologist who prescribed various medications, none of which worked at all. The only thing that helped was the prednisone. Consequently, one thing we contracted out was the laying of the 12-inch concrete blocks for the main walls, and even then my neighbour, June, and I mixed the concrete.

This was a busy year for us, what with building the barn, adding Susan to our family and looking after our ever-growing population of farm animals. We also had our first experience with haying when we baled the hay in our top field ready for the winter. Of course, my first time on the back of the wagon stacking bales, I, in my naiveté about all things country, went out in a short-sleeved shirt. Oh boy did I learn my lesson. By the end of the day my arms were covered in scratches from the prickly hay. But we got the job done (David drove the tractor) and got it all stacked and ready to go into the hay loft once the barn was completed. Toby was going to be starting school in the fall, attending every other day, and then I would just have Susan at home. I secretly hoped the teacher would survive Toby.

We also had another addition that year. Since Cathy was 2 she had been asking for a pony. Now, if you knew Cathy, you would also know that she is a persistent person. So, finally we considered her old enough and surprised her with a little black pony that was pretty much as wide as she was long. Cathy was totally enraptured with her and soon proved that where horses were concerned, she could do anything. The pony's name was Little Black Angel, Angel for short. From that day on Cathy was never without a horse. She is now 41 and breeds Clydesdales, as well as goes on treks through the Alberta Rockies on her ranch horse (she rides western style). She rides Ruby ("Wild Rose Ruby Rose"), her first Clydesdale, English style and has even entered Ruby in English riding class at the Calgary Stampede, coming in third in her class. At that point she had only been riding young Ruby for five weeks. Wow! Goodness, I am really rambling on ahead of myself here. Pretty soon I will have a book with the end in the middle and the middle at the end—or something like that.

The summer progressed. Toby dug lots of big bear traps under the apple tree with his Tonka toys and other than this did not get into too much mischief this particular year, except for finding a can of yellow house paint in the neighbours drive shed and painting Gloria the goat yellow. It must have been her colour because she did not seem to mind. Toggenbergs are supposed to be mostly black, but hey, I am open-minded. The barn could not have been finished at a more appropriate or necessary time. As we put the last nails in the roof the first snowflakes began to fall, and our animals all stood looking at us somewhat accusingly as, I am sure, they felt we should have timed things a little better. This was too close a call for them. Well, we were able to open the doors and they were all ushered in to their nice, new stalls. I felt a little bit like Noah at that point, getting the animals safely out of the elements.

Winter came and went; the children were all doing well at school; David was still driving to work every day and I was becoming more of a farmer. By this time next year I had more pigs, ducks, a milking cow and some young calves. In the morning after the three older children had gone to school, Susan and I would go to the barn to do chores. I had a new pen with fresh straw where I would put her to play while I cleaned out the animals and fed and watered them. When the older children came home from school they were expected to collect the eggs and give the suppertime feed and water to the animals. These were pretty easy chores as I did all of the major stuff in the morning. Fortunately, they enjoyed this and it taught them responsibility. By now I was providing all of our own meat, vegetables and fruit and made our own butter and baked our own bread, so we were pretty self-sufficient.

Looking back I don't know how I fit all of this into my day but I just loved our life at the farm. Certainly there were some hard times. One particularly harsh winter the water line to the barn froze, so I had to carry two five gallon containers of water from the house, climbing up the snowdrift swirled around the house, across the snow that was level with the branches of the apple trees and down the drift swirled around the barn. I supplemented this with shovelfuls of snow that I melted in the water in the troughs. David was no longer able to do any of the farm work and his hands were becoming more and more deformed. However, he more than made up for this with the fun things he did with the children. He had always been interested in scouting and by now was the district commissioner for Maitland District. At the same time I was district commissioner for Guides. Cathy was in Brownies and somehow I just ended up with this position. When it came to Dave and me going to meetings it was a case of who could get to the calendar first!

One winter night we had a really bad storm with the wind blowing strongly from the east. I decided to check on the animals in the barn before going to bed, only to find the oblong widow high up in Angel's stall had blown in and she had snow on her back. Fortunately the hay wagon was parked along the wall of the barn below this window. So, armed with some thick polythene and a heavy-duty staple gun I climbed up on the wagon and stapled a cover over the window frame. By this time it was eleven fifteen p.m. and the temperature without the wind chill factor was about minus 30 degrees. There was no way David could have done this but that was okay. I was only five foot and about 112 pounds at that time but I was strong and healthy. True partnerships cross all boundaries.

We continued to have zany things happen during our time at the farm but it would take another book to explain them all. Richard tells his daughter, Jenna, our funny farm stories and has suggested I should write a book about them for the grandchildren. Now should that be "Funny" Farm Stories or perhaps "Funny

Farm" Stories! Hmm, I wonder. I will relate a couple of incidents: One—our 450 pound calf had a cough so we talked to the vet, who gave us a needle for him. "What do we do with it?" Dave asked. "Just stick it in his rear," the vet said. So back home we went and got the calf. We figured he wouldn't like it, so David suggested I hold him 'round the neck. Bad move! In went the needle, off went the calf—I hung on 'round his neck and the neighbours had the greatest show in a long time. *Then* they told us how we *should* have done things. At least we city slickers brightened up their lives.

Incident two: Gloria adopted a pet chicken, just a wee little fluffy thing. At night it slept under her chin, all cuddled up to her and during the day sat on her back while she wandered around.

Incident three: I had to write a note to school for Toby explaining that yes, the goat really did eat his homework, and no, this was not just the workings of a fertile imagination trying to cover up for work not handed in.

Incident four: I raised some baby pigs at the same time we had a litter of kittens. I would call, "Here, kitty, kitty," and both the kittens and the little piglets would come running for some milk. Once grown, two Mennonite farmers tried to load two of the pigs onto a truck. Nothing worked. I offered to help and received a disgusted, "No thank you." One hour later I stepped onto the truck. I called, "Here, kitty, kitty." The pigs came running onto the truck, and the farmer threw his hat down in the mud and muttered, "Now I've seen everything!" I got the impression he was not very happy with the pigs or me.

Well, I could go on forever, but, dear reader, perhaps you get the picture, and indeed I will one day put all of these many, many funny stories into a little book.

15.

My Little Business (the Entrepreneur)

When Susan was about two-and–a-half David, the children and I went to visit some friends in Waterloo. Ron and David worked together and I had met Ron's wife, Sharon, many times. She was artistic and always experimenting with something new. This time it was silk screening. I was fascinated with what she showed me and in the space of two hours I had the technique down pat and was dying to try this myself. My idea was to make pretty note cards and such to put in the church sale. Before coming home, Sharon gave me a screen, some ink, a squeegee, film and developer, enough for me to try my hand at silk screening. The first things I made were some fall-themed notelets that turned out really well.

Never in a million years had I envisioned that people would take such an interest in what I was doing, and pretty soon I was being asked if I could print team patches for sewing on jackets.

Next it was T-shirts. At first they were small orders for family reunions and such, but then the orders became larger and for more varied uses. David was very good at design layout (he was, after all, an engineer) but I also did graphics, something I had never done before but found quite easy. The one weak spot was the quality of the shirts that were available, and it did not matter how good the design or printing job was if the quality of the shirt was poor. So I did some thinking. This was dangerous because the problem with this "thinking" thing was that it always ended up with me jumping in where angels feared to tread—feet first!

I found a solution. I went to the mills in Hespeler and investigated the possibility of buying bolts of lacoste fabric at a wholesale price. They were accommodating and explained that they had odd rolls leftover from big orders, and these were in various colours. Or, for a big order I could order a dye lot of several bolts, and I could also get either matching or contrasting trim for the neck and sleeves. Now I was getting really excited; my plan was coming together. Back I went to my farm and told David about my plans. As always he was totally supportive of what I was doing.

Next I came up with a business plan to effect what I wanted to do. The one end of my big, farmhouse kitchen had become my workspace but there was only so much I could do here, so that needed to be addressed. It was satisfying that the whole family was excited by and involved in this process. Cathy came up with the name for the business. She decided on "Grey Mouse Print-Art", a name very much in keeping with the seventies era. Next I applied for a business licence and then put an advertisement in our weekly newspaper for ladies with overlock stitch sewing machines who were interested in sewing T-shirts. The response was fantastic. This was a farming community with a lot of young mothers who had children in school and men in the fields. There was no work available, but to be able to work from home in their own time suited them fine. Naturally I went and interviewed them and explained what I would need. The process would be that first I would phone them and see how many shirts they could take. I would have all the parts of the shirts cut out ready to sew, drop them off at the ladies' homes and then pick them up when they were done, paying so much per shirt. It was a good system for me and provided a small income for the farm wives.

Pretty soon I had a newspaper reporter requesting to interview me, and she did a front page article with photos, which was featured in all of the *Wellington County* weekly newspapers. Now that really opened up the flood gates! My phone started ringing with requests for some really big orders, and I soon found I had a full-time business on my hands. The funny part of all this is that I never considered myself anything but a housewife who was just dabbling for fun, but I guess that was not how other people viewed me. This was especially true of Ernie, a businessman from Listowel who himself was a real go-getter. He owned several bowling alleys and was also involved with the Kinsmen. Every year the Kinsmen sponsored a big St. Patrick's Day parade in the town of Listowel, and so Ernie gave me the order for all of the "Listowel Paddyfest" T-shirts. I ordered a dye lot of green fabric and stocked up on white trim.

The children were ecstatic when the shirts were made and it was time to print them. By this time I also had a supplier for ink and poly-blue film and developer, and just seven miles down the road from where I lived was the Bell Thread Company, where I could order large cones of thread in any colour. Well, the night we did the printing was truly a family affair. As I made my own patterns I was able to accommodate any size, from an infant's size two up to as large as was needed. So as I was printing, the children were running all over the house finding room to lay out the shirts to dry. Our house was a sea of green shirts with a full front design in white. There were even shirts on the stairs! Finally we were done and I was able to clean my screen and equipment, and after a well deserved drink and snack we all went to bed, tired but with a sense of achievement.

By the next morning the shirts were all dry and looked really good … except for some tiny paw prints where our kittens had run across the wet ink. Oh no, now what? Well, kittens weigh very little, so their prints were just sitting on the nap of the fabric. Out came the masking tape and we were able to remove any signs of feline frolicking. We folded the shirts and packed them in boxes, and they were ready for pickup and I was ready for a nice cheque. Over the years Ernie became my best customer, and he was great to deal with. I priced the shirts according to quantity and there was never any haggling; he was always happy with the results and he always paid on pickup. What more could I want? His customers were so happy with the quality of the shirts that one gentleman, who was an overall big person, had me make him six new T-shirts every summer in size XXXL. The choice of colour was left up to me and they were just plain, no printing, but he liked V-necks with no sleeves. Well, everything was custom-made, so why not?

My little business was rapidly growing out of my house and it became obvious that I needed to find some dedicated space. Our little village of Kenilworth was just a cluster of about eight houses, a church, a corner store, a garage, a school, a feed mill, one building that housed the bank (open once a week on Wednesday afternoons) and three or four apartments. It just so happened there was an empty, good-sized ground floor apartment. It had a bathroom, one bedroom, a nice-sized living room, a bright kitchen and a big, closed-in heated sun porch. This was just perfect for my needs so I established what was, for the era, a very progressive cottage industry. The bedroom was the office and design room complete with drafting board, the living room became the cutting and sewing room and the kitchen was where I made up my screens and did the printing. David made some racks for the wall so the T-shirts could be stacked vertically to dry.

This meant some changes for the ladies. I bought an industrial sewing machine and cutter to go with what I already had and the ladies now came to what we called "the shop" to work. However, I let them set their own hours, and the sunroom was turned into a playroom for my Susan and any other children who were not yet at school, or who only went every other day. As they were still paid by the piece, the ladies could stop to tend to their children and were able to go home to fix a midday meal for the men coming in from the fields. Everyone was happy with the flexibility as they could work to earn some money and at the same time take care of their children and commitments at home. I stocked the kitchen with tea, coffee and snacks along with a toaster and a tea kettle so the ladies could get a drink whenever they felt like it. Boy, did the productivity ever go up! Sometimes one or another person might choose to come back in the evening to work if that suited her better. Another positive was that the school was right next door. My children would go to school on the bus in the morning, but after school they walked over next door to me.

The orders just kept on coming. I never once had to advertise. After receiving my manufacturing number I had my own labels made to go into the shirts, and soon after that Ernie was ordering shirts with his own labels but my manufacturing number. By now I had several salespeople ordering from me plus I had my own sales representative on the road. Many orders were pretty big and from well-known sources. There were schools, hotels, the Fergus Highland Games (an annual event), various groups plus a well-known worldwide distributor of cola products, along with a big Toronto brewery whose product label is a household name. Soon I was shipping overseas, and I started all this with just $5.00 out of my pocket.

Just for fun I made some shirts with a silhouette of a big city skyline, and under this I put Beautiful Downtown Kenilworth. This was a big hit with the locals, and soon I was doing Beautiful Downtown Damascus (another dot on the map) plus the same for several other little villages. At Christmastime I made little white pyjamas and nightgowns with red trim and with a big picture of Santa Claus on the front. Along with these went a little white and red nightcap. Well, I could hardly keep up with the orders for these and repeated the product each year. The funny thing was that in my mind I was still a housewife who was fooling around with a hobby.

Meanwhile, David's health continued to decline rapidly, and there were many things he found hard to do, but not for one minute did this stop him from trying. I should also mention that David's mother, or Nan, as the children called her, continued to visit annually, usually staying for several months. She was an absolute blessing and the children adored her. She taught every one of them to swim, and she was a great help to me. She also taught me many things I had not had the opportunity to learn when I was growing up.

I had been working out of the shop for some time when David came home one day and told me his company was moving to Ottawa and he could either move with them or be laid off. Well, there was no way we were moving to Ottawa, but what would we do? David was one of the top engineers in the company and earned good money. He was pretty worn out before he got this news, and looking for another job would be stressful. It is also well know that stress is one of the worst things for arthritis.

That night, after the children were in bed, we talked about our options and came up with a plan that would be a blessing to both of us. To everyone's delight David was going to take a year off and work with me in the shop. No more having to get up so early; no more driving more than an hour each way in all sorts of weather to get to work and back and the added bonus of not having to wear a suit and tie! Our finances would be tighter but we figured we could do it. Of course, if David had applied for his unemployment benefits as he should have things would have been easier. Unfortunately, he was notorious for not doing government paperwork, not even our income taxes. I had to resort to endless prompting (okay, nagging) to get this done. Sometimes it would take me a year and he would just not do it. Part of this was because of his disease, but I know that in part it was a quirk of his nature.

There had been times when he was just totally wrapped up in his little world, and although this did not alter his interaction with the children, at times I felt as if he just did not know I was there. One day Susan said to me, "Mommy, Daddy's name is David, but what is your name?"

That was when it really struck me that he never, ever addressed me by name. He had given me a new name (Chris) by which everyone knew me, but he would not use it to address me. He just launched into a sentence, and when introducing me it was, "This is my wife," period. But he had been taking prednisone since he was 27, and this drug can really mess with a person's perceptions.

Before I moved to the shop there was a day when just Susan and I were home. It was summer and the cows had calved, but the big Charolais cow who led our neighbour's herd seemed to have been usurped by a western beast with big horns. By this time my neighbour and I had come to an agreement that each year he would bale my hay for me and stack it in my hay loft in return for his cows being able to graze on my bottom pasture field, an arrangement that worked very well. He would open up the fence along his side of the laneway to give his cows access to my bottom field. My top field, which contained the barn and house, was fenced all around with a gate onto the laneway.

One day I heard a commotion and came out of the house to find a young calf inside my fence and just about strangling itself by pushing its head through the square hole in the wire fence, trying to reach its mother. What to do? The little thing was in dire straits and the herd outside the fence was getting agitated. Susan was told to stay on the doorstep of the summer kitchen and I went to pull the calf's head out of the wire. The next thing I knew, the western beast burst through my gate and attacked me. I ended up draped up over its head, holding on between its horns while it proceeded to ram me repeatedly into the fence, which had barbed wire along the top. The rest of the herd followed through and all turned on me. For some reason I don't remember feeling any pain from the barbed wire, and I was extremely calm. What I do remember is looking down our long, long laneway and thinking, *So this is how it's going to end.* I did not expect to survive—I was helpless.

Just then my friend Dorothy drove up the driveway with her 16-year-old son. Young John saw what was happening and came and booted the beast in the rear. I dropped to the ground and rolled, cowboy style, under all the hooves and out of harm's way. Dorothy was holding Susan, who was screaming, and John got the cows out of my gate, including the errant calf. My friend took me into the kitchen and made me some tea, but I was pretty badly beaten up.

When David arrived home from work I said to him, "I was almost killed today," and told him of my injuries. His response was, "Oh," and then, "What's for supper, love?" That hurt much more than the bruises and cuts ever could. By rights I should have been taken to the hospital, at least for a tetanus shot, but that was all he said.

For the next three weeks I could hardly move, but he never said another word about what had happened and again seemed totally unaware of my many cuts and bruises and the fact that I could hardly walk. How to explain this? I couldn't, other than to hope it was the result of his medication. All I can say is that his total dismissal of the event stayed with me for a very long time. No matter how I tried to rationalize this away, it still hurts, and perhaps this was the start of my feeling like a non-person.

But the year at the shop went well. An added bonus was that David could volunteer to go on the school trips with the children. He also went into the school and taught a few classes on science experiments. The classes especially liked it when he made ice cream from dry ice and commercial soft ice cream mix! Party time! His design expertise and innovations were a great help with the business, as was his dealing with some of the customers. Best of all, we were together every day for a whole year. This ended when he was actively recruited to be the chief engineer at an electronics company in Stratford. Unfortunately, although this was a good position with an excellent salary, it also meant he was back to driving one hour and fifteen minutes each way, which really started to take an even heavier toll on his health.

The time came for Susan to start school. Her birthday is in November, so she was still not quite five years old. When I went to enrol her I was approaching forty, and it seemed strange to see all these (from my perspective) children enrolling their children. It made me feel a bit like a grandmother.

On Susan's first day of kindergarten, I didn't know what to do with myself. I'd had at least one child at home for the last 13 years, and here I was on my own. It was the most unproductive day I'd ever spent and I was at a total loss as to what to do. As with all things I soon adjusted and began to enjoy my every other day of freedom from motherhood responsibilities.

This was September, and by November David's health had taken a dramatic turn for the worse. We went to see our doctor, who advised us that if he did not cut out the travelling, especially with winter upon us, David would be in a wheelchair by spring. So that was that. We had no alternative but to move close to his job. My friend Dorothy and I drove down to the Stratford area one day to look at the rental properties, with David also checking the market. By the end of the week we had a place within 15 minutes' drive of David's job, so we immediately closed everything up and moved.

It broke my heart to leave our farm after putting in six years of hard work getting it to our liking. It was my dream home and I loved the farm. I closed the shop (the business would be relocated in the big, old farmhouse we had rented), and fortunately, my customers followed me. We had some friends who were boarding their horses in our barn for the winter and we arranged for them to look after Angel and Gloria in return for this when we moved. Our other animals we sold to our neighbours who were happy to buy them, especially my young heifer. Her mother was a big Holstein cow that we had bred Charolais, with the resulting calf being a pale, misty grey all over. What a beauty! She was my pride and joy and I had named her Misty. That farm had so much of my personality imprinted upon it, especially the big, old wooden back doorstep. I had painted the door and step a bright yellow, but in the process the kittens kept running across the wet paint. So I gave in, and using black paint I painted little kitty paw prints running across the step into the house. But this was me—my personality—and I had to leave it all behind. So that was that. We turned down the heat in our farmhouse and left, also leaving behind the many happy memories and our good friends.

16.

A Necessary Move (the Repurposed Wife)

Our new location was about one-and–a-half hours' drive south of our farm, but whereas we left snow and what was already winter, here the grass was still green. I could not believe this short distance could make such a difference in the climate—and they said this was snow belt country. They obviously did not know what a real snow belt was like! The farmhouse we had rented was considerably larger than our own and I would estimate that it had been built in the 1930s. At one time it must have been quite lovely, but time and neglect had taken its toll. Upstairs were four large bedrooms. Richard and Cathy had their own and Sue and Toby shared. At our own place Cathy and Sue had shared and Richard and Toby had their own rooms, so I thought it was time for Cathy to have her own space. Downstairs was a small kitchen for cooking, complete with a dumb waiter that came up from the basement. Then there was a good-sized eating kitchen, a living room with pocket doors to separate it into two rooms and a downstairs bathroom. The one upstairs had never been renovated and was unusable.

From the back veranda one came into a large room where the washer and dryer were kept, and it made a great place for taking off winter boots, etc. Beyond this was yet another room I think must have been used for storing wood. This made a perfect room for Gloria the goat when we transitioned her down here, and Angel was able to go out in the field for a while before going into the rather dilapidated barn. David's mom and Aunty Olive had come from England when we moved and were invaluable in so many ways, either with cooking a meal or watching the kids or just whatever. They also helped me set up my workshop in a closed-off portion of the living room (those pocket doors were very handy) so I could keep the continuity of my business.

By far the most appealing aspect of the property was the land. The front driveway was lined with mature trees and a good-sized front lawn. Beside this was a field leading down to a meandering stream that wound its way through the length of the property. David and I would often walk beside it through what had been an apple orchard. Now the trees were gnarled and had been left to go wild, but the apples were wonderful. Of the many varieties, there was not one that tasted like the produce in the stores, and I believe they were probably heritage varieties. The tastes were strong and distinctive, with some tasting like wine. On a small bluff overlooking the stream we found the remains of what must have been the original house on this land. The children loved digging around for old treasures. Perhaps they felt the same sense of discovery I'd felt as a child when I was digging in the diamond dump.

Although I tried to make this place feel like home, it did not have the welcoming feel of our own farmhouse. It did not have comforting vibes. On our first day there, Richard had an asthma attack and we had to take him to Stratford Hospital. We were seen by a young Dr. Parsons, who advised we would need a family physician and offered his services if we were interested. He was our family doctor for 25 years, and I believe it was meant to be that we met him during an emergency that night. David and I were totally puzzled by this sudden asthma attack, but some years later Richard confided to me that he hated that house.

It was November 24 when the children started school, and this happened to be Susan's 5th birthday. She was not impressed when her teacher wanted to give her birthday spankings on her first day! For their first year in this area the children went to school in Mitchell because of the school boundary lines, so they were all together. After being schooled in Kenilworth they were all way ahead of their classmates. David was able to get to work in about 15 minutes, a big help for him. However, apart from his unchanged attitude toward the children, I found him living more and more in his own little world. He joined the local Scout Group, which was good for him, but like everything else he did he gave it his all. It did not include me. On Sunday morning he liked to listen to a radio music show called "Eclectic Circus"—for three solid hours! This would have been fine if at the same time he had some conversation with me, but he didn't. One Sunday I broached the subject and he flew into a rage, unplugged the radio, took it outside and threw it in the garbage bin. Now this was really extreme and even though I could see it was the medications that were affecting him, it still did not hurt any less. Later I went outside and retrieved it.

David also joined the Freemasons and once again gave it his all. Our evenings evolved into eating supper, my getting cleaned up and putting the children to bed while David was out at one meeting or another. When we first came to Canada I stopped dancing. David would not dance and I would sit at his work parties, sometimes close to tears, watching all the other couples on the dance floor. Dancing had been a big part of my life. By the time we moved to the rented farmhouse I had pretty much stopped singing. In the evenings I felt very much alone.

One evening I sat down alone at the kitchen table crying—I felt so isolated. I had a pencil and paper and within fewer than five minutes wrote the following as all my feelings came tumbling out.

"Dim memories, fragmented thoughts,
A tired soul's weak yearning.
What's done is done, what's passed is passed
But my thoughts keep returning.
Frail circling of dreams half dreamed.
Thwarted by dawn's sure breaking,
Suppressed within the day's demands
Of pushing, striving, taking."

These are some thoughts that arose unbidden in my consciousness, feeling like a raw wound. How had I reached such a bleak, dark place in my life? What had changed so drastically in such a short time? It was not as if there were not lighter, happier periods of time during this season of my life, but I could feel my spontaneity and joy in the moment slowly but surely slipping away. I think I was beginning to feel the start of the weight that was, through the years, to build on my shoulders, and not recognizing this at the time I was fighting against the restructuring of who I was.

Winter turned into summer and by this time the children had established local friendships. It was a quiet, rural area, so the three older ones were free to go off on their bikes and do what children do. Not far from us was a tiny village called Motherwell, and through the village ran the Thames River. The local children would all gather here and paddle under the bridge. There was also a little general store where they could get a treat. Motherwell was in a hollow with the road running steeply out of the village in both directions. On top of the hill and overlooking the village was what had once been the schoolhouse. It was a huge, impressive-looking red brick edifice that some years before had been totally renovated into a house with no expense spared.

As fate (and my innate curiosity) would have it, I was driving past one day and saw a white, official-looking notice on the front door. Of course I had to stop and have a look. Well, the place had been repossessed by Canada Mortgage and Housing and they had it listed for sale. How could I not look into this? After telling David about my find we agreed I should arrange for us to look at it with a realtor. Wow, the place was absolutely fabulous. Originally it had been bought and renovated by the Lancasters, who then sold it to a young couple who lost it when the interest rates hit 22 percent. All CMHC wanted out of it was what was still owed on the property.

David wisely went to City Hall to find out what this was, and then offered about $5,000 less. CMHC accepted our offer and we were able to move in almost right away. What a difference this made to us all. There was so much space (more than 4,000 square feet) and with five bedrooms, each of the children was able to have his and her own room. This was the year Susan was turning six and David and I forty-one. So that was also the summer before Richard turned fourteen, Cathy thirteen and Toby eleven. My goodness, they were all growing up so fast and I don't know where the time went. If any of you dear readers are young mothers, love your babies as much as you can and enjoy this time. Before you know it they will be all grown up and you will miss those early years.

But back to our new house. Are you ready for another tour? On my honour this will be a quick one! Unfortunately there will be no tea or scones at its conclusion; this is Canada. Perhaps a coffee and a doughnut? Anyway, the main level was actually the upper floor as the basement was at ground level. There were two doors at the front, with one leading both upstairs and down to the basement. The other front door was inside an enclosed sun porch, and inside the door was a beautiful, wooden spiral staircase leading right up to the attic level, where there was a lovely room built right under the bell tower (still complete with bell). Partway up was a door that led to the main level. Now this upstairs room was to be Richard's domain. What more could a teenager want? He had his own front door and a "secret" staircase leading straight up (well, actually spiralling) to his room. On the main floor was a bright kitchen, a computer room (as soon as they came out David bought a TRS 80), main bathroom and three good-sized bedrooms. These were for Toby, Susan and David and me. Now for the living room. It was 26 feet by 35 feet and had six chandeliers. It was so beautiful and had a big picture window looking out over the fields and three side windows, outside of which was a mass of tall lilac bushes.

Everything except the kitchen and the bathroom were carpeted, including the entire enormous basement. This was where Cathy had her bedroom plus a two-piece bathroom. There was also a carpeted laundry room and the furnace room, which contained two huge oil tanks. Being at ground level there were two doors leading directly into the garden. There was a fence all 'round the property that I would guess was about one and a half acres. In the front there was a row of six big old maple trees and in the back the original swing set and see-saw from when this had been a school. Everything was manicured and lovely with just a few flower beds, the rest being lawn. Whew! Did I do okay? Good! Coffee and doughnuts will now be served, so you must take a break from reading and go put on the coffee pot.

We settled in well here and everyone seemed to be much happier. In the fall, Cathy, Toby and Susan went to South Perth Centennial School in the country, while Richard started high school in St. Marys, a town with a population 5,000. During the day I would be at the old village church I had bought to house my ever-growing business. I bought this while we were living at the rented farmhouse. It had been repossessed by the Federal Business and Development Bank and I purchased it for a song. Considering this business started with just $5 from my pocket I don't think I did too badly. The church had formerly been bought and turned into a recording studio, with a two-piece bathroom, kitchen, waiting area, control room and large studio downstairs. This was ideal. The control room with its big, soundproof window became the office and the studio the workshop for cutting, sewing and printing. The studio people had built a loft with two bedrooms and a full bathroom for bands who needed to stay overnight, so I stored fabric up there. It was a quaint old church with a pretty garden. At this point we had the farm (which we had put up for sale), the schoolhouse and the church. I can quite clearly remember David telling the children, "Now remember, if you see a fire hall for sale, don't tell your mother!" As if I would—now really!

While we were at the schoolhouse David's eldest brother, Bob, came to visit from New Zealand, along with his wife, Pat, and daughter, Gillian. Gillian was somewhere between Toby and Cathy's age. I could not help but notice how frail David was compared to Bob, who was seven years his senior, but we had a great time. Then Nan came in the summer and was still there to spend Christmas with us. She became really good friends with the local ladies and went to Women's Institute with them, as well as on day trips, shopping and visiting. It was so nice to have her here. Our routine was that when David came home she would sit and chat with him over a cup of tea while I made supper. After supper she insisted on making tea for David and me while she and the children cleaned up. They really loved their Nan and when she went home, we all missed her.

Richard did well in high school. He had a good brain and chose to use it, so when he found a Dungeons and Dragons club at school, he quickly joined. This is where he met Jonathan Ryder. He was a year older than Richard but they became best friends, and now, 29 years later they are still connected. Jon lived right in St. Marys, but one day it was arranged that he would come home with Richard on the school bus and have supper with us. His parents were going to drive out later in the evening to pick him up. Ruth and Gord arrived to pick Jon up about seven thirty and we naturally invited them in for coffee and dessert. This was instant friendship that has endured throughout the years. Have you ever had that happen to you, when you meet people and feel you have known them forever? There was no initial shyness or clumsy conversation, we were just totally comfortable. Ruth was (and still is) very attractive and vibrant with a ready laugh and a sense of humour. Gord was the quiet one, content to sit and smile and be more of a listener. David and Ruth had a common interest in photography and computers and could chat for hours about things technical, but Ruth and I also had a lot in common. It was great for David to have someone he could talk to who understood his passions.

From here on we visited back and forth to each other's homes just about every weekend and somehow never ran out of things to talk about. The fact that Richard and Jonathan were best buddies was a plus for us as well, and at that time they joined air cadets together. They loved it. There is one particular sunny, Sunday afternoon I remember well. Ruth and Gord had come to visit, but instead of preparing a dessert ahead of time we all went for a walk and gathered tiny, sweet alpine strawberries from the side of the road. Once back home it took only a few minutes to make some pastry and prepare the strawberries, and voila, we had fresh strawberry pie and thick cream. Umm, I am positively drooling at this memory. Life seemed so much simpler then, and I have to wonder how, as I have aged, my life has become so complex.

Although I still treasure simple things there seems little time left to enjoy them anymore. Despite his health problems, David and I were happy at the schoolhouse. If he was stiff and sore we would go for a quiet country drive, but otherwise we would walk to some woods just up the road and look for trilliums to photograph. I remember one beautiful summer day when we went walking. We were on a grassy bank where the woods abutted a cornfield, and we sat down to enjoy the peace and the songs of the birds. Before we knew it we were making love right there on the grass. This is a treasured memory that I have never mentioned to anyone before this. Because of David's health and his level of pain, our intimate moments were becoming few and far between. Throughout all but the earliest years of our marriage I had let David initiate our lovemaking, but I always welcomed these most precious times when we were so attuned to one another. When a couple truly love one another these times are sacred.

Susan was about seven years old when David arrived home early one day. The look on his face told me something drastic had happened. He had been fired on the spot and escorted from the building. Apparently something had gone terribly wrong and the company comptroller and the general manager said David was to blame. He was totally innocent and knew he was being used as a scapegoat. I guess they (inaccurately) thought that because he was friendly and considerate of others, he would just buckle. They obviously did not know the will of steel he had against anything corrupt.

After hiring a lawyer he took them to court for wrongful dismissal and won. I believe the fact that he stood up to them and took this action was a completely unexpected shock. Pretty soon the comptroller and the general manager were being led out of the company and were charged with criminal activity. Lesson: don't mess with my husband's integrity. He may have been laid-back, but he was cleverer than the lot of them put together! Within a short time David had become successful as an engineering and managing consultant, working for himself. He would go into a company that was about to go belly up, streamline them and completely turn them around. By the time he was done they would be in the black and have orders on their books. Soon his reputation as a problem solver spread and he did very well indeed.

My business was continuing to grow and I would often go back to work after cooking supper. If there was a rush order for the next day I would print until perhaps one in the morning, sleep at the shop until five a.m. and then get up to fold and package the now dry shirts ready for an eight a.m. pickup. After this it would be home for breakfast and then spend a meaningful Saturday with the rest of the family. For years I existed on four to five hours' sleep a night with no ill effects.

But this little "hobby" of mine had reached a point where I needed to make a major decision. Either I had to be willing to go really big and forgo family time or quit and be a mother. My heart lay with David and the children, so I decided to sell. Before I knew it one of my employees offered to buy the business, the name and the equipment, etc., but she did not need the building. So I sold the business to her and separately put the building up for sale. I also agreed to help the new owner from time to time if she needed input or had a rush order.

Well, the church sold and I was once again what I had always considered myself: a wife and mother. It was wonderful. There was time to go shopping and visit with my friends. Once a week we would gather at my place for the afternoon to work on our personal projects while we chatted and had tea and goodies. We rather irreverently called it "The Stitch and Bitch Club." I so enjoyed this time to be just me and even joined the Women's Institute. David had long since needed to give up Scouting so now he gave his all to the Masonic Lodge.

One has to have an outlet. I believe it was God's plan that I should have this carefree interlude because heaven knows that within six short months the storm clouds began to gather darkly. This was when even the laughter stopped. There would be no more breaks for me.

17.

Changing Roles (the Working Wife)

It was now July 1985 and the children were growing up. Susan was still only 9, but Richard was 17, still passionate about air cadets. He had won many awards and was planning to make a career in the military. He had had his licence to drive for a year and a half and was proud to be the designated driver when he and his friends went out. His car was an old, red Pacer and he was able to help out if Dave and I needed him to pick up one of his siblings from a friend's house. Cathy was 15 and had been accepted to go to the Philippines for a year as a Rotary exchange student. She was a quiet but intelligent girl with a strong character and even stronger will. Nothing daunted Cathy.

Toby was 14, but I must back up a little here. When he was 12 we received a phone call from his music teacher, Mr. French, who asked if we knew what an incredible talent Toby had for singing. We did not, and this took us aback. His adoption information indicated he came from a musical background and that his biological father was a well know African American singer.

Next we had a phone call from his friend Jamie's mother. Jamie had been singing since he was 6, but his mother heard Jamie and Toby singing together in their yard and called us all in a flutter (she was rather a dramatic type). "Did you know that Toby has the most amazing voice?" She then contacted Jamie's teacher, who was considered "the best" and was selective about whom he taught.

Next thing, Toby was taking lessons and after only three months took the Ontario Medal for best in his class. Then he and Jamie (who had a fantastic voice) went against each other in competition, and despite his never having failed before, Toby beat him and took first prize. After that his mother did not speak to me for a while. Ah well, c'est la vie. I would like to interject that Jamie is now a talented and well known opera singer. He and Toby were never at odds about the competition and are still connected today.

The next thing we knew, Toby's teacher Mr. Wood had submitted a tape of his singing to the America's Boy Choir. Each year they chose the 12 best from across North America and went on tour throughout Europe. You guessed it—my most mischievous child was chosen as one of the 12, and all of a sudden there was a flurry of newspaper reporters calling and the radio station wanting to interview him. He toured France, Germany, Belgium and Holland and apparently made quite an impact with his solos as a boy treble. Once back he was in great demand to sing at various functions and at different churches, but at home he was still "our Toby," with a knack for getting into all kinds of mischief. This was not intentional, but with Toby around things just happened! At school he received the Perth County Board of

Education Award for Outstanding Achievement, which goes to one student in the county each year. Next came a photo session and more newspaper reporters, and a large portrait of Toby was hung in his school. But I must get back to July 1985.

David was working with a company in London that had been having some serious problems. They had resorted to changing their company name more than once in order to avoid going under, and it looked as if they were heading that way again. Their biggest problem was that the business employed family members in key positions, and that rarely works out well. However, he went in and made good progress sorting out the company's issues. David's health was a big concern for me, but he seemed to have the stamina and determination to keep going. He really enjoyed what he did and was a creative problem solver. Unfortunately, this company asked him to be more creative than the law would allow, so he told them exactly what he thought of their ethics and walked out. This would upset anyone, but with David it just seemed to knock that last bit of resolve right out of him. When he arrived home he told me he just could not do it anymore, that his health had finally given out to the point where he could no longer work. What surprised me was that he had not given up sooner.

The next day we went to his appointment with Dr. Parsons, who also said that anyone else in David's position would have stopped working years earlier. Right there and then he filled out the necessary government forms stating that David qualified for a full disability pension. However, we all know that "the wheels of justice (and government) turn exceeding slow." Ultimately, even with there being no question he qualified, it took nearly two years before his monthly pension started to be administered. So what were we going to do in the meantime? As David had been self-employed he could not claim unemployment insurance, so the reality was that all income ceased on the spot. If there is one thing I can say it is that I have a strong sense of responsibility, and in that moment when he came home and told me he could no longer work, I knew it was now up to me to do whatever it would take to provide for the family.

After seeing Dr. Parsons, I had mixed emotions. Although I was relieved David had retired, I was also concerned about how this would affect his psyche. His health was a big worry. The only medications that gave him any relief were prednisone and aspirin, which he had now been taking for 17 years. The rheumatologist had tried every other medication available, sometimes in combination, and nothing worked. Already he had sustained dozens of fractured bones due to osteoporosis, as well as having surgeries and ever more frequent bouts of pneumonia. There was no question that I would have to get a job, and quickly. What I needed was a steady, guaranteed paycheque.

That evening we talked things over and agreed this was just a role reversal. For many years David had been the breadwinner and I the mother. Now it was my turn to go to work and David would be home to deal with the family. We had always worked in partnership with each other, and this was no different. The children, who were not so little anymore, accepted the fact that we would all pull together as a family unit and did not seem at all fazed by this change. Life goes on and we do what we have to do.

The next morning I did something I had never done before—I went to the unemployment office down in St. Marys to talk to a job counsellor. We discussed my qualifications and education, and then I was asked what I would like to do. My response was, "Anything that will give me a paycheque at the end of the week." As it happened, there was a job available at the local Association for Community Living. It was a full-time job as a support worker assisting individuals with developmental challenges with their daily living. An interview was set for the next day, and to say I was nervous was an understatement. Here I was, 44 years old with a husband and a family to support, with everything hanging on gaining employment.

The two ladies who interviewed me could not have been more pleasant. I found it was almost unheard of for them to have a full-time job opening, so someone was watching over me that day because I was offered the job. What's more, they were starting me at level two on the pay scale instead of level one. The hours were three forty-five p.m. to one a.m. Monday to Friday and one weekend a month, which would either be eight a.m. to four p.m. or four p.m. to midnight. How did this happen? My very first job interview and I landed a full-time position. This was Thursday and I was to start the following Monday, working along with someone to get orientated. On Friday I received a phone call to ask if I would work that weekend as they only had one staff instead of two. So on the August 8, 1985, I started work on the eight-to-four shift. Talk about putting the horse before the cart.

The building where I was to be working housed four apartments, each occupied by one person needing support. In two of the apartments were men who did not need full-time support. In the other two were ladies with whom I would be working. Theirs was a different story, as they both needed 24-hour support and extensive input with their daily living. Other than the apartments there was an office, a staff washroom and a laundry room for the tenants.

When I arrived on that first Saturday morning the occupants were all still sleeping, so I had a chance to chat with the other lady who was working. She had been with the association for several years. During our conversation I mentioned that I had been asked not to read the files until I had been there three months. My co-worker was horrified and said she had never heard of such a thing and that there was something I should know. The one lady with whom I would be working was extremely aggressive and could go from pleasant to full-on attack mode in a split second. Apparently it had hitherto been impossible to find staff to work with her for this very reason. So this was what was being kept from me. Now I understood and was grateful I had been warned. Obviously there was something my interviewers did not know about me. Once I commit, I do so 100 percent, come what may.

I took an instant liking to this lady. She had the understanding and verbal skills of a two-year-old and had built a wall around herself. I had my share of attacks from her over the years, but once I managed to get behind that wall (it took about three years) I found a warm, loving person with incredible empathy and a great sense of humour. We got on really well, but I guess she came to realize that no matter what, I would be there for her. Ultimately I was to work with her for 14 years, during which time I came to understand her issues and persisted in finding out what her diagnosis was. It turned out the psychotic rages were part and parcel of her medical problem. So instead of trying to change her I advocated for changing her environment to one that would better suit her. We were truly very good friends and had fun together. I would take her, along with her friend, for annual vacations at a cottage on Lake Huron, and I loved these times with her.

Will I never learn? Dear reader, I am way ahead of myself again, so my sincere apologies, but we must go back to 1985 (how do you like being a time traveller)? This new job really suited me, and I quickly learned what was necessary. At the time I started, the association had just lost the team leader who would have been responsible for the staff on the teams where I worked. For whatever reason, the manager had not gotten around to doing a job posting for this position and no one had been allocated to fulfill the team leader responsibilities. Although I was not formally asked, I realized what was not being done and started to assume responsibility for the month-end reports. This fairly quickly turned into my taking on more of these responsibilities. It was either that or the tasks necessary to running the teams and the office would not be completed. I did this willingly as I like a challenge and it gave me something to do once everyone was asleep and my daily report was done.

My team mates told me I was being used and asked why I would do a team leader's work for support worker's pay. I just shrugged and said, "I don't mind," but I had a plan. As far as I could tell, all these ladies had husbands who worked, and for them (they were all part time), this was just pin money. For me it was a different story. I had a family to feed and support, and I was determined to climb as high as I could and therefore earn as much as I could. This team leader position was not posted for six months, during which time I had taken on all the responsibilities. So when it was posted I applied. Well, I was doing the job anyway—how could they not offer it to me? In less than a year I was the team leader, with the pay that went with the position. Not bad. I had strategised my job like a chess game and now my team mates were working for me.

On the home front things were running smoothly but money was tight. Our house was 4,645 square feet and was expensive to heat. On top of this I was paying for Toby's singing lessons. Another problem was that I left for work before the children came home from school and then did not arrive home until well after one a.m. Consequently they were off to school before I woke up so

I did not see them all week. Neither was I home to see how things were going for David. During the day things seemed fine and he was cooking good suppers for the children, but years later Susan said she could pinpoint this as the time when he started to act strange. She was only 9 but was bright and perceptive. For years David managed to control behaviours in front of me that he did not bother to hide from the children. At this point it was actions that were just a little odd and comments that were just not quite as rational as they should have been.

But life carried on, with the children growing with the changing seasons. With winter came the snow and ice, and it was no longer safe to take the back country river road to work and back. If I were to go into a ditch after one a.m. there would be no one around to help, and the farms were few and far between. Despite our reduced income we had a wonderful Christmas. Nan had come from England and was there to celebrate with us.

On New Year's Eve I nearly had a heart attack. Richard and Toby decided to go up onto the roof (a tremendous height) and go into the bell tower to ring in the new year with the old school bell. I was in a panic that this would disturb the neighbours, but I was wrong. Apparently they found it a wonderful surprise and the best possible way to ring in the new year. The bell echoed all over the valley and had everyone reminiscing about when it rang to call them to school. It had been silent far too long.

Another lovely memory of the Christmas season was when Ruth, Gord, their two boys and Ruth's mother and aunt came over to visit and we all gathered at the big old Victorian grand piano. While I played, our families all sang Christmas carols together. Somehow it felt so much more relevant and enjoyable than the more commercial Christmas activities.

Spring arrived, and soon it was time to celebrate Victoria

Day. Although it was a statutory holiday, my job was in human services and I had to work from four p.m. to one a.m. that day. Once everyone was settled for the night I went into the office to write my reports. Outside it had become dark and the fireworks were starting down by at the park by the river. Looking out the window I could see all the different coloured flares and sparkles lighting up the night sky. It was beautiful.

That was when my nightmare began. I heard a noise. Instantly I was in full panic mode—my heart was racing, I was in a cold sweat and trembling and the hair stood up on the back of my neck and on my arms. What could I do—where could I run? What if the whistling stopped? *Oh please no, don't let it stop over me!* But it did, but I was still alive and not obliterated by a falling buzz bomb whose whistling had stopped directly over my head, indicating it was now going to fall after its horizontal flight. Unsteadily I sat down to try to control my trembling and collect my thoughts. By now I realized that what I had heard was a new kind of firework. However, the pitch and volume were absolutely identical to those most dreaded of bombs. This fear was something that must have been embedded in my subconscious since my days as a small child in World War II, and yet I do not remember being afraid as a child. So do these old experiences affect us? Yes, most definitely yes, and at times and in places where we least expect them. Finally I realized that I was not unscathed by the war but was a scarred product of my early environment. So now the question was, what other unpleasant memories or experiences from my past might suddenly be thrust into my consciousness by some totally innocuous sound or event? One o'clock came and I drove home in the dark to the sanctuary of my own home and the comforting presence of my husband asleep beside me in our bed. All was well.

By summer Cathy was off to the Philippines for a year. This would be another $100 a month I could ill afford, but this opportunity was worth every penny in experience alone. Richard went to cadet camp, where he met a girl named Edie. Apparently there were some issues at home and Richard had said to her, "If you ever have a problem our door is always open." Oh, my dear son! A true product of his parents. You have probably guessed, dear readers, one day, right out of the blue Edie arrived on our doorstep from a great distance away. So we lost Cathy and gained Edie. Of course we immediately contacted her mother, who agreed it would be good if she could stay with us for a while. That "while" turned out to be a full year, during which time we mediated between Edie and her mother, gradually getting them to talk, then visit and finally for Edie to go home. Whew! I must admit she was something of a handful and at times tried my patience to the limit. None of my own children were manipulative and I did not take kindly to this trait. But, to quote the Bard, "All's Well That Ends Well."

By now money was really tight. There was no way I could earn anything near what David had made. Pretty soon we had gone through all our savings and cashed in our life insurance. David and I talked it over and decided to put the house up for sale. It would not sell quickly, as it was a unique property and would need to appeal to the right kind of buyer. Winter was on its way and I knew heating the place was going to be really tough. We had the opportunity to buy a second-hand woodstove cheap so we installed this in the basement. It was now getting tough to even find enough money for food. Fortunately I had learned to cook in England, where, due to the war, we had to be resourceful enough to make really good meals out of very little. Nothing was ever wasted.

My job was going well. I worked conscientiously and was wholeheartedly committed to the people for whom I was responsible. I had received some nice pay raises, but it was still not enough. We were living payday to payday (once every two weeks), and by the time the next one was due I was scraping change together just to buy bread. But somehow my family was always fed. After I arrived home at one thirty a.m. I would have some tea and toast and then bake muffins so there was something to put with the school lunches.

As yet another winter approached we had many wild wind storms. I remember driving home along the river road with branches from the big, old trees raining down everywhere. It was somewhat scary and more than a little dangerous, but I turned this to my advantage. On my way home the next night I stopped frequently and loaded up the trunk with as much wood as it could hold. This would be used for the wood stove in the basement and would give us some free heat. As I said, nothing was wasted.

One night when I was at work, I knew we were out of toilet tissue and there were still two more days left until payday. The staff cupboard was packed with toilet rolls and it would have been easy to just put one in my bag. Darn my conscience—I just could not bring myself to do that as I considered it stealing. No one would have know, or probably even cared, but I would know and I couldn't do it. Instead, I took just enough off the roll in use to see us through. This I could live with.

That Christmas I was totally surprised to receive a gift basket from the Salvation Army, quickly followed by various beautifully decorated food baskets and gifts from all kinds of friends and neighbours. Please excuse me, dear readers, but I suddenly find myself sobbing, for the first time ever, with gratitude and relief over this generosity. In writing this I have finally succumbed to the realization of the severity of our situation. I must take a break here and have a cup of tea. This emotion came out of nowhere and hit me hard.

Well, here I am back again and somewhat more composed. I never did find out who was clued in to our situation or had called the Salvation Army and our friends. I was unaware anyone knew. This made me stop and think that from the time David first told me he could no longer work it never crossed my mind to go to the food bank or ask for welfare. This was my family, and as far as I was concerned it was my responsibility, and whatever it took I had to do it. But that was a good Christmas.

So time passed and we struggled on. The house was up for sale but we were not holding our breath for a quick result. Cathy returned from the Philippines after having experienced going through the revolution there. Trying to get her back was an issue as she would have liked to stay there, but finally the day came when we all went to Toronto to meet her. It had been close to a year and a half since she'd left as a teenager of 15. Now she returned as a self-possessed young lady of 17.

Richard had just finished high school and was about to apply to the Canadian military, Toby was in high school and Susan was in her final year of grade school. At this point, right out of the blue, the schoolhouse sold.

18.

Times of Change (the Professional Wife)

What a relief. David and I were now going to be free of the expenses that went with living in our large schoolhouse. Our plan was to find a smaller house in St. Marys that we could afford on my wages. Quantitatively we would be decreasing our lifestyle, but in terms of quality we would be so much better off. Living with the stresses of our large, beautiful but costly home, I had reached the point where I would wake up in the night and find myself screaming. Now I was going to be able to put this behind me, although the memories of the hardships would be with me for a very long time.

We looked at quite a few houses for sale in town, finally settling on a brand new semidetached three bedroom with a garage. It also had the unique feature of being built on a hill, so the front door was at street level but there was a walk-out basement with patio doors at the back. The only problem was that the living room was very small, so we planned to have the back wall removed and build on a large, all-glass sunroom. And the best feature? This all fit within our budget. An added bonus was that my place of work was just a five-minute walk down the street so I would not need to use the car, thereby saving on mileage and gas.

It was 1988 when we moved into our new house on Church Street in St. Marys, and we were there until June 1996. During that time there were so many changes in our family, what with some of them growing up and leaving home and others coming. Others coming, you ask? My, do I have a tale for you, my dear reader!

As I mentioned previously, Richard had applied to be accepted into the Canadian air force. He took his tests with outstanding results and was accepted for officer training, was told that the whole field of options were open to him and that he could learn a language in half the time it would normally take. The only drawback was that he took the tests in January when he was just 19, and the courses at Kingston Military Academy did not start until the fall. He was filling in time working in a factory, and this was certainly not his cup of tea, so he opted to join immediately and go as a regular recruit. Actually, he never did live in our new house, although he was stationed in London nearby for a while and visited on weekends. It was while he was in London (and we were still at the schoolhouse) that he met Lynn, a beautiful young lady whom he married when he was 21. By then he was stationed in Germany, coming home for just one week to get married. In all he lived in Germany for seven years and, at least physically, was pretty much out of the picture.

My children were growing up so quickly right before my eyes. How could this be? It seemed like only yesterday I was taking my small little souls across the field at the farm to collect wildflowers.

My house was full of them. We would pick one of each kind and then identify it from my wildflower book at the house.

So my eldest son had left the nest. Next to leave was Toby, although for several years he seemed to be attached to a piece of elastic and kept bouncing back. At 15 he had, a little defiantly, announced he was not going to sing anymore. I suspect he thought I would say, "Oh, no! Please, please don't give up your singing." Instead I said, "Well, that's your choice. It's not part of the school curriculum so you don't have to do it," and that was that. By 17 he could no longer contain himself and set off for England to explore his singing. He had dual citizenship (as do all my children) and was able to work there. He also had plenty of relatives with whom he could stay. He was fortunate to meet up with a very talented musician who was several years his senior. Together they produced Toby's first album under the duo's professional name of "Eden's Lore." He was gone for many months.

Once Cathy (finally) returned home, she did her Grade Thirteen at St. Marys Collegiate before going to New York to take her entrance exam for the University of the Philippines. She took the exam in all subjects and had to do so in Tagalog, the Filipino language. Her final mark was 99-plus percent. We contacted the embassy for the Philippines in Toronto but did not seem to get past the red tape, so in the meantime Cathy opened a small store in St. Marys called "Tradewinds." She sold unusual things from all over the world, including the most beautiful Columbian leather goods. Her strategy was to cut out the middleman and deal directly with the source. This kept her prices reasonable and she was still able to make a profit. Before long she expanded into a much larger store in the old St. Marys Opera House. At 20 she moved to Toronto and became a private detective (David and I kept the store going for a while before selling it), eventually becoming the security systems administrator for all five of the Toronto Dominion towers in downtown Toronto. It was at this time that she met Bill and they moved in together before moving to Calgary in 1996 and eventually getting married.

When Toby was 19 he took another trip to England, where he did some more work on his music for a couple of months. Two days before leaving he came home and gave his dad an envelope. It contained a plane ticket to England. After much sputtering that he could not possibly go, especially at such short notice, we bundled him onto the plane with Toby. He stayed with his brother Don in the Cotswolds, but while there fit in a week visiting Richard and Lynn in Germany and a couple of weeks with his brother Mike in Galway Bay in Eire.

This left only Sue and me at home. Of course I was working and she was at school, but we had a wonderful time. By now my job was mostly administrative and I was the senior team leader and the highest paid. I had played my moves well, and after the manager left I answered only to the executive director of the association. I had been to many workshops and taken many courses and really loved my job.

Toby and David were due home a couple of days before Christmas, so Sue and I had free reign to shop and decorate the house however we wanted. We also made a point of going out for supper once a week while the boys were gone. Depending on funds it could be a fancy restaurant or a fast food place, but we always went.

That year we had a good Christmas and I was so happy David had been able to have a nice holiday while he could still travel. It was during our time at Church Street that he began to get more frequent bouts of pneumonia. His pain was also much worse and he would take extra prednisone, which caused steroid psychosis and periods of dementia. After these episodes he had no memory of them, so we were unable to discuss the situation. I was left with the rather unenviable task of having to discuss this with our doctor in private. Dr. Parsons concluded that we needed to take a more aggressive approach to the pain control and prescribed morphine for David, warning me that if he took too much I would find him in a coma on the floor. Believe me, I watched him like a hawk! The morphine helped for a time and David began to enjoy his activities again, but there were times he still appeared to be in his own little world.

It made me happy that he continued to be involved with the Masonic Lodge. Like everything else he did he went all out and one year was the grand master in both the Blue Lodge and the Red Lodge at the same time. This led up to him being district deputy grand master from 1992 to 1993. He was also president of the Children's Aid and on the town's Economic Development Committee (EDC), and through that he was responsible for bringing a farmer's market to St. Marys. What this meant was that he was out mixing with other men, something that would have been natural if he were still able to work. But once again this put him in his own little world. He was driven by his interests to the exclusion of anything happening with regard to me. I was predictably becoming just an extension of everybody's needs.

My knees had been bothering me for quite some time and were becoming more and more painful. After seeing a specialist I was diagnosed with osteoarthritis and found to have no cartilage left in my knees. During our years at Church Street I had four surgeries, with the first one coinciding with David going away for a week with the EDC. He was so fired up about this that my impending surgery was not even a subject for discussion. Being a conscientious wife I packed his suitcase and off he went.

The next day, Toby (then 17) drove me to the hospital where, during surgery, I was found to have an even more serious problem than the X-rays had shown. A week later Toby picked me up and brought me home. David arrived home later that day. I had not had a single visitor during my week in the hospital, and to say I felt hurt and devalued was an understatement. Still, I got over it and carried on with our life, but these kinds of hurts run deep and the memories they create can pop up at the most inconvenient times, causing resentment.

The year 1991 was quite different. We were still very close with Ruth and Gord, visiting with each other every weekend. Ruth and I even bought ourselves Chihuahua puppies. Both males were from the same litter. Hers was black and white and she named him Peppi while mine was brown and white and we called him Riggs. I already had a little black and tan Chihuahua a workmate had asked me to look after while he moved. He never came back for him, so Randy became mine. Riggs was actually bought for Sue but seemed to be very much David's dog.

Toby was working at the local gas station, and with his charismatic personality everyone knew him. He had grown into a tall (six foot three, the same as Richard), good looking young man. Did I tell you he has quite a sense of humour? One day around noon I pulled into the station to get gas for my car when he asked if I would mind picking up a submarine sandwich for him. Apparently they knew him well at the store, so he told me to just tell them I was his mom. Seemed simple enough, right?

Upon entering the store, I said I had come for Toby's sub, and with a puzzled expression the lady asked, "Well, who are you?" I said, "Oh. I'm Toby's mom."

At this she burst out laughing, and I stood there feeling rather bewildered. Finally she recovered enough to tell me that when

Toby had placed his order, she had asked how she would recognize me. His response was, "Don't worry, she looks just like me." This explained everything. Toby is six foot three, slim and black, whereas I am five foot, white and, oh let's admit it, a little on the chubby side. That's my boy!

It started out as a day just like any other. We all did what we usually did and went about our business. Isn't it strange how a day that starts out in such an ordinary way can turn into one that will change one's life forever? At some point in the day there was a knock on the door. I opened it to find a young teenage boy standing there holding two stuffed garbage bags, and like Toby, he was black. I said hello and asked who he was looking for, and his answer (I shall never forget this) was, "Hi, I'm Dan and I've come to live with you."

Life with my children had always been a little strange, so I took this in stride and said, "Come in." David was home, so we sat down to talk with Dan, only to find that he was just 15 and his mother (his adoptive mother, I might add) had thrown him out of the house and changed the locks. His father had left when he was 12. Dan had apparently known Toby for quite some time and hung around the gas station when he was there. Toby had taken on a big brother role, looking out for Dan and inviting him along when he went to a movie with his friends. And of course, being one of our children, Toby had told Dan that if ever there was a problem to come to our house. He and Toby had a bond in that they were both black and both loved music. Of course we accepted Dan into our home.

The next day David contacted the Children's Aid for advice (15 was in the grey zone) and spoke to Dan's school counsellor. She was well-versed in Dan's issues on the home front and said that if he could find somewhere to go, he should leave home. Of course we phoned his mother, but she could not have cared less, so we increased our family from four children to five. That was 20 years ago, and I am still Dan's mom. We never officially adopted or fostered him and never, ever received any money from any source for his keep. He just became our son, and his mother's loss was our gain. Susan was over the moon to have a "little brother" and to this day still looks upon him that way. With Cathy and Richard having moved out, we were able to give Dan what had been Cathy's room along with the bed and dresser.

Toby's domain was in the basement, and with the big patio doors he had a nice place of his own to entertain his friends. We had let him renovate and paint (would you believe deep purple?), and he had a nice bedroom and sitting room. It was great to see how well Dan fit into the family and even better to see him realize he was important, valued and loved. The other kids could not wait to tell him not to make Dad mad as he would not like the punishment! His method was to sit down with the offending child and calmly and quietly explain, in great detail, how he or she might have done things differently. This little talk might last an hour or more, and many times the children said they would have preferred a quick slap instead of this extended dialogue. We did not believe in slapping, and once a situation had been dealt with it was never mentioned again.

Dan's first big mistake came not too long after he came to live with us, and boy it was a doozy. He asked permission to go and stay at a friend's house overnight, and we saw no problem with this. We had the friend's name and telephone number, so off Dan went on his bike. On the following morning we phoned the friend's house to see what time Dan would be home and were told by his friend's mother that Dan was not there. Also, her son was out of town for the weekend visiting relatives, so Dan was not with him. She further told us Dan had told her son he was going to a motel overnight with two girls. Well, this behaviour was something new to us. The mother gave us the name of the motel, which was a seedy little place some way from town. Dave and I got in the car. I had never seen him look so angry or grim—or known him to drive so fast!

While we were on our way, Sue called the motel to warn Dan. She asked why he did not tell us he was not going to his friend's home. First he said he did, but when she pointed out that he didn't, he said, "Well, I meant to."

Dave and I arrived at the parking lot with a flurry of whirling dust and gravel from our tires. When Dan came out, David's only words were a very sharp, "Get in the car!"

Dead silence filled the way home. Once inside the front door, Dave exploded. "What the bloody hell do you think you were doing?"

Dan's answer was that he had called Sue to say where he was. In no uncertain terms Sue told him that no, he hadn't, to which he answered, "Well, I meant to."

Instead of the usual quiet, lengthy lecture, David did some pretty loud yelling for about five minutes. Then it was all over and it was never brought up again. Dan never did that kind of thing again. What he did find was that we would champion him to the end where necessary, whether it is with the school or whatever. Now that my children are all grown up they will sometimes get together and reminisce about their younger days, and inevitably they will all have a big chuckle over "Dan's Big Mistake."

The next few years flew by in a whirl. I was working more than full time. My job description had changes with many added responsibilities and I was always constantly juggling work, home and David's health. Ruth and Gord were still our very close friends and we still got together on Saturday evenings. Somehow we always had fun and never ran out of things to talk or laugh about. These were true friends.

Also during this time we became "the place" in town where young teenagers who were having problems came for help. Sometimes we would give some child shelter for a night or even a week or two while we mediated between the child and his or her parents to sort out their issues. We jokingly said we should put a sign over the door saying "Drop-in Centre."

One particular incident I remember very well. It involved a lad of about fourteen. His parents (well-known in the community) belonged to some offbeat church, and his mother was, quite frankly, a nut case. She found her son listening to some heavy metal music in his room and declared he was possessed by the Devil. It was six o'clock on a cold, wintry morning when, on his way to work, Toby found this lad huddled in a shop doorway. He was freezing cold and soaking wet from the previous night's heavy rain. After stopping and getting his story, Toby told him to go straight to our house. We took him in, got him some warm, dry clothes and something warm to eat and then sent him upstairs to get some sleep. Meanwhile, we called the school to let them know he would be absent that day and also called his parents to let them know where he was. They did not want him. Late the preceding evening, the mother had called the town police and asked them to throw him out of the house for who knows what—this woman was delusional, and as these people were so-called pillars of the community the (excuse the expression) idiot police complied. Wrong move, gentlemen; wrong move. You woke the sleeping giant of justice that was within Toby!

On his way home from work at four that afternoon, Toby burst into the local police station full of righteous indignation and proceeded to tell all police personnel present that it was their job to protect youth and keep them off the streets, not throw them out of their homes in the middle of the night. The older officer in charge just sat and smiled as the new constable sputtered and muttered. Unlike everyone else in town, he did not know Toby.

After asking Toby his name, the constable turned to his superior officer and asked if he knew him. His superior just nodded, grinned and said "Yep."

The constable then asked, "Does he have any right to come in here like this?"

Again: "Yep."

The constable: "Are you going to let him talk like this?"

"Yep."

After this, the amused senior officer thanked Toby for doing what he had and Toby left. Before he had a chance to drive away, the young officer ran after him, opening the conversation with, "Boy, I sure like your car."

It was an old Volkswagen Jetta that Toby and his friend had fixed up. He proceeded by telling Toby he knew a lot about cars and if ever he needed a hand to fix something to just call him. Toby thanked him and peace and justice reigned. This lad ultimately lived with us for three months until his dad finally admitted he was in the wrong. I am proud to say that although my children are social, calm and friendly, there is not one of them who would stand by and see an injustice done.

Then there was Lawrence, Toby's best friend. Together they would buy old cars, fix them up and paint them (for years my garage had a faint red hue from the plastic not being hung properly when they spray painted) and then resell them for a profit. Lawrence was training to be a mechanic. It took six months of Lawrence's clothes cycling through my laundry before Toby actually admitted he was living with us. Such was life at 288 Church Street, St. Marys. Quite frankly, during this particular season of my life there was so much going on it has been somewhat of a challenge to put the sequence of events into any kind of order. What with my working, looking after the house, doing groceries, paying the bills and laundering who knows whose clothes, it was a wonder I remained sane, although there may be some, especially my darling offspring, who may seriously question that premise. Dear reader, if you're actually reading this, then I know I am not really in some locked facility and this book is not just a figment of my imagination. Phew! Perish the thought!

Now one major thing that took place while we were at Church Street was David's trip to New Zealand to visit his brother Bob and sister-in-law Pat. David's health had been getting worse, and I was concerned that within a short time he would no longer be able to travel. With this realization I cashed in some of my Registered Retirement Savings Plan and bought him a plane ticket to New Zealand. It cost me $2,000 that I could ill afford, but neither could I afford not to do this. I knew that in all likelihood this would be the last time he would see his brother. He stayed for two months and had a most incredible time. I was so happy for him. While there he saw and did everything and came home with some wonderful photographs. Also, he brought me back a sheepskin rug and a genuine Ashcroft spinning wheel. What a wonderful, thoughtful husband. This was more than amplified when he bought on older, hard-topped tent trailer for $500.00. He stripped off all the old canvas and completely remade it with marine canvas. To do this he used the old industrial sewing machine we had bought when Richard was a baby—this was the last time his hands were able to use it. We fixed up the inside of the trailer with new paint and curtains and it looked so lovely.

Lake Huron was only 50 minutes away, so we would go and spend two weeks camping in the Pineries Provincial Park each year. Toby would come along to help us get set up, as this was getting too difficult for Dave to handle, but we had the most marvellous, relaxing times there nestled among the trees of the forest.

19.

New Beginnings (the Grandmother)

The year I have reached is 1992, and I am in one of those introspective moods that cause me to look back on my life and wonder where all the years have gone. At this point, David and I were 51 and our children had come, grown and in some cases already left the nest. Life was still pretty busy at our house as we were still considered the "place to go" for the young folk in town who needed a bed, or even someone just willing to listen to their troubles. David was excellent in the way he talked to and understood young people. However, he was always careful not to put them in opposition with their parents or whomever. Rather, he would help them communicate their needs more effectively to their family and helped mediate a resolution.

Under these kinds of circumstances David was still, as yet, able to function in a professional and rational manner. The problem was when he was just dealing with the everyday things in life and could let down his front of professionalism. We began to see more and more strange behaviours—plus some of his ideas were, to say the least, bizarre. I was starting to need to watch him when we were in public and sometimes steer the conversation toward a different topic. It is sad that the people who are closest to the ones who have issues are also the last to see or accept that something is wrong. You tell yourself, "No, this is just my imagination," or else you downplay it, saying, "Oh, it's not really that bad, just a little off-kilter." After all, these kinds of things happen to other people, not you. Your family is too ordinary for such things. So, I was in effect dealing with two personalities in one. There was the rational David and the David whose pain and medication were distorting his reasoning and perception.

Did I ever tell you about my little Norfolk Island pine tree? It was beautiful. Well, a few years before, when we were out shopping, I saw these little trees in their pots. I would say they were probably four to six inches high and only cost about $2. The fronds were as soft as velvet, and when you ran your fingers down them they had a soothing effect. Needless to say we bought one. Over the years we loved and nurtured that tree, and by 1992 it stood a proud nine feet tall in our sunroom. Even after all these years I still delighted in running my fingers down its boughs. One day I went off to work, and all seemed pretty calm on the home front. The problem was when I came home and noticed that my beautiful tree was missing. Gradually my eyes turned toward a big garbage bag on the floor and found it contained the mangled, chopped up remains of my tree.

At first I was too stupefied to say anything, but I finally asked David what had happened. He very casually said, "Oh, the top didn't look right so I cut it up." What was I to say? There was absolutely no way one could argue with David these days or he would fly into a rage, so I bit my tongue and accepted my loss. His medications caused steroid psychosis and he had bouts of dementia; only afterward he had no memory of what he had done or said during these episodes, so there was no point trying to discuss or analyze what had happened. As my doctor told me, "You cannot rationalize with someone who is irrational." So life went on with no respite from work or home except the visits from Ruth and Gord.

Ultimately it was my close friendship with Ruth that gave me the one outlet that would allow me a reprieve from my concerns about David and his declining health. We decided that we would both enrol at the University of Western Ontario and work toward a degree. The thought of doing this was very exciting and not a little intimidating. Ruth was interested in starting with a sociology course while I liked the idea of doing anthropology. As we wanted to be together we decided on sociology for the first year and anthropology for the second year. These were full courses running from September to April, and as we were both working full time we did one evening class once a week. Boy did we have fun. An added bonus was that while I was studying during the week, my mind was not on my other problems. And did I study! Although there was nothing hinging on my passing the exams, I was unwilling to fail. That word is not in my vocabulary. Admittedly I was older now and had been away from academia for several decades, but during my whole life I had never failed an exam and was not about to now.

Come exam time I was a bundle of nerves and questioning my ability to have retained the knowledge I would need to pass. Well, Ruth and I both passed with good marks. Driving home in Ruth's truck that night we were ecstatic and could not wait for the next September when we could continue our studies. Ruth is a clever lady, and I must admit that on that first exam her marks were a little higher than mine. This had been multiple choice, which is not my favourite type of exam.

Now the next year in anthropology I wrote my first essay in 43 years and received a mark of 96 percent. I felt thoroughly vindicated. I lost the other 4 percent because I did not realize I had to state my case at the beginning of the essay. My professor wrote on my paper, "Cynthia, do not ever change a thing about your writing." I was so happy, particularly as I had chosen a subject I later found out was this professor's speciality. My paper was "The Effects of Revolution in a Peasant Society with Special Emphasis on Land Reform."

After that we took a psychology course, but Ruth did not continue any further. Gord passed away suddenly and unexpectedly and Ruth sold the house and moved to Victoria. After that we lost touch with one another. This must have been late 1997.

But I am getting ahead of myself. Prior to this, in 1995, when she was 19, Susan moved to Toronto. At first she and her friend Stephanie stayed with Cathy for a while before getting their own apartment. Then another so-called friend came to stay with them for a vacation and managed to sabotage the friendship, ending with Susan going to the police station in a state of confusion. The police officer called us and we went straight away. It was about a two-and-a-half hour drive and it was already evening. Well, we picked her up and took her to her apartment where the visiting girl had completely taken over. When we tried to talk to this girl she swore and screamed abuse at my husband and me so we left and took Susan home. Ultimately Susan went back to Toronto, where she met and moved in with her future husband, Jim.

It was about this time that Richard returned from Germany as the Canadian forces closed their base at Lahr. Richard loved

Germany and would have liked to stay there, but he returned and was posted to Petawawa. Just before leaving Lahr, Richard and Lynne had split up and were getting a divorce. It was amicable and they remain good friends to this day. I think that was perhaps the problem. They were very good friends but did not get along as a married couple. Life happens. Richard did not enjoy the military here in Canada, so he left the forces. He moved into an apartment and obtained an interim job here in Stratford.

Goodness, life became really complicated around this time with all the comings and goings of our various offspring! I am trying my best to keep the timelines straight, really I am, but please forgive an old lady if you happen to discover that some of them are a little muddled. Remember the "what ifs" and the "could have beens", and also the "what was real and what imagined"? Although I know the events I am now writing about are definitely real, I may have the odd date off by a few months here and there, so I ask your forgiveness in advance, dear reader, and trust that this will not interfere with your enjoyment of the story.

The date is December 1995. By now Richard had gone on to furthering his skills in computer engineering and was flying through his courses and gaining much credibility. On the morning of December 22, David and I received a phone call from the police department to inform us Toby had suffered a very serious industrial accident and had been taken to St. Joseph's Hospital in London. We could not get there quick enough, wondering all the way just what had happened and just how serious it was. Meanwhile, unbeknownst to us, news of his accident was being broadcast over the radio and flashed on people's television screens.

We arrived at St. Joseph's full of apprehension and were immediately ushered into the emergency department. The police were still there and Toby and his buddy (who had been assisting him) were both strapped to stretchers with head braces, and Toby was positioned so he could not move at all. As we went over to them we were overwhelmed with joy when we heard, "Hi, Mom and Dad." He was awake; he was lucid; he was alive! Toby's friend was released later that day with a sore neck, but at the time we did not realize he had sustained it when his quick action had saved our son's life.

Toby worked installing and fixing garage doors, most of which were industrial. On this particular morning he was working on a 30-plus-foot industrial door in London. He had already attached his safety harness and was just working on loosening the springs at the bottom of the door. It turned out that whoever had previously worked on the door had tightened the springs down by about five turns too many. Suddenly the door shot up 30 feet 2 inches, taking Toby with it. If he had not managed to unclip his safety equipment he would have been decapitated.

As it was, at more than 30 feet he thrown out 12 feet and was coming down on his back onto the concrete. Without the quick action of his buddy, who did not give a thought to his own safety, Toby's head would have smashed on the concrete and he would have been dead. His friend ran right underneath him and broke his fall. They both went down, with Toby landing on top and then rolling onto his right side. Heaven bless that selfless young man, whoever he was and wherever he may be now. At the risk of injury to himself he saved my son's life. As it was, Toby's injuries were severe. He sustained a broken right shoulder blade, his bone in his upper arm was broken in two, he had several broken ribs and had injured two of his thoracic vertebrae. Worst of all, his right wrist was completely crushed to powder.

The doctors did as much as they could for him in terms of his arm, shoulder and ribs and then let him out of the hospital for Christmas. This felt good to have him home with the rest of the family even though he had to return to hospital on January 2 for surgery to rebuild his wrist. Achieving this was going to be complicated, as essentially there was nothing left. What they did was take several plugs of bone from his hip and use this to build a new wrist. He was cautioned that if he ever did anything to injure it again, there would be nothing they could do. The doctors also predicted that he would never have more than 16 percent use in this wrist.

Toby came home with a big metal rod in his arm attached by screw into his hand and arm. Sleeping was difficult because of his ribs and other breaks so he slept in a reclining chair to be more upright and have more support. Throughout all of this he would not even take so much as a Tylenol for his pain. He did not like drugs of any kind. Now, at age 40, he has full use of his wrist, is active as a goalie on a hockey team and is full of energy. All that remains physically is a deep scar on his hand from the screw and a long scar on his hip from having bone removed. Some angel was definitely watching over him throughout his ordeal.

Let me back up a bit here to the fall of 1995. Richard had met a most beautiful young lady by the name of Eva Lok. She was a foot specialist and had her own practice. She had gone to the same college as Richard so she could brush up on the business aspects of her practice. One evening, Richard brought her home for supper to introduce us. That was it—she won me over right then and there ! Eva was born in Hong Kong but had moved to Canada with her family when she was quite young. It seemed pretty obvious to David and me that she and Richard were made for each other, and this made us very happy.

Our other ecstatic moment came about mid-October, when Susan phoned me from Toronto. In and of itself this was not unusual but this time it was different. When she said, "Mom, are you sitting down, I have something to tell you," I knew exactly what she was going to say. "Mom, I'm pregnant."

I was delighted! Sue was pretty sure this would be my reaction, and I told her that to hear of a new life coming into the world was cause for celebration. She and Jim had been planning to get married anyway, but Sue did not know that taking antibiotics took away the effectiveness of birth control pills. She was 19 and Jim was 29.

David surprised me by being equally excited (he's a bit old-fashioned about these things). He said, "Come on, let's get in the car and go to K-Mart." Did we ever have fun. There we were, a pair of would-be first time grandparents buying all kinds of little baby things. What a joy! We were bursting at the thought of our first grandchild.

On May 7, 1996, Kodiak Charles David Gwynn was born. He arrived around one a.m. after a rather difficult pregnancy and an even more difficult delivery. Although they were still living in Toronto, Sue wanted to be close to her own doctor when she delivered so was staying with Mom and Dad. While Jim was rushing from Toronto to St. Marys I was at Stratford Hospital with Sue and was definitely *not* impressed with the attitude of the staff. Susan was in terrible pain and was vomiting almost continuously, but she was having back contractions that did not show.

I shall never forget the words of the one nurse, who said, "My dear, there are more important people than you here." I think that what she was seeing was a 20-year-old black girl with no male with her and no wedding ring, and she thought Susan was just making a fuss. Finally someone paid attention and an obstetrician was called. They tried to give her an epidural but after five attempts gave up. But then Kodi was born and he was just beautiful, although it was obvious he was way overdue. By now Jim had arrived, and he and I drove home floating on a cloud.

At around eight o clock the next morning Sue called to say they were rushing Kodi to the Children's Hospital in London. He had been having seizures all night but no one had noticed until they removed his swaddling clothes and saw his limbs twitching. It turned out he had suffered a stroke as the result of having waited too long during labour. He was overdue and the uterine environment had started to break up and had passed a blood clot through the umbilical cord to his brain. When they did the scans it was still a bleeding stroke, which meant it must have happened during the last 24 hours when "there are more important people than you here"! Half the left hemisphere of his brain was dead and things were looking bleak.

I have to admire Sue's strength in the way she handled all of this. For one thing, she was not allowed to ride in the ambulance with Kodi but was discharged from Stratford Hospital, told she would have to make her own way to London and then would be readmitted. Wrong once again. Because she had been discharged, not transferred, they would not readmit her. Talk about bureaucracy—the girl had just gone through hell! Kodi was in hospital for several weeks before being considered stable enough to come home.

Once back at Mom and Dad's with Kodi, Sue could finally relax and within minutes was fast asleep on the couch with her baby lying on top of her, also fast asleep. The prognosis for our little grandson was not good. He was not expected to walk, talk or to be able to function independently. May I just say that at 15 years of age he is in high school? He is tall, dark and handsome with long black lashes and dark eyes that have all the girls swooning.

He is athletic and can run like the wind, skateboard (he has two broken teeth to show for this) and takes public transit just like any other teenager. Underneath this apparent normalcy he has a stack of neurological disorders, but unless someone told you, you would not think there was anything wrong with him. In so many ways he really lucked out. It also pleased everyone to see that Kodi and Grandpa had an unbreakable bond between them, but later we will see just how close to tragedy this bond brought Kodi.

We visited Sue and Jim in Toronto to see our little grandson when he was a few months old. Believe me, it took something this important to make me venture onto Highway 401 in anything less than an armoured tank. As far as I was concerned that road was a manic death trap. Of course it is possible I could be a little, just a little, neurotic in heavy traffic, but I would rather put it down to an overdeveloped sense of self preservation. Upon seeing my darling little grandson, all fears were dispelled. He was so happy and lively. Even at a few months he was holding on to the back of the couch and jumping up and down with incredible energy. We quickly nicknamed him "Tigger." Dave took videos of Kodi and I wish I knew what he did with them. Like many things, David did not seem to have a sense of the future importance of things. He did not like sentimentality in any form. Sue and Jim told us they were planning to move from Toronto back to our sleepy little town of St. Marys. It appears Sue was pregnant again and preferred to be closer to home. Jim would do anything for his family so this was not a problem, and within a short while they moved into the top half of a house not far from us and Jim found work.

On March 17, 1997, our darling little Cameron Daniel Gwynn was born. This time Sue was in the high-risk maternity section at St. Joseph Hospital in London. Cameron was so tiny, just 16 inches long, but perfectly healthy and just 10 months and 10 days younger than Kodi.

Sue's labour came in the middle of a blinding snow storm with the police blocking off roads, and visibility down to zero at some points. Somehow I found a way through and we arrived at the hospital safe and sound. She was in labour for five days, during which time my best friend Ruth took a week off work to look after Kodi. Incidentally, Cameron is now 14 and the spitting image of his mom. He is tall, husky and is a lance corporal in army cadets. Oh, and he wears a size 12 shoe. So much for our teeny, tiny baby.

Let's back up to 1996 again. This same year David, Toby and I undertook a joint venture that I must admit was my idea. Was it a brilliant idea? I don't know. Maybe it could have been. Was it a stupid idea? Perhaps, but one has to try and we cannot just sit back and play it safe forever. Was it an innovative idea? Definitely. A little way out from the edge of town and backing onto a beautiful conservation area stood an old, empty nursing home with five acres of ground. The owner had been trying to sell it for ages but this was a problem because of the zoning, which was institutional. Of course I had previously owned a farm, a schoolhouse and a church, and David had warned the children not to tell me of any fire halls that were for sale. He had not, however, said anything about not buying a nursing home, so I figured it was fair game.

The three of us sat down and discussed this at length and arranged to go and see the place. It had not been well maintained as a nursing home; in fact, it was downright awful, but it would be great for our purpose, although it would require a great deal of work. That's right, dear reader, I did not tell you about our master plan, did I?

After his accident, Toby was not able to continue with the job he had been doing, and although the Workmen's Compensation Board sent him for retraining this was just not his thing. Toby has many attributes, but the ones that really stand out are his incredibly high energy level, the fact that he can do complex mathematical equations in his head before you can even get a calculator out of your pocket and a talent for singing and song writing that is quite phenomenal. Yes, I know I am his mother, but this is also everyone else's opinion. Add to this a charismatic personality and you have something really saleable. So our idea was to sell our house, buy the old nursing home (more than six thousand square feet) and turn it into a school for the performing arts. I would continue to work as well to maintain our income, Toby would teach voice and we would expand into other areas pertaining to the performing arts and hire the appropriate teachers. As for the zoning being institutional, it was a perfect fit for what we wanted. At first Toby was nervous about the proposal and came on board with, I think, some trepidation. David and I would supply the down payment but it would be jointly owned by all three of us as Toby would be doing the work and spearheading the project.

Our house sold in a day to the first person who walked through it. Next came the problem of obtaining a mortgage for the new place. We jumped through hoops to get one but finally acquired one with a somewhat higher interest rate. Meanwhile, Toby had been talking to his mentor down in the States, who to our amazement said that he would match every cent we put into the place. So in recognition of his contribution we named the school after him, and it became "The Shallenberger Centre for the Performing Arts." Our building plans, which David drew up, were approved, but at first we basically camped out at the place until the work got started.

At one end of the building was to be two one-bedroom

apartments, one for Toby and one for David and me, complete with our own entrances, kitchen, bathroom, etc. By this time Dan had finished school and was living in an apartment in town with two of his friends. He was also working downtown and this was handy for him. With the help of friends, Toby worked his butt off to renovate the building and it started to take shape very nicely, but it was a big project. There were teaching rooms, an office, a reception area, washrooms and a huge drama rehearsal room. There was also a room with mirrored walls for ballet and other forms of dance. Eventually Toby installed a state-of-the-art recording studio. The biggest hold up was that the fire chief would not approve us for opening until the entire building was completely finished, even though two thirds of it was set to go. Because of this we were not able to open or generate income for a whole year. It was fortunate that I was working and earning good money as we did not finally open until 1997.

Our opening was a huge success. We were all set to teach voice, choir, piano, drums, guitar, drama, ballet and modern dance. We had a fully equipped kitchen suitable for catering for when we rented out the big drama room. Around the edge was carpet, but the middle was a lovely parquet floor that was good for dancing. The final fire inspection was "fun" in a sock-it-to-you kind of way. One of the responsibilities of my job with the association was to do the annual compliance revue in their buildings. And who did I have to deal with? You guessed it, the fire chief. He was a really good guy and certainly knew his stuff, and over the years I had gotten to know him well. Consequently, I also knew exactly what he would be looking for when he inspected the centre. Well, he could not find a single thing wrong! Secretly I think he was a bit miffed but was good humoured about it. Waiting a whole year to open had really affected us financially, but I could also see the fire chief's point of view. After all, the buck stopped with him if anything untoward happened.

By the end of our open house we had many students lined up for lessons, the majority for voice training. So we were finally off and running and able to start generating some income from the centre.

20.

Times of Trial and Error (the Mediator)

*I*t was 1998 and all was well. I was still working, and I was planning to do so until I was 65 and able to get my Canada pension. Toby's reputation as a teacher and singer/songwriter was growing by leaps and bounds and he had a waiting list of students. At Christmastime the students had put on a really good concert for their families. Talk about the world going 'round—our drama teacher was one of Toby's former high school teachers who was now retired. We put on a production of *Oliver!*, and while Toby taught the vocals his partner taught the acting. This was a good give-and-take relationship and they worked wonders together.

David and I were enjoying our beautiful property—five scenic acres complete with a meandering stream and some really big, old weeping willow trees. There was also a big barn and some little sheds, but best of all were the large flowering cherry trees outside our living room patio window. We also had apple trees

that encouraged the deer to come right up to the building for a
tasty nibble. It was enchanting. And of course we cannot forget
our two little grandsons who came every weekend and could play
in complete safety in our rural setting. On their birthdays, Sue
and Jim were able to use the drama room for their parties so there
was lots of room for all of the kiddies to play.

Time passed quickly and I was working a lot of hours.
Sometimes I would go back to my office in the evening so I could
catch up on my paperwork without the phone ringing or having to
deal with clients' crises. Perhaps if I had been home more I would
have been more cognizant of David's changing behaviours. His
health was deteriorating rapidly and I was well aware of this, as it
was I who sat in the emergency department at Stratford Hospital
two or three nights a week, either because of his migraines or yet
another attack of pneumonia. Often I did not get home until the
middle of the night and still had to get up and work the next day.
What I was not so aware of was his changing mental attitude,
especially toward Toby. At this point he was still able to control
this when I was around.

In anything he had ever done he had always "run the show"
and been the top dog. All of a sudden he was no longer the alpha
male; this was a partnership and Toby had authority as well.
Actually, Toby was doing all the work, teaching and keeping
up with any maintenance around the building. He barely had
a minute to himself and very little income. All the money went
into paying the bills.

Toward the end of the year the animosity became more
noticeable, with Dave resorting to yelling and arguing about
every little thing. He was definitely more unstable, and as his
wife I had the unenviable task of having to step in and mediate. I
totally understand where Toby was coming from and was behind

him 100 percent, but I also had to be supportive of my husband and try to put a more favourable light on his actions. This was not an easy task. As much as I wanted to rationalize them away, I could no longer ignore his behaviours.

As far as the students went, all was well. Toby entered the voice students into various competitions and without exception they always took first prize. If two or three students entered the same category they would take first, second and third prize. This was nothing short of amazing. Naturally we had our share of "stage mothers," but thankfully not too many. Problems began to arise when parents did not pay their bills or bounced cheques. As Toby could not do everything, David decided to step in and take over the finances. Bad move! He put everything into his computer with a password to stop anyone accessing anything. After a few months we were in one heck of a mess. His idea of filing was to keep stacking bills (some unopened) into big, jumbled piles. Now we all know this does not work, but he was "in control."

Things got worse when Toby's mentor had problems and stopped sending the promised money each month, so I cashed in the rest of my Registered Retirement Savings Plan to keep us going. We even hired a part-time accountant to try to get us straight, but Dave would not give him any of the paperwork he asked for. Quite honestly, I think he lost them. It had reached the point where any communication regarding the business had to go through me as he was slipping more and more into episode of dementia. I agreed with the accountant when he said there was no point in being there without David's cooperation, so he left.

David was in a great deal of physical pain and his joints were giving out and becoming even more deformed. He had already had numerous surgeries including three knee replacements, the toes on his left foot amputated and those on his right foot operated on to straighten them. Then there were the hernias and other internal problems along with an elbow that had to be replaced (because it was broken in five places) and would not heal no matter what. Can one even be surprised at his mental condition? Next I found out he was saying things about me behind my back—for example, that I wanted to kill him. This really took me by surprise. He also kept notes on his observations about me, such as how I said I cared about him but my body language said otherwise. When he was not going through these episodes it was as if nothing had ever happened and he was his kind, loving self. As he had no memory of his psychosis, I could not even discuss these issues with him. I had to pretend everything was fine. And who could I turn to? I had no friends. There was no one I could phone and nowhere I could go. This was my reality—this was it!

One day I was really upset and got into the car crying and drove to Stratford. I called my doctor from my cell phone and he immediately saw me. It appears he was more aware of David's personality than I realized. He told me David was a very controlling person, and that he knew because David had tried it on him a few times. He gave me a prescription for a medication used for severe anxiety and we agreed I would see the doctor periodically. Strangely enough, David had written a paper giving me the final say in everything if ever it became necessary, so the doctor and I were able to discuss the concerns surrounding David's health without breaking the doctor's code of ethics.

Could things possibly get any worse? Oh yes they could! Enter Enrico Bertolini! Dear reader, have you ever met a true narcissist? No? Then let me introduce you to Mr. Bertolini. I first set eyes on him when he and his lovely wife attended the 1998 Christmas concert. Their daughter had been receiving lessons all year. She was between sixteen and seventeen and had a beautiful voice.

Even now I can remember my first impression of Mr. Bertolini. He was definitely positioned in the forefront with his wife barely saying a word. She was an older version of her daughter (an only child) with those beautiful, dark Italian looks. We chatted briefly and that was that, as the saying goes. Or was it? Christmas came and went and at least we had plenty of room to have the whole family together. That year the association for which I worked held their annual Christmas dinner for staff and clients at our facility. I don't know when I ever saw so many people turn up for that event.

With the advent of 1999 Enrico started to hang around more and more often. He was getting very chummy with Toby and seemed to be wiggling his way into everything, especially our business, which was private and should have been none of his concern. But he filled Toby's head with all kinds of ideas and Toby was probably relieved to have someone to talk to. Now Toby and I had always been close, had respect for one another and understood one another, but I began to sense him closing off from me and getting quite, well, snarky is the word I would use. In this company Toby was the president and I was the vice president and David held the other third of what we jointly owned. Suddenly I was hearing things from Toby, such as, "What's this two-third bit you and Dad are using against me?" He should have known I was on his side, but I also had to keep David out of the business without him realizing it and deal with work and David's illness at the same time. Things were out of hand when David was dealing with the local businesses. He would suddenly become paranoid and start yelling and screaming, particularly at our pharmacist, and I ended up having to mend a lot of fences. I even went so far as to tell the pharmacist to make sure he called me if he had any questions, and to make sure to call me at work, not at home. On top of that

David's driving was getting really bad, with him thinking he had the right of way when he didn't. I became inventive with reasons I should drive when we were out together.

Suddenly Mr. Narcissist decided to leave his wife and daughter, take all the money "because it was his" and move in with Toby. Please understand, it was none of my business who Toby invited into his apartment, so it was not my place to say anything. Mr. N. made himself very comfortable in our place and started trying to take over everything. He even decided to take over half the basement, buying wood and building shelves for all his belongings that he'd removed from his home. Worst of all was the way he abused and damaged the things David and I had stored down there. Our things may have looked as if they were in a bit of a jumble, but everything was packed safely and I knew where everything was. Showing absolutely no respect for our property, he just heaved it across the room in a pile.

This really upset me, especially when I could not find the box containing my wedding veil. It had been carefully packed in a square box to prevent it from being crushed. The veil was a very long, traditional style and I had needed two page boys to carry it at our wedding. It was attached to the top of a pillbox hat covered in French lace, and Susan was going to wear the veil at her wedding in August. Eventually I found it—underneath a pile of rocks and totally crushed. The hat was squashed flat and the delicate strands of the veil had all snapped from the weight. The cardboard box looked like a concertina. After carefully looking after this for 36 years, I was devastated. There was no point in telling Toby and I definitely needed to keep this from David, so I mourned my sentimental loss alone.

Periodically we held staff meetings to discuss where we were and what we could do better, as well as to plan for any upcoming events. For the sake of harmony I suggested to David that I would go on behalf of both of us. I just wanted a good, productive meeting where we could maintain professionalism and be respectful of one another's views.

As soon as I walked into the meeting I could see the battle lines had been drawn. Enrico and Toby were sitting (or rather lounging) next to each other along the back wall. You could have cut the atmosphere with a knife, and their body language stated very strongly, "We are a team, we are one and we are in control." I had never seen Toby act this way before and I am not making excuses for him—he had the right to choose. But why was Enrico even there? He had nothing to do with the business. The teachers were along the side wall, and there, at the wall facing Toby and Mr. Narcissist was one chair on its own, left for me. Now I am not a stupid person and my job included my chairing many meetings, so I could see at a glance what was going on here. I had also passed a full university course on industrial/organizational psychology and this was just a transparent ploy to put me on the defensive. It did not work. I remained calm and professional even though the comments directed at me were rude, patriarchal and condescending. Paul, the guitar teacher, was looking at what was happening with incredulity. He was so embarrassed I think he must have wished the floor would open up and swallow him.

The meeting did not last long. Later I discovered that Enrico had offered to take Toby to pay three rather pressing bills to the total sum of approximately $3,000. Was he stupid enough to think this would clear the way for him to take over the business? Because I am sure that was his plan. So Toby was desperate and made a deal with the Devil. I think he quickly learned this Devil now expected him to dance to his tune. A couple of days later I went to my office in our building and found Enrico had been making himself comfortable in there. On my desk was his day book, and he'd been stupid enough to leave it open. As far as I'm concerned this discounts any expectations of privacy, so I read the open page. Listed there were all the ways in which he was planning to work on Toby to turn him against David and me. For example, he wrote, "Your parents are using you, your parents don't trust you, your parents don't care about you," and so on, ad nauseum. I took the day book up to reception and photocopied the page. In fact, I believe I still have it somewhere. Although I did not tell Toby about this, Enrico did not seem to be around too much longer. I like to think the real Toby saw him for what he was. Thus 1999 was a year of ups and downs in so many ways.

Along with the coming of spring came Richard and Eva's wedding. This made me so happy to have Eva as a daughter-in-law. She was petite and pretty, but she had a brain like a steel trap. I think perhaps she is one of the cleverest women I have known. While she had her own practice, Richard had a high profile position with London Health Sciences working with their computer systems.

Their wedding was on a Wednesday, with the date being set according to Chinese traditional signs by Mr. Chong Lok, Eva's father. For this there were just family members present (about 30 people) and afterward a family reception at a restaurant. Come Saturday there was a full, traditional Chinese reception in Toronto with probably 150 guests. What a meal! We had 11 courses and each one was fish, but with such a variety. It was incredible. Eva wore a beautiful evening gown, and as tradition dictated, halfway through the dinner she changed into an equally lovely gown. Everyone from out of town had been booked into a hotel for the night so we could party late. The next day Richard and Eva moved into their new home in London.

At the beginning of summer I had a rather unsettling phone call from my brother Don in England. At the same time but in different cities, he and my brother Sam had been admitted to hospital. Donald had thrombosis and Sam had had a stroke. They had both been tested for a genetic condition called Factor V Leiden, which had only been discovered a year before, and both of their tests came back positive. (Factor V Leiden is an inherited genetic disorder that can increase your chance of developing abnormal blood clots, usually in your veins.) Don told me that I and my biological children had to be tested right away. My doctor had not even heard of this yet but found the necessary information and arranged for me to have a blood test. The laboratory had not even heard of it either but did the test and sent it off to Toronto. It came back positive as did my daughter Cathy's test. Richard declined to tell me whether or not he had had the test or of any possible results. All of a sudden the old saying in my mother's family made sense: "If you can get past your early sixties you will live to a ripe old age; the trick is getting past your early sixties." Most of my relatives did not, so that meant we had a strong familial history of this problem. Ah well, life goes on.

At the centre we were still keeping our heads above water but were having a terrible time collecting the money owed us, so it was a good thing I was still working. By now I had been getting the maximum holiday allotment of five paid weeks per year for several years. Trying to fit the holidays around my workload was another question, but when David and I received a letter from Reg and Jean Butler, two old Scouting buddies from England, to say they were coming to Canada I really hustled to get the time off. They were going to be touring around Canada for several weeks and wanted to meet up with us in Kingston (up the dreaded highway 401) and spend a week together bed and breakfasting and touring the Algonquin and Georgian Bay area. Oh how good this sounded; a week without responsibilities and just enjoying time with old friends. David quickly booked some bed and breakfast places and we were all set.

It was a beautiful sunny day in June when we set out on our journey. I was really looking forward to seeing our old friends, but I must admit to some trepidation regarding travel on the 401, which was necessary in order to get to our destination. This highway was from Windsor in Southern Ontario right through to Montreal in Quebec and is heavily used by big, commercial tractor trailers and such. From our home it took about one-and-a-half hours to reach the 401, all of it through idyllic countryside, but once there the merge lane onto the main highway was long and nasty. I considered it worse than any other access lanes I had ever driven. Nonetheless, we merged safely into the traffic in the slow lane, though even this was going at about 110 kilometres an hour. Phew! Now I could relax a little. We had travelled for about 10 minutes when we felt a jolt from our rear bumper. This did not really alarm me until I realized our car had started to spin around and around. One second we were facing backward with a tour bus coming straight at us, and as we continued to spin across the four lanes it hit our car right in my passenger door. The impact sent us across all the lanes into the concrete median, which we hit. This impact sent us back into the lanes of traffic, where the tour bus once again hit my passenger door. Back to the median we went and somehow David managed to bring the car to a stop. Thank God. We were motionless and we were okay. If we had been hit by the bus on the driver's side it would most likely have broken every bone in David's body. My bones were strong.

Before we knew it people were running up to our car. I shall never forget the beautiful, dark lady who reassuringly said, "I am a nurse," and told me to lie still. David, thank goodness, was totally unscathed but I had taken the brunt of the hits and my car door was wedged into my right hip. If, by any chance of fate, that lovely lady should read this book and recognize herself, I want to say a profound thank you for her calmness and reassurance. Next I heard a cacophony of sirens and then there were firemen and paramedics everywhere. I had to be released from the car by the firemen due to my door being pushed in and was told by one of them, "Lady, I don't know how you're still alive." My neck was hurting but I was certainly alive and oh so thankful our merry-go–round had stopped.

Then the paramedics extracted me from the car and had me firmly strapped to a stretcher with my head immobilized. I remember seeing out of the corner of my eye photographers snapping pictures of me and feeling a little indignant. Soon the sirens were blaring and we were speeding off to Cambridge Hospital. Although I never saw it, apparently a double tractor trailer had made an illegal lane change and tipped our bumper, which is what sent us spinning. There were many witnesses and the driver was charged on the spot.

Upon arrival at Cambridge Hospital I was taken into a cubicle in emergency and the doctor immediately arrived. He examined me thoroughly and sent me for X-rays. The results came back negative but to this day I have a problem with my right hip that has worsened over the years, and I suspect there was a hairline fracture that did not show on the X-rays. By the time I was back to the cubicle Richard had arrived. I was given Ativan and Percocet and released. Boy did I feel good! I remember telling Richard, "See, I told you your mother was a tough old bird." This was okay, but apparently, from the backseat of the car, I kept repeating this all the way home. It must have been with some relief that they bundled me into bed, where I immediately fell into a drug-induced sleep. Our car was a write-off. While I was sleeping, Richard and David went to the lot where it had been towed and took photos of the damage. There were bumps and bangs on all four sides. Next they arranged for a replacement car through our insurance agency and contacted Reg and Jean at the hotel in Kingston. Apparently our little mishap along with our names was all over the news on both television and the radio, and the 401 was completely shut down for about four hours while an investigation took place.

By the next morning I was perfectly lucid. I was also hardly able to move as I was badly bruised, especially all up my right side. Nonetheless, my dear husband bundled me into our rental car and once more we set out on our journey to Kingston, following the route we had taken the previous day. I was a nervous wreck until we passed the point of the previous day's mishap, and then my internal barometer went down to extremely nervous. At least this was a step in the right direction.

Several hours later we reached Kingston and were reunited with Reg and Jean. I was so glad David had insisted on keeping our plans. We had a wonderful time taking in the places of interest and stayed at some charming bed and breakfasts. By now I was really stiff and the bruising was hurting, especially when I tried to find a comfortable position for sleeping. Reg gallantly assisted me in and out of the car but I could walk pretty well on my own. Time just flew by and too soon our lovely holiday was over and we had to say goodbye to our friends from England. We never saw them again, although Jean and I still write the occasional letter to each other.

Once we returned home things settled back into our normal routine, at least for a short while. Then I started to experience a bad pain in my lower left abdomen, along with some other strange symptoms. This led to my being hospitalized for a few days to clear up an infection from diverticulitis. After being released, the same problem recurred and back I went. This happened three times before I experienced a really bad pain. The elderly doctor who was filling in while my own doctor was away examined me and declared, "My dear, you need a surgeon." With this he wrote a note to Dr. Sorsdahl, a specialist at Stratford Hospital and sent me there right away. I was admitted and lined up for surgery. It was a major surgery that required opening up my abdomen from top to bottom. It was found that I had a perforated bowel with an abscess on the outside that kept feeding infection into my bowel. Part of my bowel was removed and there I was, back in hospital again. Oh joy, this was fun, and yes I am being sarcastic. I was in hospital for a couple of weeks and then allowed home. The hospital lined up home help for me as I was not to do anything. David really spoiled me, putting a lawn chair under the crab apple tree and piling it with pillows. Ah, it was good to be home but it was a while before I could return to work. Fortunately I had plenty of sick time accumulated plus still more holiday time.

Within a short time of being home I was getting ready for bed and experienced a very sharp pain in my lower right back. I decided to remain dressed for a while and watch some television to take my mind off it. By one a.m. I was walking back and forth in agony and had to wake David to take me to the hospital. I was immediately admitted, but no matter which way the nurses tried to get me comfortable it hurt so much I was crying out. Now this is definitely not like me. In fact, I have a very high pain threshold but I had never felt such pain as this.

Dr. Parsons came in to see me the next morning. He was

asking me how I was when he suddenly said, "Are you out of breath?"

I guess I was but had not realized it. All of a sudden there was a flurry of activity. Dr. Sorsdahl was called and I was sent for an MRI (I remember that room was freezing). The MRI showed that I had blood clots in my right lung. In other words, I had suffered a pulmonary embolism. Then came more specialists, lots of needles, and lots of IVs. They were in both wrists, which made things a little difficult, but I did not care what they did as long as I received some relief from the pain. I was kept in a private room and told I would be there for a couple of weeks. Quite frankly I did not realize what all the fuss was about, but I was treated like a princess by all the staff and specialists.

Dr. Parsons came to see me every morning before going to his office, as he did with any of his patients who were hospitalized. What really surprised me was when my executive director and another manager came to see me, bringing me a huge bouquet of the most beautiful flowers. He assured me not to worry about getting back to work but to take as long as I needed to get well.

On one particular morning, Dr. Parsons came to see me as usual but this time was different. He leaned against the wall and looked very serious before telling me that both of the problems I'd had were extremely serious. I had not realized this and was somewhat taken aback. He took his time to explain that when I had the bowel surgery I was found to have a rather exotic bug that was hard to kill. Then he explained that after surgery I had developed a blood clot in the top of my left leg that had worked its way up to my right lung, and that the chances of survival had been 50 percent.

Finally my genetics had caught up with me and I was going to be on blood thinners for the rest of my life instead of the usual six months. Whew! I'd had no idea things were so critical. By now I had a team of specialists, one of whom had the job of balancing my blood levels, and even though I was feeling good I was not allowed home for yet another two weeks until they were balanced (something that had proved to be rather difficult). Then I was home, 30 pounds lighter and looking forward to Sue and Jim's wedding in August. Dr. Parsons would not allow me back to work until September and then only for two hours a day, increasing one hour a day every two weeks after that. By now we had finished fighting with our insurance company over the car and they finally gave us $5,000, even though it was worth considerably more. C'est la vie; what can you do? Anyway, we were going to be having a lovely outdoor wedding right in our own backyard.

Our stately old willow tree was going to be the backdrop for the ceremony and we were renting a white wedding tent for the reception, along with caterers and a DJ. Sue and Jim were on a bit of a tight budget but both the caterer and the tent owner were people we knew so gave them a good deal. Cathy was to be the maid of honour and Richard the best man. Two other bridesmaids plus Toby and Dan made up the rest of the wedding party. It was so nice to be able to look forward to some happiness and pleasure after the stresses of the last year or two, and David once more showed his excellent and varied talents by making Susan's wedding dress. It was simple but elegant and I stitched a row of small pearls along the shape of the bust line. My veil was no longer an option thanks to Mr. N., but Sue had bought a pretty tiara.

The big day dawned bright, warm and sunny and all the younger generation were busy with the final touches before the afternoon ceremony. Our big willow tree was adorned with curls of satin ribbon and silk roses. What a picture it made! Early the previous evening the wedding tent had been erected and all the tables and chairs put in place, so things were looking really festive. A final touch was the row of urns holding gladioli that were placed all along the front of the table where the ceremony was to take place. This was another idea David had arranged. Now one cannot have a wedding without a glitch. Ours came in the form (or should I say swarm) of dozens of furry, flying, stinging bees! Apparently the spot under the willow tree where the table was placed was on an underground nest and the table leg broke through. So this had to be dealt with and the table moved forward. The minister and guests arrived and Sue was walked from the building to the willow by her dad. She looked stunning. She had always had the prettiest face with big dimples when she smiles.

It did not start raining until everyone was in the reception tent, so we were all dry and happy. I had collected all the gladioli and placed them just inside the door of the tent so the ladies could help themselves after the dance. Sue had left Jim to order the wedding cake and I must say his choice was simple but elegant. What a perfect day! My personal little glitch came when I was approached privately by Richard. Being the best man, it was his responsibility to disburse the cheques for the various servicers, but just ten minutes before she walked down the aisle with her dad, Sue had informed Richard she had no money to pay for any of this. She had followed the English tradition of buying the bridesmaids dresses and shoes for them and had paid for the flowers. However, being in and out of hospital so much I had not stopped to consider how Sue and Jim were going to find the resources to fund their wedding. So I did the only thing I could do at this point and gave Richard my chequebook with five signed cheques. These were for the minister, the caterer, the tent company, the photographer and the DJ and came to just about $5,000, the amount I had received for the car. Oh well, what was done was done and I was not going to make an issue of it and spoil their special day. As always, Mom would sort it out later, with my only recourse being that I would have to lease a car instead of buying one.

Come September I started back to work. The first week I followed my doctors' orders and just worked two hours each morning, but there was so much catching up to do and it was a busy job at the best of times. By the second week I was totally immersed in my work again and reverted to my full-time hours. Besides, I loved my job and was happy to be there, the only thing clouding this happiness being my worry about the centre. Sometimes I wondered, if only I could be there perhaps I could sort out some of the issues, but we needed my paycheque. Because of having had the blood clots my right lung was compromised, and by November I was feeling the effects. I was having episodes of being out of breath, especially if I had to tackle going up steps. Then an amazing thing happened. My executive director called me into his office and made me an offer. While making it clear I did not have to accept it and could work for as long as I wished, he offered me a payout of $15,000 if I would like to retire. This was unheard of and very generous, but I had been working there for fifteen years. Besides this I was also offered three years of extended sick benefits under the association's extremely generous medical plan. With David's health being the way it was this was incredible, as his medication alone ran into hundreds of dollars a month. Someone had obviously thought this out and cared enough about me to put this plan in place. For three years I would be on extended sick leave!

By now I was 59, and after consideration I accepted the offer. I did not realize what a sense of relief this would bring me, but now I could relax a little. A date was set and I was thrown the biggest party I had ever seen at the association. There was a corsage for me, flowers, a wonderful cake and photographs, and I was presented with a limited edition print in an oak frame. It had been on display in our building and someone had overheard me saying how I wished I could buy it. There was so much effort put into this party that I felt truly blessed and touched.

21.

Life after Work (the Retired Wife)

What an amazing experience it was to wake up that first morning of retirement and know my working days were over. Little did I know some of my hardest times were still ahead.

David and I had a celebratory dinner, nothing too fancy, it was probably Swiss Chalet, and bought some Christmas gifts but we were otherwise careful with the money that had come our way. Obviously some went to pay bills but from now on we would both be living off David's disability pension, which was just $1,000 a month. My doctor told me I was also eligible to apply and that if I wished he would send in the papers. But he also told me that in the current political climate they were refusing even the most extreme cases. Basically it was not worth applying, so I hoped that with the time I now had I could try to get the centre's finances back on track.

It soon became apparent that through the mismanagement of the accounts and the delinquent accounts, we were fighting a losing battle. For Toby, who had put his all into this endeavour, the one positive was that he had learned about business the hard way and by later years he had developed an extremely acute insight into the business world, along with a strong sense of compassion. This put him in a position where he achieved in a big way everything he did. By age 40 he had become the manager for the Canadian Paraplegic Association for Calgary and Region. He also had many achievements with his music, but I am getting ahead of myself here! So back to 1999.

We held Christmas at the centre where there was lots of room for Kodi and Cameron to play. They also had room to drive Grandpa's scooter up and down the halls and 'round the big drama room (actually I think their dad was having more fun than they were). I had managed to buy the scooter second-hand and very cheap. It was now necessary to have it for David to be able to get around. Some days he was okay walking but quite often he could not manage without the scooter. At least for this Christmas season all was well, and with the family gathered together to celebrate we were happy.

The new millennium arrived without the predicted problems. Computers were still working, the world had not come to an end and time was still running forward. Just kidding on the latter. Had anyone, I wondered, stopped to realize what an incredible privilege it was to actually witness the start of a new millennium? It only happens once every thousand years and I was there!

Life ticked along, and then one day in February I woke to something of an oddity. I have a rather prominent scar running from the top to the bottom of my abdomen, and to the left of this the whole side was protruding about three inches more than the right side. How strange, and no, I was not dreaming although I did not feel any pain. After a phone call to my surgeon it was straight up to see him.

Apparently my poor tummy had herniated top to bottom, left side only, if you please. When he told me I would need surgery as soon as possible and it would mean my being opened up for the fourth time I kind of suggested that maybe we could just put in a zipper He was kind of amused but decided to stick to proven methods of incision closure. Problem: I was taking blood thinners, so before I could have surgery I needed to see a specialist in internal medicine. What a small world. This doctor was very English and it turns out he had worked at the Queen Elizabeth Hospital in Birmingham, where my mother had been for so long 70 years before. He was also able to tell me that the "white leg" from which she suffered was the term they used for deep vein thrombosis (DVT). The genetics came home to roost! Dr. Gillette prescribed five needles for me, one for each of the five days before my surgery, and I had to inject them into my abdomen. Fortunately needles do not bother me and I hardly felt them.

Okay, so I wake up after surgery to find that I am fine, lots of stitches but no zipper (the doctor must have been feeling optimistic), but I was told I now have mesh stitched across from my one hip to the other to prevent any further problems. My recovery from the surgery did not take too many days, but by now I was in the hands of a very nice lady specialist who had the job of getting my blood levels balanced yet again. This took at least another two weeks, during which time I overheard the aforementioned lady doctor discussing with my surgeon what they could possibly do next and why it was so difficult to thin my blood again. Plus they did not dare let me go home until this was

achieved because I could die. Oh joy—I thought I had better be
prepared to stock up on patience, even though I couldn't wait to
get home. Dr. Parsons came to see me every day, and to be quite
honest I did confide in him that I was scared and that I did not
want to die. Looking back I believe this moment was the most
fragile my emotions had ever been. Having always been strong
enough to cope with whatever came my way, this vulnerability
took me by surprise. Finally this all passed, as things do, and I
was able to go home.

Being home was wonderful, but now I once more had to
pick up the family reins and face the gathering storms. David's
health was rapidly declining and he now needed physical help for
such things as getting out of the tub or getting up from a chair.
It was becoming difficult for him to hold things because of the
deformities in his hands, plus he did not have a lot of strength
left. Despite this he continually wanted to try different projects,
so this ended up with him calling me every few minutes to hold
something, undo something, lift something, etc., etc. So in fact
his projects were being done through me, with my interests being
set aside all the time so I could help him. Finally I just gave up
trying to do anything for myself as it was coming to the point
where I could not call my time my own. My perception of myself
was as just an extension of everyone's needs. Although the one
thing I did do was stick to my university studies. Why? In spite of
any academic achievements in my early life, I had never received
any praise for anything I had accomplished, so I believe I did this
to prove to myself I was not stupid, because deep down inside I
had started to believe I was.

Once a week we bought the *St. Marys Journal Argus* that came
out—you guessed it—once a week! Hmm. In looking in the late
March edition I'd noticed a disability unit for rent at the local co-

op housing complex. David most certainly qualified, so I decided to look into this. It had everything a person with a wheelchair or other problem could possibly need. The bathroom was huge, with a conventional tub and shower plus a separate shower for rolling in a bath chair. Off the living room was a large second-story deck accessed through patio doors. There were no front steps at all, just a gentle slope up to a covered front porch that was large enough for a bench and flower baskets. A plus was that there were two bedrooms—a huge master bedroom and a smaller one—plus a big basement with patio doors leading out to a little garden. At the front and side of the porch were also gardens. To top it off it was right on the edge of town and looked out across a field and a little stream. David really liked it, and pets were allowed so we could take our little dogs with us.

Back at the centre the writing was on the wall. It was not going to survive despite Toby's incredible efforts and his enormous success with his students. He was burned out and stressed and David was not helping matters, so removing him from the situation would help. We were accepted at the co-op and moved there in May, but the woman who was temporarily running the office told us there were no more geared-to-income allocations available right now, so we would have to pay market rent of about $700.00 a month. This would leave us with $300.00 between us to get through the month. But you know what? I did it, and paid our utilities, although I had to be pretty inventive with our meals. It was not until about nine months later that I found out disability units get rent geared-to-income regardless, and our rent went down to $250.00 a month. Now *that* made a big difference. But let me back up a little. I discussed our idea about moving with Toby and he agreed it would be best. He would stay on at the centre to close things up and put the building up for sale. Once done he and a friend moved into a rented house in London and he continued to teach privately. At the same time Toby was dealing with a former adult student who wanted to buy the building, but he kept stringing us along, and the bills kept piling up.

Here I am going to leave the timeline of my story and jump ahead to May 2001. The centre finally sold, so at least we did not have to face the ignominy of having a foreclosure. After all was said and done we paid out the mortgage but had not a penny left between us, and Toby, David and I were faced with having to declare personal bankruptcy as we were unable to pay the centre's bills. Toby and I had to hand back our leased cars, but Toby went way up north to Timmins to pick up an old but very good car for me from his friend's garage for $200.00. Boy was that car nice and warm in the winter. In November 2001 Toby moved to Calgary, Alberta, and stayed with Cathy and Bill while he found a place to rent. Cathy had lined up a job for him ahead of his arrival.

We enjoyed living at the co-op. It was very much a community, with neighbours dropping by to chat and all the children playing together. Of course there were always one or two miserable people, but that occurs wherever you are. Everyone who was living there was there for a reason. No one had money and all were struggling because of some kind of crises in their lives, and camaraderie and helping one another was the order of the day. Our little gardens were small enough to handle but big enough to enjoy, and this gave David great pleasure, as did taking our two little dogs for walks across the field to the stream.

Within two weeks of moving there I was elected to the board of directors, and then the rest of the board immediately elected me president of the board, a position to which I was re-elected annually for four years. To be truthful, I enjoyed this as it was right up my alley. Previously it had not been run well or according to the bylaws, with the members of the board using their positions for personal gain for themselves or for friends who were looking for a place to live. That is, they were queue jumping. Also, there was a total lack of confidentiality. No more. I ran that board with compassion and ethics and to the letter of the bylaws. Breach of confidentiality was not tolerated and was dealt with immediately. And you know what? We had a good, happy board that pulled together, and bit by bit the co-op was running according to its mandate. Previously it had been like a powder keg—one spark and there was uproar among all the members. On the whole I put in at least four hours a day, five days a week. As I was retired I had the time and was always available, plus it gave me a purpose. My only conflict was with David, who, now being more controlling than ever tried to run the co-op through me. It became necessary for me to be diplomatic, firstly to not let David influence me (yet not appear to be disregarding what he was telling me to do) and secondly to maintain confidentiality. David was not a member of the board.

On the home front Susan and Jim were now in an apartment in Stratford, which was just twenty minutes' drive away from us. They came for supper every Sunday and spent the day with us. Grandpa had all the time and patience in the world for both Kodi and Cameron, as well as the other children in the co-op, and he never had a harsh word for any of them. Somehow he managed to teach them all kinds of things without their realizing they were being taught—and this went for *all* the children he knew. Unfortunately, with me he was having episodes of being less and less patient and had started to yell at me, something he had never done in all our married life. Apparently when he was in his psychotic states he saw me as the enemy and as being against him. One Christmas it came back to me that he was going around telling people that I hated him and wanted to kill him. Thank God I had the wisdom to see this for what it was. This was not David speaking, it was his illness, and I was certain in the knowledge that he still loved me. It was the little things that counted, like always bringing me a cup of tea in bed in the morning, or covering me up with a throw if I lay on the couch to have a nap. Now this was the real David.

September 21, 2000, brought us enormous joy when Eva delivered a baby girl, our very first granddaughter. She was named Jenna Elizabeth Redfern. This is such a beautiful name, and Elizabeth was my mother's middle name. David, Sue and I went to see her at the hospital the next day, and what a beautiful baby she was. Somehow there is a special relationship between grandmas and their granddaughters, and I sat and held her, drinking in the joy of watching her little face. Mom and Dad were doing fine and Jenna and Eva would be going home the next day, just in time for Mommy's birthday on the twenty-fourth. To top things off, Susan was two months' pregnant with her third baby.

Our years at the co-op seemed to blend into each other with the changing of the seasons. In between David's mood changes, they were happy times. David said that being there was as close to living with his neighbours in England as it could get. We had many community events and impromptu barbeques where everyone joined in, and we all watched out for each other's children. At Christmastime we had a community dinner, with Santa coming and bringing gifts for all the children. On Victoria Day the dads all took care of putting on a big fireworks display. This was true community.

In the fall of 2000 an incredible thing happened. We had a call from my old friend John McCaw to say he and his wife, Jean, were coming to Stratford for a few days. Apparently their son, Andrew, was the assistant lighting director with the Stratford Theatre and was involved with the production of *A Midsummer Night's Dream*. They were going to be staying at the Queens Hotel in Stratford and wanted to get together with us for dinner one night. What a lovely surprise. Although we spoke on the phone occasionally I had not seen John for 43 years (I still visualized him as 18) and I had never met Jean, so was really looking forward to getting to know her.

Well, the day arrived and I suddenly realized how old I looked and started worrying about silly things, such as would we recognize each other and what would we say after so long. No need to worry. We walked into the hotel bar where we were to meet and John and I immediately recognized each other. He was just an older version of the same John. It was so nice to finally meet Jean; she is such a lovely person with sparkling blue eyes, a ready smile and an easy manner. While she and David talked, John and I seemingly just picked up where we left off. It was as if I had just seen him only yesterday. As we walked the block to the restaurant, Jean and David were deeply immersed in conversation. She and John were both doctors of medicine and she appeared genuinely interested in David's health issues and his medications.

John and I walked a few paces behind and had a great time catching up. I'm not sure what we talked about but I know somewhere along the way we did some reminiscing about when we were young. At the restaurant we were joined by Toby, so there were introductions, laughing, dining on a wonderful meal (thanks to Jean and John) and much taking of photographs. Time flew by and the evening was over, but the next day Jean and John planned to come to St. Marys for the afternoon so that David and I could show them around. It really is a picturesque little town with its old, stone buildings built with stone from the local quarry.

The next day when they arrived, the sun was shining, the birds were singing and we all had a really happy time. Although the town is small (population 5,000), there is a great deal to see in the way of historical buildings, plus we were able to walk across the old Sarnia Railway Bridge that had been made into a walkway spanning the Thames River. After there was just time for a quick stop at Tim Hortons before they had to head back to Stratford for dinner and an evening performance at the theatre. They were leaving the next day, so we said our goodbyes, but the following morning John dropped by to have a last cup of tea with us before flying back to Victoria 3,000 miles away. However, friendships had been revitalized and communication became more frequent.

On April 29, 2001 (I think it must have been a Sunday), Sue, Jim and the children were visiting. We adults were sitting on the back deck watching Kodi and Cameron play with their friends in the field. Suddenly Kodi started screaming and running toward the house. Sue dashed out the front door and, nine months pregnant, jumped down the tall retaining wall to get to Kodi. He had stepped on a nest of red ants and they were crawling all over him. While Sue stripped off his clothes I turned on the hose and washed them all off him. Phew! No harm done. We all went and had some more lemonade on the deck. At about four o'clock Sue announced that she needed to go to the hospital as she was in labour (amazing what jumping down a four-foot retaining wall can do). Off we went, Sue, Jim and I (neither of them drive), leaving the two boys with Sue's friend. Within about four hours we had another baby granddaughter.

Her name was Hannah Rose Gwynn, Hannah after her mom's original name of Hannah Marie, and Rose after Grandma Cynthia Mary Rose. Rose is a traditional name in my family, with someone from every generation carrying it. Now Hannah was taking up the tradition. What a beautiful baby she was, but unlike Kodi and Cameron she was white, like Jim. Sue said she was her little white toast. That summer they all moved to a three-bedroom house at the co-op, just three doors away from us. Jim and David had always gotten on well together and enjoyed the closeness so they could visit and enjoy a coffee. Jim was also very good at helping David with things that were physically beyond him. Every night after supper, we would go to Sue and Jim's for an hour for a coffee and David always read a bedtime story to the children. Little Hannah adored her grandpa and would lie in his arms looking up at him. I don't know, he just had a very special rapport with children and they all loved him, although there seemed to be an extra special bond between Kodi and Grandpa that never diminished.

Days turned into weeks and the weeks turned into months and then years. Our time at the co-op seemed to just blend into a series of vignettes. I was getting pleasure from sewing for the children, especially Hannah's little summer dresses, although I also made things for the boys. Each year I made all the children's summer and winter pyjamas, and for only a fraction of the cost of buying them. I even made David's nightshirts—he found pyjamas a challenge to get on these days and so preferred the nightshirts. In fact I had to make the boys nightshirts "just like Grandpa's." As time progressed I needed to help David with his dressing and undressing as his hands no longer functioned. He spent much of his time in bed sleeping and there were days he was just too sore to move. The trips to the hospital with migraines or pneumonia increased, with the latter always needing him to be admitted.

Now I must admit that although it sounds callous, I sometimes welcomed those periods of hospitalization so I could just get a rest from the constant needs and revitalize myself a little. He had taken to having episodes of yelling at me, saying, "I know you don't want me so I'll leave." Rationalizing with him did no good, so I would end up leaving the house and just driving and crying at the same time. But where was I to go? There was no place to go, no one to call and no one in whom I could confide. Eventually I would go back home and everything would be normal. After theses periods of dementia or psychosis David had no memory of what had occurred, so there was nothing I could do but accept that the abuse was something beyond his control.

I tried some different things to give his life more meaning. One day I signed him up for Sumi-e Japanese ink brush painting that was being taught by Nancy, a lady here in town. The cost was extremely reasonable, and not only did he enjoy it, he was extremely good at it. His first art piece was so good that I have it framed. What a man! Was there anything he could not do? Nancy also taught the art of oral storytelling, so I took this course. At the end I received a certificate saying I was a qualified member of "Spellbinders." Very excitedly I called Richard to let him know, to which he responded in typical style: "Congratulations, Mom, I'll buy you a new broom." Kids. Huh! David and I became friends with Nancy and her husband, Louis, and we visited back and forth with each other for dinner or dessert and coffee. Because of my course I started to go once a week to the kindergarten class at the school and spent 20 minutes telling the children a story. This was fun and a nice outlet.

Talking of outlets, for three years I ran the Grade Three children's gardening club sponsored by the St. Marys Horticultural Society. The town allotted us land at the cemetery where we had a huge garden in which we grew food for the food bank. My assistant (and good friend) Nettie and I were there for three hours every Thursday, and during that time we had three groups of children come to work for one hour each. The garden was sectioned into three plots and the children were split into three groups, each assigned to one of the plots. They were encouraged to come up with a name for their group, and we had such things as "the Busy Bees" or "the Scarecrows." Little hands can achieve so much, and the results were quite amazing. For me and Nettie it was hard work doing three hours in the hot sun, but we were paid extremely well (and we could do with it), and we loved what we were doing.

The children did everything from planting in the spring, weeding and watering all summer and then harvesting in the fall. Sometimes I would cancel the class if it was either too hot for the children or else raining. Nevertheless, Nettie and I were out there doing our thing. We got on well together and had a good laugh when we got soaked and covered in mud. Now this reminds me of the time it was pouring with rain but there were dozens of tomatoes needing to be picked. So the intrepid twosome set off in raincoats and wellies to do their duty—except we ran out of baskets before we had finished the picking. Hmm, what to do. While I was thinking, my eyes travelled up the enormous stalks of the Giant Russian sunflowers the children had planted just for fun, to their huge, tropical sized leaves. Aha! What did people do before they had baskets? To Nettie's puzzlement I started breaking off some huge leaves and handing them to her. "We're going to use these for the tomatoes," I said through the rain running down my cheeks. She looked at me as if I had lost my mind and then broke into uncontrollable laughter. We were all but rolling on the ground, but you know what? It worked.

Meanwhile, in Calgary Toby had met and fallen in love with a young lady named Tara. Tara was obviously very focussed, and even though she was a few years younger than Toby she already had bought her own house. I had not yet met her, but to find someone who was compatible with Toby's personality, she must be quite something, and indeed she was. On October 11, 2003, Mason Levi Redfern was born. What a thrill this was to David and me—another grandchild, and even more amazing, Toby a father!

It was not long before David and I went out to Calgary to visit them. Mason was the exact image of Toby except for his curly hair being blond and his eyes blue. Tara was such a delight, at six feet tall with hazel eyes and gorgeous, thick auburn hair she took everything in her stride and nothing ever flustered her. David was thrilled with Mason and would sit with the baby asleep on his chest. By now Cathy and Bill had a brand new upscale house only about half an hour away from Toby and Tara. We were only there for a week, and although we left green grass and warmth in Ontario it was already cold and snowy in Calgary. Nevertheless, Cathy took us out to see all the places of interest and we had a wonderful time all around. I had visited Calgary once before, in the middle of the winter, when Cathy and Bill first moved here and were living in a little rented house. At that time we could not do too much because of the weather, but Bill did drive the three of us to Banff so I could see the mountains.

My next visit to Calgary was in 2004 when I took Kodi with me to visit his aunts and uncles for a week. He was such a joy to be with and was so interested in all the new sights and activities. If I remember right he stayed with Aunty Cathy and Uncle Bill while I stayed with Toby and Tara. Kodi got to do everything (and of course Grandma went along), from horseback riding along trails and through rivers to going to the Science Museum and exploring Banff. Bill is excellent with kids and left Cathy and me to shop while he and Kodi climbed a mountain. They came back with all kinds of fantastic tales about bears and mountain lions and how they had even conquered a grizzly bear!

When I arrived back in Ontario a writer from the Toronto *Globe and Mail* contacted us about writing an article on grandparents travelling with their grandchildren. Apparently it is a new trend. Well, Kodi and I ended up with a full front page article in the travel section of the *Globe and Mail*. Wow, he was one proud little boy.

Having Sue, Jim and the grandchildren living almost next door was good in so many ways. Neither of them drives so it was both convenient and social for Sue and me to go shopping together. Also, Jim worked quite some distance away and used his bike to get back and forth, but if it was close to his finishing time and I could see it was pouring with rain or snowing then I would just drive up to meet him and bring him home. We had a lot of give and take as he and Sue helped David and me with things we could not manage.

By now David's cervical vertebrae were in a state of collapse and he could hardly hold up his head. Mostly it rested on his shoulder. He had seen a specialist at London University Hospital who was supposed to operate on his neck, but this doctor just kept putting him off and finally did not return his calls. I believe it was a case of this problem being beyond his expertise, but to have admitted that would have looked bad so he just avoided doing anything. On top of this, David's surgery to put in a replacement elbow would not heal and we were going back and forth to a doctor at St. Joseph Hospital in London. What a difference. This surgeon was excellent and went all out for David. He did skin grafts and everything possible to close the wound, but 37 years of taking prednisone was preventing any healing.

Most of the time David slept—it was too painful for him to sit because of his neck. If we went to visit Richard and Eva in London for supper, I would recline his seat and give him pillows, and he would sleep all the way there. It took about 30 to 45 minutes. That way he could wake up and have a nice (though fairly short) visit and then sleep again on the way home. Eva (her actual name is Yi Wah) knew how much David liked Chinese food (the authentic stuff)! And she would prepare a fabulous meal that he could really enjoy. She would deliberately cook way too much and then send us home with all kinds of packaged meals. What a sweetheart.

By now we had a new vehicle. I had gone through the daunting task of going to look at it and taking it for a test drive myself as Dave was not well. But what did I know about cars? Well, I guess I knew enough to listen for a smooth gear change and a few other things, and the seller was more than fair. It was a Ford Aerostar seven-passenger van, enough space to carry Dave and me plus Sue's family. It was a 1998 with low mileage and only cost $500.00. The seller was not short of money. On top of this, he offered to have the vehicle fully serviced for me before I took it. Well, it turned out to be a great vehicle and so useful.

Christmas 2004 arrived and we were all excited and looking forward to the holidays. I had taken to making most of my gifts the past few years for the sake of economy, but this Christmas I was just a little bit better off so had lots of toys for the children. It was ten a.m. on Christmas morning when Kodi and Cameron came running to our place barefoot and in their pyjamas in the snow. They were screaming, "The house is on fire, the house is on fire," and I could immediately smell the smoke on their pyjamas. We hustled them inside and then Sue and Jim arrived to bring Hannah and the pets before heading back to their house. By now the fire trucks were here, and oh, what a commotion. The chief was out of town for the day but his guys worked efficiently at getting things under control. As president of the co-op I had to get out there and sort out what was happening. Apparently the fire started in the basement of the town house next door, but it turns out the fire wall between the two houses was compromised and the flames just went right up between the walls. Later the firemen found that the fire had spread between the upstairs floorboards right underneath Hannah's bed! The house and everything in it was a total write-off, but thank God the family and the pets were safe.

What a day! The first thing I had to do was contact the co-op's insurance company, so between getting the turkey in the oven and trying to give some normalcy to the day for the children, I was back and forth dealing with insurance folks, journalists and the fire department. Sue and Jim had lost everything, including their clothes and the children's gifts. Fortunately Santa had left a whole pile of things under Grandma and Grandpa's tree, so they had lots of things to unwrap and play with. There was another empty three-bedroom unit the family would be able to have, but it would take a little time to get it ready, so in the meantime they all stayed with us.

One thing about living in a small community is that everyone pulls together, and believe me, the whole town was involved. Before long Sue and Jim had everything one could possibly think of. Our Mennonite neighbours even gave them the most beautiful handmade quilts I know take days of work to make as well as requiring the skill to do it. On Boxing Day (December 26) I met with the fire chief and the insurance company representative, and then it was paperwork, paperwork and more paperwork. The damage estimate for the two houses was horrendous, but life went on and soon Sue and Jim were settled in a house across the road from us. It had been a tight squeeze with us all together but we did it. My concern was the psychological effect it would have on the children.

Winter turned into spring and it was now 2005. With the collapse of his neck, David had gone from six feet two and a half inches to five foot eight and was in a terrible state. When his elbow specialist saw him, he was far more concerned about his vertebrae and called in several other specialists who were in the building right then and there. In Calgary Toby mentioned his dad's problem to a friend, who was also a medical specialist. He asked Toby to get an MRI sent to him immediately and David's elbow specialist took care of this and sent it off to Calgary. By now David could hardly eat or swallow and was suffering from severe sleep apnea. I would lay awake in bed at night listening to his breathing. When he stopped I would count the seconds until he took that big gulp of air and breathed again. He was also quickly getting to the point where if he did not have surgery, he would be paralyzed from the neck down. Wonder of wonders, Toby's friend had contacted one of his colleagues who was the only surgeon in Canada qualified to do the operation David needed, and he was willing to take this on.

There was just one thing. We would have to move to Calgary.

22.

Moving West (the Nursing Wife)

*H*ow many times in our life had David and I moved out of sheer necessity? It started way back when we had to move from the farm because of David's health. Oh how I wish I could have just stayed there! I loved that old farmhouse with its fields and my animals. It seems that everytime we started to put down roots, our life took another twist or turn. How many gardens had I planted just to have to leave them as they started to mature? Then it was on to the next place and start all over again. Our garden at the co-op was without a doubt one of the prettiest we had ever grown, and now … another move. I recognized we had to do this and fully accepted that fact, but I must admit to some trepidation about moving to a city of a million people. Then there were my grandchildren. When would I see them again?

We planned to move in July, and this was now early April, so we had time to sort things out. By now Toby and Tara had bought a new house in the northeast of Calgary, backing onto a park and with a view across the fields of the Rocky Mountains. Immediately Toby and Tara took up the reins and started working on our move by looking at numerous houses and looking into moving companies. I really have to give them both the credit for facilitating this move. Their plan was for us to buy a house, and they would do this by putting down the down payment for us and making sure we would be accepted for a mortgage and have a way to pay it. Toby had developed a real head for figures and Tara was right there with him. Toby asked me what kind of features I would like (although he knows my tastes very well) and started to send David and me photos of different properties by e-mail.

Finally he and Tara narrowed it down to just two houses, one of which was a brand new "spec" house. That is, one that was not built to order but that the builder just constructed and then "speculated" on selling it. As soon as I saw the photos, that was it! It had everything we could ever want, including the cutest little bay window above the kitchen sinks. This would be great for my plants. There was also a big, wide, covered front deck where we could put our bench and enjoy a cup of tea. By now I was starting to get excited, as was David. Never in a million years had we ever expected to own our own home again. How could we? But somehow my dear son had managed to pull this off for us, although I knew I would remain nervous until we signed on the dotted line. After all, "It ain't over 'til it's over."

Did I tell you my son has a head for figures? The realtor was asking $192,000.00 for the house, so Toby decided to be cheeky and offer $175,000.00. He fully expected to bargain back and forth, but lo and behold, they accepted the offer on one condition: that we take possession on May 1. By now we were well into April, but we accepted this and started to hustle. We had accumulated so much stuff over the years that we held a massive yard sale. As we were shipping our things to Calgary we needed as little weight as possible, but Dave's perception of "needed" was a little different than mine. Like he needed a whole bunch of tools he could no longer hold, but they went anyway.

At this time we were faxing all the legal papers back and forth to be signed and time was flying. One evening I was presiding over a board meeting when there was a knock at the door of the board room. It was David, who handed me a paper and left. Toby had e-mailed us a colour photo of the keys to the house. I couldn't believe it; it was ours; we had a house and it was ours. I showed my board members and they were all laughing, crying and cheering. Wow! In the co-op we were all pretty much in the same boat and everyone understood what an incredible thing it was to make it out. The plane tickets were arranged for David and me plus our two little dogs, Snuggles and Riggs, plus the cat. We left mid June but not before the community threw us a big outdoor party. I was very sad to be leaving the grandchildren, and the last thing I remember as we drove off to the airport was Kodi's sad little face. This just about broke my heart, but really, we had no choice.

Touchdown. We were in Calgary, and there to meet us were Toby, Tara, our dear little grandson Mason and our daughter Catherine. We reclaimed our baggage and our critters and off we went to see our new house. It was right on the next street to Toby and Tara, just across the park, and was everything we imagined it would be. Our dear son and daughter-in-law, knowing all our belongings were in transit, had made sure we had everything we could possibly need. They had brought over a couch and a television for the living room, a picnic table and chairs for the dining area and had put their futon bed in the master bedroom. On top of that was a telephone, linens, a toaster, tea kettle, garbage can ... the list could go on and on. We were sparsely furnished but lacked nothing. David and I were home in the house of our dreams. Our van was arriving soon by rail, but in the meantime we had a car at our disposal.

Before moving it had been arranged that we would babysit Mason while Mom and Dad were at work, and this would give us a nice bit of income, plus, at the beginning of December I could start receiving my old-age pension. We were going to be all right. Having Mason around was the best possible thing for David, as he read him stories and invented all kinds of games for him. His favourite was fishing—on the living room floor. Yes, you read that right—fishing. David got a cardboard box for Mason to use as a boat and then gave him a piece of dowel to which he tied a piece of string. On the end of the string was a magnet. David had cut out a bunch of shiny, orange plastic fish and to each of these he clipped a metal paper clip. Voila, we spread the fish around the floor and Mason used the magnet to catch them. Simple, right? My dear husband had an incredible mind.

On a more relevant note we had been put in touch with a family doctor who had agreed to have an interview with us. How could we be so fortunate? His whole demeanour and personality were just like Dr. Parson's, whom we had had for 25 years. This doctor could see the seriousness of David's condition and accepted us right away. We gave him the letter from Dr. Parsons noting all of David's medications and the reasons for taking them, and he was quite willing to prescribe morphine for him. We had an appointment with the surgeon in September, but meanwhile our new doctor kept a very close eye on David. He had also taken me on as a patient.

Eventually our goods arrived, but they were pretty broken and knocked around. Toby had contracted a very reputable company, but it appears they subcontracted our order out, and we had quite a battle trying to get compensation. But when all was said and done we loved our new home and were happy there. We had fun planning how we were going to do the garden, which at present was an empty lot, and agreed that although it was somewhat small it was plenty for us to handle. As we were able we would get our fence and our deck built and then be able to get the sod laid for the lawn. We even figured out where we wanted our little flower garden to be and what we would like to plant in it. By now it was just a waiting game until we saw the surgeon, and David could not do much physically, but we had fun doing our planning, and I had now set up our things in the house and it felt very much like home.

September came, and David and I went for his appointment with his surgeon. The first thing I noticed was how young he looked, or perhaps it was the perception of an old person like me, but he proved to be brilliant. He was also very friendly and down to earth and treated us with great respect. Our appointment with him lasted for about two hours, during which time he asked David many questions and talked to him about just how incredibly serious his condition was. In explaining the risks he did not gloss over any aspect of what to expect or what the outcomes of the surgery could be. Without doubt, he explained, if David decided not to have the surgery he would very soon be paralyzed from the neck down, and with David's pneumonia that would complicate the scenario. He had already explained the risks of having the surgery, that things could happen and he may not come through it. But now, having all the information, it was David's choice to make an informed decision.

There was no hesitation on David's part. He was not prepared to go on the way he was, and, he said, "As far as my life is concerned I prefer quality over quantity." So that was that, and I stood beside whatever decision he chose to make. My husband's bravery was incomparable. The date was set for early January and there would be two surgeries. The first would be nine hours and on the front of the neck. Three days later the second one would be a twelve-hour surgery on the back of his neck. There were five cervical vertebrae that had just crumbled away, and these had to be removed and a titanium tube put in to replace them. His head was quite literally falling off. Afterward he would not be able to turn his head and therefore be unable to drive, but considering all that he had gone through this was a minor detail.

One day in October I had a phone call from Toby. He was at work (he worked in social services with developmentally challenged adults) and one of his co-workers had a problem. She had such a gentleman living with her (known as a "supported roommate") who during the day went to another person's house to be cared for. Now I was somewhat familiar with this system as Toby and Tara had such a person living with them, although their roommate went to a day program. Well, it appears the co-worker had a problem with the daytime caregiver and wanted someone for two or three days until she could work something out. Toby had told her this had been my job for many years and that I might be able to step in until she solved her problem. Of course I said I would help. Why not? I was home with David anyway, so it was arranged.

I will call this gentleman Larry for the sake of confidentiality. The next morning he arrived at my door by cab, along with his backpack containing his lunch and his needs for the day. He was a diminutive person who was middle aged and nonverbal. Fortunately he understood what was being said to him. The next couple of days went well and I was asked if I would like to take on this job. It was Monday to Friday from eight to four and paid well. I was certainly not going to pass up this opportunity, apart from which Larry really liked David and my pets. He would break out into a big grin when he was happy and this was almost reward enough in itself. Larry did have some behavioural problems that could be quite severe (believe me, I had dealt with worse), plus he most times chose to be incontinent. These are the things that prevented him from going to a day program; anyway, he preferred to be in a home setting. Quite frankly I really enjoyed Larry. We all settled into the routine very nicely and all was well. As this came right at the time Mason was starting nursery school, it meant we still had some income, and I would start getting my pension in December.

One Sunday evening in November I received a frantic call from Sue in Ontario. They had been around to a children's birthday party at a friend's house when they had a call to say their house was on fire. This was the house they had moved into after the Christmas day fire 11 months earlier. Sue and Jim dashed home to find their house engulfed in flames that were quickly spreading to the units on either side. Fortunately, a neighbour had been able to save their little dog and one of their two cats. They again lost everything. After this the whole co-op came under close scrutiny and was found to be at risk for disasters in many areas. It was established that the fire had been caused by faulty wiring in the living room wall. Just how much more did this family have to take? Kodi suffered from seizures that rendered him comatose due to his stroke, and Cameron had been diagnosed with Asperger's Syndrome, a form of autism. The only good thing was that after the last fire Sue and Jim had doubled their fire insurance. Smart move! That night they moved in to stay with their friend whose party they had been attending.

Meanwhile, back here in Calgary the phones were in full use as all the siblings were informed. Richard was in London, but by now Dan was working in Toronto and had his own nice little apartment. We all discussed the situation and thought that with the money they would be getting it might be a good opportunity to move to Calgary and buy their own house. Also, there was very little work where they were and Jim's job was low paying and was affecting his lungs. He worked at a factory that made tortillas and pizza dough and he was getting baker's lung. Mind you, they would miss him because he was the one person who could do anything with any machine, including shipping or maintenance or whatever came up. Plus he has always been a very hard worker and would need to be tied down to get him to miss a day of work.

I believe it was Toby who put this to Sue and Jim and explained how it could be beneficial to all of them. They did not have the insurance money yet, but then they had nothing to ship anyway. The brothers and sister got together to sort out the airfare, and on December 15 they arrived in Calgary. Naturally Grandpa was ecstatic that the children would once more be close at hand. What a wonderful Christmas this was going to be. Dave and I had three bedrooms, so they would be staying with us. Our house was going to be full, but that was okay. I already had a guest bedroom set up with a double bed, and in the other bedroom was a single bed, so we borrowed Cathy's camp cot for little Hannah and put it beside the double bed Mommy and Daddy would use. In the other room we split the other bed into box spring and mattress and this made two beds for the boys. We also had a good size guest bathroom they could all use. Dave and I had our own ensuite bathroom.

I remember Christmas Eve so well. We all put on a new pair of

Christmas pyjamas and watched the movie *The Polar Bear Express*. Having Sue help with Christmas was a bonus for me. Apart from anything else she is a fantastic cook, and it was good for Grandpa to spend time with the family before going into hospital.

23.

Separation (the Visiting Wife)

Way too fast it was time for David to be admitted into Foothills Hospital. After changing into one of their wonderfully haute couture gowns, he was taken into a small room that contained a specialized bed that only fit into the room if it was put on an angle. Next arrived a team of highly specialized medical personnel, all under the direction of the surgeon's second in command. They then proceeded to attach something called a halo (which is used to manage cervical spine injuries to minimize neurological damage) to David's skull (the only comparison at all to a halo is that it is round and designed to encircle his head with a few inches to spare). This halo had to be physically attached by drilling four holes into the skull, two on either side at the front and two to correspond at the back, and then screwing the device into place.

I stayed with David while all this was done and can only

imagine what the drilling must have sounded like inside his head. Of course they had given a local anaesthetic to his skull before starting the procedure, and although I could sense he was scared, to his credit he lay still and did not make a sound. From here they tried to attach a weight to the halo to try to straighten his neck before surgery, but with it being so badly compromised they had to forgo this procedure. So that was that. He was settled into his room, and eventually I left for home. Cathy was planning to meet me at the hospital at six o'clock the next morning, and we would accompany David as far as the operating room.

Fortunately for me, Susan had taken the role of back-up for Larry and was able to step in and have him dropped off at her house. I did not sleep well that night. It's funny the things that go around in one's head: flashes of old memories, worries about the next day and also after 39 years of marriage I was not used to sleeping alone. Well, I guess I would have to get used to it for a while. I am not sure if the morning came too soon or not soon enough as I had very mixed feelings about the coming day. Anyway, I was up at four thirty to get to the hospital. Unlike me, Cathy did not live more than 15 minutes from Foothills, so she was there waiting when I arrived.

The time had come, and Cathy and I were allowed to accompany David into the room right outside the OR and stay with him until he was wheeled through. This took a little while as he was checked thoroughly and asked questions. Whoever the doctor was we were dealing with, he was wonderful. He was chatty and humorous and talked to David like an old friend. Once again, I have to admire David's courage, knowing what lay ahead and the uncertainty of the outcome. Then he was taken in and I watched as he went through the doors and into the hands of the surgical team. Cathy and I were shown to the ICU's waiting room. It was a comfortable place outfitted with computers and the necessities for making tea or coffee along with a stocked snack cupboard. Fortunately Cathy had thought to bring some snacks along for us. It was going to be a long day.

Time moved slowly, with us taking breaks by walking out to the lobby to stretch and have a different view, and then back to the waiting room to sit again. Although there were books and other reading material it was hard to concentrate on any of these. Cathy spent some time on the computer but mostly we talked, just small talk about this and that. The day stretched interminably on and I seemed to have a problem keeping my eyes off the clock.

Finally the door opened and there was David's surgeon calling my name. We went out to speak with him and he reassured us everything had gone according to plan and that David was going to be taken into the ICU. David was not conscious, so we would not be seeing him, but that was okay. Now we could relax and go home, knowing he was in good hands.

Visiting the ICU was restricted to close family, and even so one was required to go to the ICU waiting room and use the phone provided to see if we could visit. The nurse assigned to my husband would either say yes or tell us they were in the middle of a procedure and to check again in 20 minutes. When I saw David the next day he was not really aware I was there. He had tubes and wires running all over his body and was on a ventilator to help him to breathe. I had not brought anything for him as nothing was allowed into that unit. Each patient had his own nurse who had a stool and a computer at the bottom of their bed. It was certainly high-quality care. He was scheduled for his second surgery in just three more days and that was going to be the really tough one.

In the meantime, I visited each day, with some small

glimmering of awareness from David. Of course during all this I stayed in touch with David's brothers to keep them informed of what was happening. One was in England, one in Eire and one in New Zealand. Sometimes I would phone one of them and they in turn would get in touch with the other brothers. Of course Jean and John contacted me from Victoria. Being doctors they could both appreciate the impact of what was being done.

Monday arrived, and once again Cathy and I met at the hospital at six a.m. Today David was scheduled for the twelve-hour surgery on the back of his neck. This was to complete the procedure of removing five of his cervical vertebrae and installing a titanium tube. So David was once more in the OR and Cathy and I were in the waiting room. I can't say how much I appreciated her presence and calmness during all of this. If there is one thing I have discovered, it is that my daughter has great internal strength. As this was going to be a longer wait we broke it up by going to a restaurant for lunch. It was just across the road from the hospital so we were able to take our time and relax a little. After that it was back to the hospital and the eternal waiting. That morning we arrived in the dark and it was well dark again before the surgeon came to find us. David had come through the surgery, but from here on there was a long way to go, and there were no guarantees. He would be in the ICU for several weeks and we would be taking things one day at a time. Naturally the big concern was David's lungs. He had Chronic Obstructive Pulmonary Disorder (COPD, also known as emphysema) plus a chronic history of pneumonia.

To be quite honest, my recollections of the events of the next year are not completely clear. It was just one big jumble of visits to the hospital, looking after Larry thrown in with the stresses of David insisting on coming home. So I will try to put the events into some kind of chronological order, but that year I was stressed beyond imagining and (as my doctor told me) totally exhausted. After David's second surgery I continued to visit daily, although I was not the only one. The other family members who were in Calgary also visited. Eventually David was more aware, but at first he had to communicate with a pad of paper and a pencil as he could not yet talk. One day, not too long after the surgery, I went in to visit and noticed he was oozing large amounts of brownish-coloured blood from the wound site at the back of his neck. Now David had not had any kind of immune system for years, and now he had a massive infection in his neck. Back into surgery again and the back of his neck had to be reopened and completely cleaned out to get rid of the infection. This done, he was returned to the ICU. He was still having trouble with his breathing and was being fed and given his medication through a tube in his nose that went down into his stomach.

By now I had been back to looking after Larry for some time. The way I worked this was that I would be up by seven a.m. ready for when he arrived and take care of him all day. His ride usually picked him up between four and four thirty, at which time I would jump into the van and was off to the hospital, right in the middle of rush hour traffic! During the time David was in ICU I could not visit for too long, but later, when he was out of there, I stayed until visiting hours were over at eight thirty to nine p.m. Then it was back in the van, pay my parking fee (it was so expensive), drive home, cook a bit of supper, relax for a while and then off to bed. Then the next day it would start all over again. On weekends I visited from noon until about four p.m. for a bit of a break. I did this for a whole year, with the only break coming after a few months, when Cathy picked up on visiting her dad on Tuesdays on her way home from work.

About four o'clock one afternoon David finally made it out of ICU. At eleven p.m. I had a call from his doctor to tell me he had been rushed back into ICU. He was having trouble breathing and had to be given a tracheotomy. The next day I talked to his doctor while visiting and he told me straight out that things did not look good. He said that if a person had to be readmitted to the ICU, his chances were cut by 50 percent. Not quite the news I wanted to hear, but I knew David and I knew his strength of will. He was a fighter and he did beat the odds. Finally he was out and sent to a special floor. Not quite ICU but definitely more observation than on a regular floor, and after a while he was put in a private room. It was nice and sunny and had a stunning view of the Rocky Mountains. David was not able to read well because he had cataracts on both eyes (another future surgery), but I had bought him some large-print books. Cathy had brought him a CD player/radio. Also, I made sure I rented him a television, as most of the time he was just lying down and still wore the metal halo.

Out of the blue, another problem appeared. A thoracic vertebra in David's back broke and required surgery. This did not involve so much waiting, but the difficulty for the OR staff was trying to position him on his stomach when he could not turn his head. The surgeon glued his spine so that it was fused at the break. When he came out to talk to me he explained that by fusing the vertebrae, it would put more stress on the other vertebrae and he was concerned about this. He also told me just how bad his osteoporosis was. He said, "If you took a piece of David's bone between your finger and thumb and rubbed it, it would instantly turn into powder." With all being said, he was in the process of complete spinal collapse. As predicted, a week later another thoracic vertebrae crumbled, but this time they chose to leave it alone.

April arrived and the second was to be our fortieth wedding anniversary. As I recall it must have been a Saturday, as all the family were gathered at the hospital. I had bought David a pair of moose-hide moccasins with a rubber sole. He was getting up and moving around a bit now, although he still had the halo and the feeding tube. However, he was allowed little sips of pop or whatever, but he had to be careful not to get it into his lungs. I arrived and walked into his room and could not believe my eyes. There in a huge glass vase were 40 long-stemmed red roses! How had he worked this? I was floored. So we did our gift and card exchange and then I found out David had arranged to use one of the nurse's rooms to have a party. Someone brought pop, another brought chips and I think it must have been Sue who baked a cake—yummy!

We wheeled David's chair through and the party began. He could only sip pop with help but he was so thrilled to have all of the family together and to see the grandchildren. Next came another surprise. David handed me a little gift bag, inside of which was a velvet jewellery box. I opened it to find the most beautiful pair of diamond earrings. I was truly stunned. But just a minute—I didn't have pierced ears. No problem. David had already bought me a gift certificate to get them pierced and had arranged for Tara to take me to get this done. I found out that Cathy had made arrangements with the florist for the roses, Toby had bought the earrings in Edmonton and Tara had sorted out the gift certificate. Now I know why David wanted his Interac card!

The next big surprise was for both David and me. Cathy and Bill produced a *huge* package. It was really heavy and proved to contain a very large, framed Robert Bateman print of a bison. It was called "The Chief." We were both delighted with this as we love nature and animal pictures. But Bateman? How could we be so lucky?

We all had a lovely party with our chips, pop and cake, but David was getting tired and it was soon time to leave. What a wonderful anniversary! David had gone all out and I was wondering if he was thinking that this may be our last.

Along came summer, and although David's halo was off, he still could not swallow. By now his surgeon had gone to Australia to teach his techniques there, but he had left David in the very capable hands of his second in command, a brilliant surgeon in his own right. My husband had been told no one had ever gone longer than six months without regaining the ability to eat or drink, but it looked as if he was the exception. When he tried to swallow, a piece of metal at the back of his throat prevented him, so they put a permanent feeding tube in through his abdomen and up to his stomach. By now he was barely 110 pounds and was frail and thin.

The time had come for the doctors and the community liaison nurse to talk to him about his future. They did not think his health would ever be good enough to go home and that perhaps he should start thinking about an option in the community where he could get long-term care. That did it! David was *not* going to hear any more talk about community support and told them he was going home—*now*! They did not expect this, but then I could have told them this would be his reaction. Throughout his six months in hospital David had been cheerful, considerate and pretty much very pleasant to be around. I guess they did not realize he also had a will of iron. When asked who was going to give him his nursing care he said, "My wife will take care of me." They tried to explain that right now he needed a great deal of care, which was being given to him by several people working in shifts.

No matter, his response was the same: "My wife can do it." Oh boy, we really had a situation on our hands. Believe me, I would dearly have loved to have him home. Six months alone after 40 years of marriage was enough for me. But could I do it? You bet I would give it my best try. I had already been through periods where I had nursed him, given him morphine needles and taken care of his arm dressings and medications. Fortunately, my job had required me to take a pharmacology course, so this was not new to me.

Upon hearing the dreaded words "long-term care," David wanted home as fast as possible. Once there he believed he would be safe from the system. So I met with the community nurse to set things in motion. I was going to move our queen-size bed into one of the smaller bedrooms for myself, and there would be a hospital bed, feeding pole and hospital table set up in our big, bright bedroom. The bed would have sides, but I would put it against one wall and turn the rest of the bedroom into a living room, complete with armchairs, etc. I would put my dresser in the spare room and move the drawers from there into David's room to hold all of his supplies and dressings. The medications would be in a locked box high in a cupboard in the kitchen. This way folks could visit with him and the atmosphere would be more like a living room. There would be home help set up for each morning and evening to get him bathed and dressed, and later to get him ready for bed. He would also have a community nurse come in once a day. She would show me how to set up his feeding bag and how to inject his medications through his stomach tube. I already had a pestle and mortar (originally for my herbs) that I could use to crush his pills before mixing them with water to be injected. The nurse would change the Fentanyl patch on his back and I would do the calcitonin-salmon spray in his nose. His supplies would be delivered from the hospital as needed. Phew! All set to go.

Everything David would need was requisitioned and arrived at our home the next day. I must admire the efficiency of the way everything happened so quickly, as this meant David could come home. I must admit to some trepidation about how I would cope with his needs, but this was his home as much as mine and I had certainly missed having him around. So with much joy he arrived home and was so happy to be out of the hospital. It had been a long haul, although his health did not look as if it would ever get much better than it currently was.

As arranged, the caregiver came twice a day. She was great and David really got along well with her. It transpired that she lived just around the corner from our house, so that was handy. The nurse came each morning to check his elbow and change the dressing, but the hole was getting bigger instead of smaller, and the flesh around it was starting to turn black. We could actually see the prosthesis, but David's arms were so thin there was little flesh left on them anywhere. On top of everything else he was no longer able to raise anything up as far as his lips as his neck was rigid and his hands and arms did not work. Without exception, every doctor who saw him said his was the worst case of rheumatoid arthritis they had ever seen.

Life with David was certainly busy. There were medications to be given at various times throughout the day and sometimes in the night. Much of the day he slept (this was when I was looking after Larry from eight to four), but in the evening he was more alert and therefore his needs were greater, plus I needed to be ever-vigilant for any sign that he might be getting pneumonia. For him to just sip a little water through a straw I had to hold the glass for him and then he had to be very careful not to get liquid into his lungs.

Getting him to the washroom was something of a trial but we managed. Unfortunately, it was during the night that he seemed to need help with things and I would be awakened by him calling, "Chris, Chris" several times while I was sleeping. Then there was his liquid food that needed to be put into a bag on an IV pole and then a tube attached to a valve in his abdomen, which was quite a ritual. First the tube in his abdomen needed to be flushed clear with two syringes of water. After this the valve had to be flushed and cleaned and then the area around the valve usually needed care. Only then could I attach the tube that would give him the liquid food supplement.

Throughout this time, since his admission to hospital, I had kept in touch with David's brothers, but also Jean and John had kept in close contact with me as they were quite concerned. They were also a great support to me. In trying to remember how long David had been home when I received a surprise call from John, I think it was perhaps two weeks. As I have already stated, during that year one day ran into another and I am finding it difficult to pinpoint exact dates and times. In thinking back I look for clues, such as was it summer or fall? Ah, it must have been summer as we had a barbeque at Toby's and were all dressed accordingly. As I remember David's help did not come on the weekends, so I took care of things myself.

But you must be wondering what the surprise call from John was all about. John and Jean had been talking about David being home, and as they were both doctors were cognizant of the impact this could have on me as the caregiver. Now I was happy to have David home (and also not to have to drive to the hospital every day), but I have to be honest and admit that I was worn out. But he was my husband, and not only did I consider this my responsibility, I loved him very much.

Apparently after talking to Jean, John had said he would like to visit for a few days and see for himself how things were going for us. Fortunately I have a guest bedroom and bathroom that are always kept ready in case of unexpected company. The bedroom is a bit frilly for a man, but that was okay. John was planning to arrive in the evening on Friday and leave during the day on Wednesday. David and I were thrilled to be having him visit. It would be someone for Dave to chat to who understood his problems, and I could take him out to visit our various offspring while David was resting. Actually, like any mother, I could not wait to show off my children and grandchildren. Over the years we had chatted back and forth in our letters about our families, so this would be great.

It turns out John could not have chosen a better weekend to visit as his help was definitely needed. Thinking back I am still so grateful for Jean and John's thoughtfulness in arranging this visit, and also for Sue being willing to take Larry for a few days.

Friday evening arrived and I rushed off to the airport to meet John. Well, I waited and waited at the end of the airport by the West Jet arrivals. Everyone had disembarked and there was no John. Up I went to the other end to the Air Canada exit—still no John. By now I was in quite a tizzy wondering what had happened. Back I went to the other end (quite a haul) and still no John. After looking around I scooted the length of the airport arrivals and was almost back at Air Canada when a gentleman caught my arm and said in a joking manner, "Well, I never! You didn't even recognize me." Now that was the John I knew. Being so distracted, my eyes had been dead ahead when they should have been looking up. John is a tall man and I am a vertically challenged five foot nothing. Of course I knew that now I would be teased all the way home, but it was so good to see him. Our home was only 10 to 15 minutes away from the airport, so we were soon there, with David waiting happily to see our visitor. This was going to be so good for him. After showing John his room and bathroom he went to chat with David while I made us some tea. At this point I was glad I had set up the bedroom like a living room as it made it comfortable for socializing. Before we knew it the evening was over and John retired while I got David settled down for the night before wending my way to bed with our two little dogs Riggs and Snuggles. They were both almost seventeen years old now and, like David, slept most of the time.

Saturday morning arrived, and I got up to get David's medications and feeding tube ready and to get him washed up for the day. After this I got myself ready and wandered downstairs. What a wonderful surprise! John must have heard me puttering about because when I got downstairs he had made himself at home in the kitchen. There was breakfast, all ready on the table. There was grapefruit, boiled eggs, toast and tea. Now that, dear readers, is a true friend. You know what else? I was really touched that while I was busy with David someone thought about me. As I think I mentioned, David sleeps a good deal in the day, so I put the phone on his bed and turned on my cell phone and took John to show him around the neighbourhood. Sue had arranged for us to have supper with her and her family that evening, so during the day we spent time with David.

At four we went over to visit with Sue, Jim and the children. This was so nice to be able to introduce John to Kodi, Cameron and Hannah. Sue's house is always a bit of a zoo, but one immediately feels at home there. Plus, she is a fantastic cook and can whip up the most marvellous meals with seemingly no effort. We did not stay too late because of David but we had a good time. Fortunately it took fewer than 10 minutes to drive home. Following his usual pattern David was livelier in the evening, so we gathered in the "sitting room" before bed. Just once in the night David called out for me. I am a very light sleeper and was at David's door when John poked his head out of his room to ask if everything was all right. I assured him it was and went to take care of David's needs.

Sunday dawned and once again breakfast was prepared while I took care of David. I could definitely get used to this! I was being spoiled. That summer Cathy and Bill had built a lovely deck for us off the kitchen, and subsequently I had had the yard fenced in, with wide gates at the front and back in case David should need a wheelchair or a scooter. So far I had marked out my garden, but it needed to be dug as it was still what had been prairie. While I was puttering around clearing up, John found the gardening tools and set about digging the garden for me. Something as simple as this meant a great deal to me as neither David nor I could do this. Thank you, Jean, for letting me borrow your husband! Toby had invited us to his home for a barbeque that afternoon. He lived on the next street with just a little park between us, so we could walk there in five minutes.

We went over mid afternoon and Toby and Tara had invited a bunch of people to join us, so we had quite a party, and the bonus was that I could get home in the blink of an eye if need be. The day was warm and sunny so we were able to gravitate from the house to the deck at our leisure. Mason thought "Uncle John" was funny (it's easy to tell when someone is already a grandpa). All in all we had good food, good company and a chance to relax with a drink. Everyone wanted to know how David was, so I took the opportunity to chat with the ladies while I noticed John was having a good time with Toby and all the other guys who were there.

Later in the evening we went back to spend time with David. He had good days and bad days but rarely complained, but I knew he was enjoying John's company. We all grew up not far from each other in England (even though I did not know my husband as a child) and it seems we had all played at the same local spots and knew all the same landmarks. John said goodnight and I saw to getting David all settled down with his medications and feeding tube, and then I tucked myself in with my two furry little canine friends and hoped for an undisturbed night.

Unfortunately, wishes do not always come true. It must have been about two or three in the morning when I heard a terrific bang and a crashing noise. I was already out of bed and moving when I heard, "Chris, Chris, help me." By the time I reached David, I heard John coming out of his room about thirty seconds behind me. My dear husband must have decided he was going to try and help himself and not disturb me, but he somehow ended up on the other side of the room on his back. His hospital table and IV pole were knocked over and he had pulled out tubes and goodness knows what. If we ever needed a doctor in the house it was right now. David was bumped about and bleeding all over. From years of taking prednisone his skin was like tissue paper and literally tore at the slightest touch. Immediately John stepped in and checked him all over. There was already a swelling in his chest from a fractured sternum and I can guarantee he had several broken ribs.

On my own I would never have been able to get him up off the floor, but our kind "house doctor" was now all business and we got David back into bed. From here I just did what I was told and gave John the dressings and other things he asked for. David needed to be bandaged in various places, but this time, for once, I could relax in the knowledge that it was not all up to me to sort things out. Without John I would have had to resort to calling 911.

After everything was over we all settled down for what was left of the night. The nurse was coming in the morning and John wanted to talk to her. It was his opinion that David needed to go to the hospital, but understandably that was the last place he wanted to be.

Come morning, John had checked David and assessed him before the nurse arrived. He was still of the opinion that David should be hospitalized but would not overstep his bounds. With the sternum being fractured there was now the added concern that David would also get another bout of pneumonia. The community nurse arrived mid-morning. She talked to David about his accident in the night and suggested he needed 24-hour nursing care, with the usual response of, "No, my wife will do it." John took the nurse aside and had a few words with her, after which she told David he really needed X-rays and the kind of care only the hospital could give him. Finally he capitulated and the ambulance was called.

When it arrived, there was a problem. The paramedics said he would have to go to Peter Lougheed, the closer hospital. I told them all his specialists were at Foothills and that it was imperative he went there. I got the same answer.

Then the nurse cut in and said, "This gentleman is a doctor, and he thinks he needs to go to Foothills." Whoops—gutsy young lady! All of a sudden the paramedic said, "Let me call my boss." The next thing we knew David was going to be whisked off to Foothills.

After the nurse left John and I followed the ambulance to Foothills Hospital, which is a good half an hour's drive at the best of times. David was already in a private room in the emergency department and being examined by a doctor when we arrived. We were ushered through and shown to the room, where John stopped outside the door. I asked him to come in but he had not wanted to intrude, but then David called out and insisted he come in with us. This was definitely a plus because he was able to explain things to the attending physician in technical terms. Actually, I had not a clue what they were saying. The one thing I ascertained was that there was no question David was being admitted again. In one way this was a relief to me, but on the other hand I really felt bad for David and could only imagine how bad he felt about all this. We stayed and visited with him and made sure he was settled in a room before we left. Time had fled and the day had all but disappeared.

Cathy and Bill had invited us to have supper with them that evening. They did not live far from the hospital, which was a good thing as we were running a bit late. I was happy to introduce them to John, and it was a chance to sit and relax after all the crises of the last day. It must have been about nine p.m. when we arrived home. In retrospect it should have felt strange having John there without David, but after growing up together I guess we were more like brother and sister, so it seemed quite natural. We watched the news while we had some tea and a snack, and then I think we were both done in so called it a night. At least I and my two furry critters would not be disturbed this night.

This had not been the little vacation I had hoped it would be for John, but I guess that had not really been his purpose for coming. He told me he had not realized just how bad things were until he saw with his own eyes. Tuesday was going to be his last day here, and we both slept in a bit after the stress and sleepless night with David. After a casual breakfast we took our time and read the papers and sat out on the deck, heading out to visit David after lunch. Once again he was settled in a private room and from the way the doctor was talking they did not think there was much chance of his overall condition improving to the point where he could go home. He still needed a good while at Foothills, but I was told that eventually he should be going to a long-term care facility. His needs were just too great for one person to handle. Of course the trick would be to get David to agree when the time came.

As it was John's last night here the whole family was all going out for a special supper with John. Toby made the arrangements, and if I remember rightly he had booked us all a table at Earl's Restaurant. What a nice, relaxing evening this turned out to be. Of course a glass of wine or beer helps things along, that and Toby's naturally social personality. Actually, John was quite impressed by him. Time was getting on when we arrived home and John needed to pack for the next morning, so we sat like a couple of old fogies and watched the news before calling it a day.

The next day was Wednesday and time to drive John to the airport. And then, just like that, he was gone. But thank goodness he was there when David fell. I will always appreciate what Jean and John did for us by having John come to Calgary to see for himself what was going on, as this was no vacation, even though my various offspring took the opportunity to entertain us.

Life now went back to the even tenor of my looking after Larry during the day from Monday to Friday and visiting David in the evenings, except on weekends, when I would visit David during the day. Sometimes David would insist I take a day off, but I only did this once in a blue moon. In spite of the surgeon's predictions it had become apparent that my husband would never be able to eat or drink again. He had the odd little sip of pop but that was all. As well, his elbow was becoming worse and he now had a sign outside his room stating that no one could enter without a gown and mask. The MRSA staph infection in his elbow was highly contagious for anyone dealing with it.

Following my usual pattern I phoned David's brothers to keep them updated about his situation. Mike, his youngest brother, decided he was going to come over from Galway Bay in Ireland to visit for a long weekend and see David for himself. Now, Mike (Dr. Michael Redfern) is an astrophysicist and at this time was head of the physics department at Galway University, hence his short visit. When he arrived, one of the first things he did was go out with Tara to buy David a male budgie. If you did not know the history this would seem a rather strange thing to do, but their dad always had a budgie and he loved that little bird, and with David being so like his dad—hence the cage and the budgie. He was named Peter, and Mike hung his cage from the ceiling next to David's favourite recliner in the living room. This way it would be right where his brother would be able to see and talk to it anytime he was home.

We spent as much time as possible with David, and Mike, being an extremely brilliant man could, I am sure, see the fragility of the situation. While we were driving to the hospital one day he told me he would rather come now and see David while he was alive than come to his funeral. There was no point in that. I totally agreed with him, and apart from anything else it was a wonderful surprise for Dave to see his brother. It cheered him up immensely, and I must admit it cheered me up to have my brother-in-law to talk to. Cathy had always been close to her uncle Mike. Theirs was a rare kind of rapport, where she could converse with him on his level. Finally, thank goodness I keep a guest bedroom and bathroom always at the ready for visitors, expected or otherwise!

24.

Changes (the Solo Wife)

In trying to pinpoint the dates I have pretty much figured it out to early October 2006 when I had a call from Jean and John. They invited me to spend some time with them at their home on Victoria and have a break from all the running around. I talked to Dave about this and he said that I was to go and enjoy myself and that he would be fine. After all, there were the rest of the family still around.

So with Toby's help (I had not travelled for years except to come to Calgary) I booked a flight on West Jet that would take me straight from Calgary to Victoria. All told the visit would be for five days. I was so nervous about flying by myself; I even worried about getting on the wrong plane and getting lost! No, I was certainly not a seasoned traveller, and not knowing what I would need I took far too many clothes.

Jean and John met me at the airport, and it was so lovely to

273

see their smiling faces. Their house is beautiful and right on the ocean in Oak Bay. Jean had set up a lovely bedroom for me and had even put a vase of fresh roses from the garden in the room for me. I also had my own bathroom, which was great. For supper, Jean, who is a superb cook (as well as a doctor and an artist), had prepared a pork roast with the crackling still on—yum, my favourite. They had put a great deal of thought into planning what we were going to do while I was there, and I was spoiled rotten. We went to a party at a friend's condominium and I had never seen such a place. It looked like something out of a magazine. We also had friends over for supper at Jean and John's house as well as them showing me all around Victoria.

I arrived on Monday and was leaving on Friday and had left my hosts' telephone number with Toby … just in case. On Wednesday afternoon we were sitting having tea and some of Jean's famous shortbread when there was a call for me from Toby. He said, "Dad is being released and coming home." The doctors had talked to him about long-term care again and that was enough for him. He told them, "No, I am going home. My wife will look after me."

My first thought was, *Oh, no,* and the bottom fell out of my stomach. All I could see was my life going right back on the merry-go-round with no way off. Quite unbidden I started to cry, and when I got off the phone I told John what had transpired. Jean had gone to the kitchen for something but came back to see what was wrong, and I remember John telling her, "Cynthia is a little upset. David is coming home." She just said, "Oh." Jean fully understood where I was coming from. I know I should not have felt that way but I was just so tired, and now in the middle of this lovely break I found out that when I returned I would have to start all over again. I would pick him up from Foothills on Saturday, the day after I got home. Once again the home care and community nursing care was put in place, although this time David was able to get dressed some days and come downstairs. This was nice, but he was so thin and frail. At this point he was down to 110 pounds.

October 18, just a few days after coming home, was David's sixty-sixth birthday. This was great and could not have been better timing. He was home and we could celebrate! I arranged a party with the family arriving at about four p.m. and staying for a buffet supper. David could not eat, so I bought an ice cream cake with Happy Birthday, David piped on the top. It was very pretty and he could have a little of this as it was basically liquid and would easily slip down his throat. He was so happy to have all the grandchildren around him. They were all dressed up and Hannah wore a brand new dress with a coronet of flowers in her hair. I made sure I took lots of photographs of this event! To top things off, Toby and Tara told us they were expecting another baby in April. What a memorable day.

Within two days the ambulance was once more at the door. David had pneumonia in both lungs and his blood oxygen level was way down again. Off we went to the Foothills, and of course he was admitted. Subsequently I met with his doctors and care team to decide the best course of action. Once he was over the pneumonia he no longer needed a bed at the hospital but was not considered a candidate for being sent home. There was absolutely no doubt that David needed 24-hour care, which meant going into a long-term care facility for the rest of his life.

Years before, David had made out his will, leaving everything to me plus giving me the authority to make all decisions on his behalf, even if this was not his personal wish. Well, I agreed I could no longer care for him at home. My nerves were shot and

I was exhausted physically and emotionally. Also, David still had times when he had a warped view of things and thought I hated him. Fortunately I have always been able to separate the true David from the delusional one. When all was said and done, it was deemed that David's signature was necessary as he still understood what was going on. I was certainly not going to override this; it was David's right to choose. On the other hand, I did ask that the team try their best to persuade him that this was the only feasible course of action, and I would talk to him as well. He really knew what needed to happen, but in typical David fashion he had been exercising his control.

So it was done. I felt a profound sense of loss knowing David would not be coming home to live anymore. I also felt a whole lot of guilt for having, from my perspective, forsaken him. My common sense told me his needs were far beyond anything I could handle, but that did not make it any easier. The search for a suitable facility led me to a beautiful, brand new place just 10 minutes' drive from home. This meant I would be able to pick him up to go out for a drive or to the coffee shop and he could come home for the day whenever he liked. Of course, this place (which was like a five-star hotel) was full, so I put his name on the waiting list. Now he would have to go to the first available bed wherever it was until a place opened up at his first choice of residence. A few weeks before Christmas there was an opening at a facility next door to the Rockyview Hospital, clear across the other side of town in the southwest. It was an attractive location with beautiful gardens backing onto Glenmore Reservoir, a popular boating spot. Because of the distance I could only visit on weekends, but I made sure he had a telephone and could call me whenever he wanted to.

In all my life I had never seen a place run so sloppily as

this facility. The caregivers had no respect for the manager and just sat around talking with no pretence of hiding what they were doing—or not doing, as the case may be. For some time now, David had been taking horrific amounts of pain medication on top of his prednisone and other pills, and they had to be given on time. Just for pain alone he was on twenty milligrams of hydromorphone every four hours with a breakthrough dose of eight milligrams as needed. This was along with Didrocal, calcitonin-salmon and a two hundred twenty-five microgram Fentanyl patch on his shoulder.

One morning he called me at ten a.m. to say he still had not been given his eight a.m. medication. I raised a little Cain and told them to administer the medications *now* and then call me back when it was done. When this happened a second time I raised a whole lot of Cain and instituted a system whereby I called at eight every morning to see if his medications had been given. If not, I told them in no uncertain terms to "Do it now and call me back to report that the medications have been given!" Pretty soon we were on track—or were we? I had visited David several times and walked around the gardens with him, but it was December now and getting too cold for going outside.

Late one night I received a phone call from the care centre. It was eleven p.m. on December 15, and the person at the other end of the line told me I had better hurry and get up there as my husband was non-responsive and may not make it through the night. He had been transferred to Rockyview Hospital right next door to the care facility. I immediately called Toby, who said he was coming right around to pick me up. At this time of the night the roads were pretty clear and we made good time.

Upon arriving at the hospital we were immediately shown into a private section of the emergency department, where the doctor was with David. When we went in he explained to us what had happened, and boy, was he angry. As I mentioned before, David had 225 microgram Fentanyl patches on his shoulder for long-release pain medication. I knew the protocol as I had been administering them when David was home. They are changed every two days and put on alternate shoulders. The old one must come off before the new one is applied and they *must* be dated.

What the doctor had found was that David was wearing two patches and now had a very serious drug overdose. He showed us the patches he had removed but I did not notice any dates. Now, did the staff not follow protocol and put on the new one before removing the old one, and then forget to remove it? Or did they misread the instructions and instead of giving one patch gave two? Who knows! The doctor had done all he could, but David was in a coma so he'd been put in ICU to be cared for. It was three days before he showed any signs of coming around, but at least he had made it.

The morning after this debacle I was on the phone to this care centre, but they had already circled the wagons. "No, no, we did not put on two patches." So what, the tooth fairy put them there? I saw the patches. I insisted on speaking to the doctor there, expecting to have an intelligent conversation. No such luck. She totally denied that David had been given two patches. Now this really boggled my mind as the doctor in emergency had the proof. But no matter what I did or said she totally denied any responsibility for either herself or the staff. At this point David was still in a coma and they were running scared. When I visited David, I went next door to the facility to talk face to face with the doctor there. You know, I was beginning to feel like Alice falling down the rabbit hole. Just how many times can a person say, "No, it wasn't us," when the proof was right there? It was no wonder the staff were lax—attitude comes from the top.

When David was finally lucid he still had to remain in the hospital for a couple of days more, but thank God he was okay with no apparent lasting damage. On Thursday, December 21 I had a call from Rockyview saying I could come and get David as he was ready to come home. What!! After explaining that he was in long-term care they assured me that no, he was supposed to be released to home. Now their computers were not hooked in with Foothills or they would have known. On the other hand, was the facility next door not contacted to take him back? It has just struck me that perhaps they were and did not want him? Another lie perhaps? Who knows?

Anyway, I arranged to pick him up that afternoon, and Susan was going to come with me. By now I had sent his hospital bed back and put our queen-size bed back to once again make the room into a bedroom. But that was okay. David was somewhat mobile now and it would be nice to not have to sleep by myself anymore. The only problem was that at the beginning of December I had found it necessary to have our two little dogs put down. I had discussed this with David at the time so he knew about it. They were both 17 years old and having bad health problems. But now what to do? David doted on his pets and I could not have him come home and not have a little dog to sit on his lap.

Susan and I scoured the newspapers and found an advertisement for Chihuahuas that were just ready to go. The address was not far away and I arranged to go around at six o'clock. Next step, I got David home and settled in and then told him I just had to run an errand and would not be long. The puppies were adorable and I chose a little tan-coloured male, 9 weeks old, and off we went home $500.00 poorer, but it was well worth it. We came in the door and I asked David to close his eyes. Then I put this tiny little critter on his lap and said he could look. Oh the joy on his face! It was the most wonderful thing to see and it was instant love. David named the puppy Billy and kept him cuddled up on his lap.

Between us we managed to take turns being with David and still finish up getting ready for Christmas, which was just four days away on Monday. How amazing it was that my husband cold be with us for Christmas, and what a wonderful Christmas it was, complete with our little Billy. Somehow David had sorted out getting Christmas gifts for me. For my birthday in December he had bought me a new set of luggage (via Cathy). This Christmas Tara had been given the task of buying me a pair of deerskin moccasin slippers and Cathy my stocking stuffers. Oddly enough they were all related to travelling. My gift to David was a gold pocket watch, one where you could see the movements working inside. He could no longer wear a wrist watch so I thought this would be a good alternative. And the children—what a delight it was to see the joy on their little faces when they opened Santa's gifts. We kept things pretty low key but still made it to Susan's for a little while for Christmas dinner. David was not able to eat but I certainly enjoyed it.

Boxing Day was calm and quiet for us and I finally wrangled out of David the mystery of all the travel items. It seems he and Cathy had been spending Tuesday evenings planning a trip to England for Cathy and me. Apparently Dave figured it was time I went back to visit Sam and Lynette, my brother and his wife. I had never told David about my past history with Sam. But this was going to be exciting because first we were going to stay in a sixteenth-century house that was now a bed and breakfast. Plus we were going to see Shakespeare's birthplace and many other tourist attractions, ending up in London before coming home.

After phoning Sam and Lynette and asking if I could visit and stay overnight, the answer I received was, "Well, we are rather too busy to entertain." After all, I was only going to be travelling 5,000 miles to see them after nearly 40 years, so what was the big deal? Excuse the language, but "bugger them!" On the other hand, David's brother Don and his wife, Rene, couldn't wait to see us and have us stay with them a while. What can I say; my brother Don and my niece Carole were also looking forward to our visit. We were leaving on Friday March 2 for two weeks. My husband was certainly doing his best to make me happy.

Unfortunately, by the next morning he was full of pneumonia again and I had to call the ambulance to rush him to Foothills Hospital. They were completely puzzled about him being discharged to home instead of long-term care. By early February 2007 David was placed into another long-term care facility, this one quite a bit closer to home. He seemed fairly settled here. We all did our best to make his room like home. There was a brand new flat-screen TV for him to watch, pictures and photos of the grandchildren on the walls and I bought him his own telephone with extra large numbers so he could see to call home whenever he wanted. In the centre of the building was a glass-roofed courtyard about three to four stories high and it was full of really huge tropical plants and trees, and there were dozens of different birds singing and flying around. Beside it was a little coffee shop where we would get a drink and then go sit under the palm trees. Naturally David knew the Latin name of just about every plant in there! On weekends I had David home all day on Saturdays and Sundays, although he could not stay overnight. Still, he spent the weekends with the family and that was nice.

David had been at the care centre for about three weeks and was settling in nicely. As long as I visited him and brought him home at weekends he was more accepting of the situation. He shared his room with another gentleman about the same age and they hit it off together and had good conversations. The next Saturday he was home and we had a nice time, although lately he had become a bit concerned about how I would manage if anything happened to him. Of course I reassured him that (a) nothing was going to happen to him and (b) I was okay. I had an income looking after Larry and being government it was legally non-taxable and non-deductible. I had a vehicle and I had a house, so what more could I want? Because of his health David had never been able to get health insurance or mortgage insurance, but so what. I am a survivor, and if I need to work I will.

Anyway, this was all hypothetical and we were going to enjoy the day. It was cold outside but we had huge windows that let in all the sunlight. The bird was chirping and little Billy, as usual, was curled up on his dad's lap. There was a certain time David needed to be back, I think it was seven thirty p.m., but by this time he was tired anyway.

Next morning I picked David up and took him to spend Sunday at home. Up until three p.m. everything was fine, but suddenly he said, "I don't feel well," though this was not unusual considering his poor health and lack of an immune system, so I asked him what was wrong. He took me by surprise when he said, "I think I had better go back now, I really don't feel good." I got him into the van and back we went. By four p.m. I was helping the nurse get him undressed and into his nightclothes. After tucking him into bed and making sure he was settled in, I kissed him goodnight and said, "I'll see you tomorrow," and off I went home. My life with my husband had been full of these kinds of events over the years, so although I was concerned, it did not impact me overmuch. I heard nothing more that evening.

Larry arrived at eight the next morning, and once he was settled I called the care centre. I was put through to David's staff and asked them how he was this morning. The staff answered in a cheery voice, "He's not responding right now." There was no hint of alarm in her voice and I said I would call back later. Sounded like the same old, same old and I suspected pneumonia.

Access Calgary picked up Larry at about three fifty, a little early, and so at exactly four p.m. I called to see how David was. Once again I spoke with the staff who told me, "The nurse is with him right now, just hold on please." When the nurse came on the phone, I repeated the question and she quite bluntly answered, "Your husband died at four o'clock." For a moment I had to stop and take in what she had said, and then because she was not saying anything else I said, "I guess I had better come up then," to which she responded that she would appreciate my coming as soon as possible. I said I would.

The first person I called was Toby. He said I was not to drive myself and that he and Tara would pick me up. They just needed to find someone to watch Mason. Next I phoned Richard, Cathy, Susan and Dan and I am so glad to be able to say there were no hysterics because right now I was staying strong. Because of the time difference there was no point in calling David's brothers right then. I think it was Richard who said he would call them all for me in the morning. For Mike and Don it would be the middle of the night and there was no point waking them. Bob was in New Zealand and I had no idea what time or even day it was there.

Toby and Tara picked me up and we drove to the care centre. Thank God for Tara's calm, capable manner. Before I went in we sat in the car and discussed the need to contact a funeral home to come that evening. I certainly did not know any but Tara got on her cell phone right away to make arrangements. Meanwhile I went into the centre. Toby stayed in the car. He even found it difficult to visit his dad in hospital and I suspect this was too much for him. They were very close.

Well, here I was, so I went up to David's floor and found the nurse. Her concern was that we move the "body" as soon as possible as the roommate wanted to get into his room. Next I went in to see David. He looked peaceful. There were no tubes or anything anymore, although I could see the indentation on his face from where he had been wearing an oxygen mask. His arm was outside the covers, and I remember gently rubbing his arm. Then I pushed the hair back off his face. All his pain was gone. It was February 26, 2007, and he was 66 years old. We had been married 40 wonderful years. My visit was not long. I told the nurse he would be in the care of McInnis and Holloway and that they would be here shortly. Then I turned and walked away. It appears my husband died from the Norwalk flu. How ironic after everything he had survived.

Toby and Tara took me home and wanted to know if I was going to be all right alone. I reassured them I would. They were taking me to the funeral home the next day in order to make all the necessary arrangements. How glad I was to be home. First I called the lady with whom Larry lived and explained that I would not be able to have him for a while, and then I think I called Jean and John. My necessary tasks done, now I could sit and cry. Now I was alone. Now I was a widow.

25.

Rediscovering Cynthia (the Widow)

*O*n the following day Toby drove me, along with Tara and Susan, to the funeral home so I could make the necessary arrangements. Although I may have wanted some things done differently I followed David's wishes to the letter. If that was what he wanted, then that was what I would do. His desire was to be cremated, not have a funeral with a viewing of the casket but instead to just have a party to celebrate his life. Oh, and "don't spend any unnecessary money on a fancy casket!"

When I met with the funeral director he was most helpful. We agreed my husband would be cremated and there would be no viewing. Therefore, if the casket was going to be burned and not viewed we did not need anything fancy or expensive. He showed me a choice of suitable caskets and I chose one that was mid-range. It had a really nice lining and pillow, and although it looked nice it was actually made of pine.

Next I needed to choose an urn. Now this was where I would not skimp. After a lot of looking and thought (my children pretty much kept quiet and encouraged me to go with my feelings), I chose a rectangular container of beautiful, highly polished, dark-green marble. The top was actually gently sloped upward so the top was a little smaller than the bottom. Next I had to choose lettering style and what I wanted inscribed on the top. I chose an elegant script that read "David John Redfern" and then underneath "October 18, 1940, to February 26, 2007." Then I asked them to put the Masonic symbol beside the script and asked for the lettering to be in gold.

So that was that. They said I could come and view David the next day, Wednesday, and I had already brought in his suit, shirt and tie. He was a handsome man and I wanted him to look his best. The urn would be ready on Thursday morning and the celebration was being held at Toby and Tara's that afternoon. I had a message that the Grand Lodge in Toronto wanted to send two representatives (a sign of how highly David was respected), but there was not enough time to arrange that.

On Wednesday Toby and Tara took me to the funeral home to see David one last time. They did not come in, but the staff put a chair for me beside his casket so I could spend some time with him. He looked smart in his grey suit and very peaceful. No more pills, tubes, patches and needles. Now he was out of pain and at peace. After a while I stroked his hair one last time and then turned and left. He was in God's hands now. My work was done.

Outside, Toby and Tara were waiting to take me home. Richard, our eldest, would soon be arriving at the airport after flying in from London. Only Dan, our youngest, could not make it from Toronto. Richard was going to be staying until

Monday, so he would use the guest facilities at my house. Out of all the grandchildren David's death hit Kodi the hardest, as he and Grandpa were particularly close. Kodi was also the eldest grandchild.

Toby picked his brother up from the airport. Meanwhile, I was sorting out some of David's things to be displayed the next day. I still had his regalia and medals from when he was district deputy grandmaster of the Grand Lodge in Toronto. This was really something to see. All the intricate embroidery was done with real gold thread. Besides this, there were all his scouting awards and memorabilia, plus I wanted to display a photo of our wedding. Grandest of all was the gold framed photograph of David in his white tie and tails, wearing all the regalia that would be on display. If I remember rightly, that evening Toby took us all out to a fancy restaurant, where their speciality was ribs. It was then I realized that the day after the celebration I was supposed to be flying out to England with Cathy for a two week vacation! Oh my stars. How could I do this? My husband had just died and I was going on vacation? Actually, he had planned it all for me, but somehow it just did not seem right. Well, I would do what Scarlet O'Hara did and "think about it tomorrow."

My wonderful daughter-in-law Tara had everything arranged for the next day. Flowers had started to arrive at my home on Wednesday, but when I reached Toby and Tara's the house was full of arrangements. She had organized the food and drinks and taken care of who to invite, so all I had to do was set up the display of David's things. I had brought my camera and photographed every single one of the arrangements, they were so beautiful. How could there be so many people who cared so much?

Bob, David's eldest brother, took on the role of head of the family and wrote a wonderful eulogy that he e-mailed me to be read at the gathering. Toby and Richard slipped out to the funeral home to pick up the urn, and in the meantime people started to arrive. There were so many I could not believe it. The boys arrived back and put the urn in place and it was now time for a toast to David. Who would have thought of it but my kids? In Ontario, David's favourite drink was a pop called Wink, which was not available in Alberta. Somehow Richard managed to bring several bottles and we all toasted David with Wink. How he would have loved that! I'll bet somewhere up there he was having a good chuckle.

People were happy at this gathering, which is just what was intended. No morbidity here; it was a celebration of life. The conversation turned to the trip that Cathy and I were to take the next day. Everyone was telling me I should go, but I didn't think I should. Then my ever-practical Tara said to me, "What are you going to do, sit and watch the flowers die?" Now that put it in perspective—I was going. I gave Richard a house key and the key to my car and he had the house to himself.

The next day Cathy and I were off to England. The last time I had visited was for Richard's christening when he was 18 months old. It was going to be a nine-hour flight to London where Cathy's friend Dave and his girlfriend, Susan, were meeting us and driving us to our sixteenth-century bed and breakfast in the little town of Bewdly on the River Severn. This was their home town as well so it worked out well. Dave was going to take two weeks holiday just to chauffeur us around. He had stayed with David and me in Canada when he was visiting Toby and said it was the least he could do. From his comments I gather he'd had the greatest of respect for my husband. Actually, this trip was David's last gift to me, so I am glad I was persuaded to go.

Cathy did all the leg work, and in booking the B and B, I

told her I wanted old, quaint and big old beams. Believe me, this place was absolutely made to order. It was called "The Pewterer's House" as it was built in the 1500s by the local pewterer and it was from here he made his living. Our hostess was a lady who was originally from London. She was middle-aged, educated and a lot of fun. When I saw our bedroom I thought I was in heaven. It had huge oak beams, deep stone window wells with leaded glass and was beautifully decorated. The only modern touch was a bathroom that had been added. There was also an electric kettle and the means to make tea or coffee plus some snacks.

We slept like logs that night and in the morning our cheery hostess served us the most magnificent English breakfast in the fifteenth-century dining room. Dave and Susan arrived and we were off to Stratford on Avon to see Shakespeare's birthplace and Anne Hathaway's cottage. Our lunch (or cream tea) was at a centuries' old inn that, I imagine, looked much as it must have done at the time Shakespeare was wandering these cobbled streets. And oh joy! I was able to buy a little teddy Shakespeare for my teddy bear collection. That day it poured with rain, but that's England. For supper we all went to a little, old restaurant in Bewdly and I was thrilled to be able to order steak and kidney pie and chips—real English chips!

Over the next two weeks we did and saw everything. I ended up with (amongst other things) a Paddington Bear actually bought at Paddington Station, a Tower of London Beefeater bear and on our final day a rather big Sherlock Holmes bear actually from Twenty-Two B Baker Street. My daughter shook her head, gave me a look of defeat and said, "Mom, if that thing does not fit into your suitcase, *you* are the one carrying it on your lap on the plane."

Halfway through our two weeks Cathy and Dave went hiking

for three days in Cheddar Gorge. This was not quite my cup of tea so they dropped me off at David's brother's house in the country. Don and Rene made me so welcome and spoiled me completely. Rene is the most fantastic cook and made the most marvellous meals. David had wanted each of his brothers to have something of his, so I took Don his gold signet ring with the initials DR inscribed on the front. As Don had the same initials it seemed appropriate—I think he was a little overcome by having it. On top of everything else it had been made by their uncle, who was a goldsmith.

We went to different places of interest, all of them just exactly my kind of thing, but they kept it low key for me. Perhaps—no, I am sure—they realized how worn out I was. One afternoon before tea Rene said to put my head down on the sofa for a bit. Next thing I was asleep, and I vaguely remember stirring as Rene gently covered me with a warm blanket. How kind she is. Before leaving there we went shopping in the little old town close to where they lived. Rene and I were looking at some clothes and they were really lovely and quite different to Canadian style. In particular I liked one blouse, but it was expensive so I did not get it. Before I left Don and Rene's, they said to me "We've got a little something for you." Lo and behold it was the blouse I so admired. To this day it is the pride of my closet.

Don drove me back to the bed and breakfast, with me arriving a day before Cathy. This gave me a chance to explore this very old town. I had supper at a real English fish and chip shop and then found a sweet store that still weighed what you wanted out of big glass jars. What I wanted was jelly babies! Yummy! They also had traditional sugar pigs and sugar mice that I bought to take home to the grandchildren. That evening my brother Don (yes, the same name) picked me up and drove me to Birmingham where he, my sister-in-law Margaret and my niece Carole and her husband, Derek, all went out to a pub for a traditional English pub meal. How I love English food.

It was quite late when I arrived back in Bewdly, and Cathy was back as well. We were to leave the next morning, but before going our hostess gave each of us a little souvenir. For me it was a fridge magnet with a picture of Bewdly, and for Cathy, a souvenir ruler. There is a story behind this. When we arrived Cathy was commenting to our hostess about the English roads and said, "Nothing is straight around here." Hence the ruler. Our last three days were spent in London seeing all the sights, and then it was off to the airport and back to Canada. And no, Sherlock teddy did not sit on my lap.

When I arrived at the house and went in it felt very empty. Lily, my cat, was glad to see me (the neighbours had been watching her for me), and the budgie was chirping, but something was lacking. I finally put my finger on it. I had nothing to do, no responsibilities. Basically I had lived by myself for the last year, but there was rarely a day I did not see David. He had been my focus of care for so many years that it caused me to question, "Who am I?" I had been the wife, the caregiver, the problem solver and the extension of everyone's needs. But who, deep down inside, was I? It struck me I did not know, and suddenly I was very alone and rather scared. There had not been time to make any friends or join any groups. There had not been time for hobbies or recreation. There had not been time for me. Susan, Toby and Cathy all lived close, but let's face it, life goes on and they all had their own lives.

Anyway, Sue and Jim did not drive, so I only saw them if I went to their place. Something told me I was so out of touch with everything that it was going to be a tough road back. I was not a person who readily socialized, and anyway, where would I start?

The next morning I went to Susan's to pick up my dog, Billy, and find out how things had been with Larry. Well, apparently the company that gave Larry rides had refused to give him any more due to his behaviour, so it took some figuring out between me and the person he lived with to find a way to get him back and forth. He lived quite a distance away. We decided to meet halfway on a mall parking lot, but by the end of April I was asked if I would like to take over the full twenty four/seven care of Larry. This meant a good wage every month, so there was no way I was going to refuse, but this put me back in the caregiver role again. Still, I had a mortgage to pay. Before this happened, on April 17, Tara gave birth to another baby boy: Brody Kale Redfern had arrived. Everyone was thrilled to bits, especially big brother, Mason, and I now had six grandchildren. Brody was the only one who would not have known his grandpa.

Time passed and I was still at a loose end. There was nothing to do and no one to see and I was starting to get quite depressed. Larry went to bed early and I pretty much sat and looked at the walls. By midsummer I went to see my doctor to talk about this. He was not surprised. We talked about David and he said his was the worst case of rheumatoid arthritis he had ever seen. Then he added, "And you were totally exhausted." The end result of the visit was that I was given antidepressants. No ifs, ands or buts about it; he insisted.

I have to admit they did help a lot. In fact, I did two positive things. The first Christmas we were in Calgary David and I sponsored a little girl through World Vision. The letters back and forth were a blessing to me and I looked forward to hearing from her. So, number one, I sponsored another child, and number two

I went to the Meow Foundation to adopt a rescue cat. Talk about love at first sight. He was the last cat I looked at and he just came right to me and cuddled. That was it. I took him home and named him Farley. What with his big, blue eyes and long, creamy fur he was gorgeous. Apparently he is a Flame Point Himalayan.

It was one day in July when I heard the doorbell ring. This in itself was unusual; no one ever came to my house. I opened the door to find two young men on my doorstep. Having had two such young men spend so much time with David nearly 40 years ago, after one of his surgeries, I immediately recognized them as missionaries with the Church of Jesus Christ of Latter Day Saints. How could I not invite them in? We had a lovely chat and they explained a little about the Mormon faith. Actually, I was quite interested and when they asked if they could visit again the next week I said yes. Well, this became a weekly event and the young men and I had some interesting and intellectually stimulating conversations. When they asked me if I thought whether the Book of Mormon was true, I said I had thought so right when I had first met them. After all, if miracles could happen 2,000 years ago, why couldn't they happen at a future date? Of course the question arose of whether or not I was interested in joining the church. I was, but before making such a life-changing commitment I had a whole lot more questions and intended to read the entire Book of Mormon.

All through the summer I looked forward to these visits, and through having these discussions I began to gain a bit more confidence in myself. Other than looking after Larry, not much was happening in my life. John and Jean phoned me frequently, and throughout the next few years I visited them several times. Sometimes it was in the summer when they were at their cabin on Salt Spring Island and sometimes in the fall when they were at home in Victoria. But no matter where we were, we always had a wonderful time and did many interesting things. They are a lovely couple.

Getting back to 2007, in the fall I heard about a storytelling group similar to the one I belonged to in St. Marys. It was The Alberta League Encouraging Storytelling, or TALES, for short. One night I decided to go along to their storytelling session, but halfway there my nerves started to get the better of me and I almost turned back. Thank goodness I didn't. When I arrived I was welcomed warmly and introduced myself as Chris Redfern. One of the first ladies I met was Anne Cowling, who happened to be very English like me. She is quite a bit younger than me and has two talented teenagers, but we became instant friends. Anne came from Coventry, about twenty minutes away from where I was born in Birmingham. So, throughout the years Anne and I have developed a tradition of meeting for lunch when we are able, and we dine at our special Swiss restaurant. It also sells imported gifts and food, so after eating we have a good wander around to look at all the beautiful and unique items. Anne was my first friend and has remained very special to me. Recently she started a new job that is quite demanding, so we have not seen each other so much, but we still stay in touch.

Well, dear reader, I seem to be doing a bit of time travelling here, back and forth to the present day, but quite frankly, after David passed away my life was pretty much a whole lot of nothing. One thing I did work on was the backyard. I was determined to have it look the way David and I wanted it, even to the bushes and the flowers that I planted. If I do say so myself it was a picture. The garden shed, which I had custom-made, looked like a little cottage with flower boxes under its windows.

In September 2007 Toby borrowed my van to move some

furniture. It was a seven-passenger and the back seats could be removed. Upon returning my vehicle he told me he was concerned about my driving it through the winter and thought I would be safer in a better vehicle. The cost of fixing this one would be more than it was worth. Before I knew it we were at the Nissan dealership. Toby knew them well and did a fair bit of business there. Well, sitting on the lot was a pale gold Altima—a lease back just come in. This car had not yet been detailed but was immaculate. It was a 2003 with only 27,000 kilometres on the clock. I fell in love with it. Toby bargained a good deal for me and it was mine. It was registered to Cynthia Redfern.

From 2007 into 2008 the missionaries continued to visit me. By now I had worked myself through several sets of these dedicated young men. However, I needed to be at a point where I'd had all my questions answered to my satisfaction. Finally I surprised them one day by saying, "Okay, I am ready to be baptized into the Church." I think they were a little bit in shock. My family supported me wholeheartedly and all came to my baptism on July 26, 2008. I was baptized as Cynthia Mary Rose Redfern. Little by little, Chris was fading into the background. I was beginning to like being Cynthia. That was my name.

Shortly after joining the church, the bishop invited me into his office. Here he introduced me to Sister Perks. Apparently she needed a ride to run an errand as she doesn't drive. This was not a problem and of course I said yes. We arranged a time and a day and I went to get her. Her name was Beverly (Bev for short). She and I hit it off as friends and have become very close. Bev is the sister I never had. In fact, people often mistake us for sisters.

This meeting was meant to be, and I am sure it was part of heavenly Father's plan. We can tell each other anything, and I do believe we are a great support for each other. Both of us love writing, and she has encouraged me throughout the year it has taken me to write this book. On October 18 of the year I was baptized, I went to the temple with the other church members, and my husband received a baptism for the dead. This would have been his sixty-eighth birthday. This also meant that in October of the following year I could be endowed at the temple, and the following week David (by proxy) and I were sealed in the temple as man and wife for eternity. Oh, I think I forgot to tell you, I keep his urn on my mantelpiece over the fireplace and underneath his picture.

As that year wore on, Larry's behaviour was worsening and he was slipping into dementia. I had been looking after him for three years during a time I was the only person willing to take him. After meeting with his doctors it was decided he should go into a facility, and by December he had moved.

At that time Toby said he wanted to talk to me. He said, "Look, Mom, you are 68 now and have worked as long as I can remember. I really think you should start enjoying your life." He took me to the bank and we had the mortgage changed into a home equity line of credit, and this meant my monthly payments dropped substantially and I would manage easily on my pension. My house belonged to Cynthia Redfern.

Toby had diligently taken on the role of looking after me. Richard was the eldest but he was 2,000 miles away. I discussed this with him and he was fine with it. Next I was helped by one of Toby's friends who is a lawyer to make out a will to safeguard my wishes, and I named Toby as my executor with Tara as a backup. Somehow, bit by bit, I was getting an identity, something I had relinquished many years before, and it felt good!

January 2009 started with a big celebration. Toby and Tara decided to get married in Cuba, and more than 20 people flew down there for the wedding. I was the only one from our family, but I chummed around with Tara's dad and stepmom Gary and Kathy. They are nice people and we had a good time. The actual wedding was midweek, on Wednesday. It was breathtaking. It took place in a gazebo on a grassy knoll overlooking the ocean and palm trees. Of course Tara looked stunning. She is six foot tall and beautiful, with thick, dark auburn hair, and Toby is six foot three, the epitome of tall, dark and handsome. The resort put on the wedding and the reception and did a great job. Although some of the guests were staying for two weeks I just stayed for the one week, but I still managed to get in plenty of sightseeing, including a trip to Havana.

Oh—I must tell you about a funny thing that happened in Varadero. I was out with Gary and Kathy and jokingly said I wanted to meet a tall, handsome Cuban man and get a kiss. Please, dear readers, take heart to what I am about to tell you and be careful what you wish for! Tara's parents and I were sightseeing and had just had a wonderful meal of lobster. Across the road was a botanical park, so we decided to have a look around. Well, there was a tall Cuban man with a camel. Of course Kathy and I decided to go for a ride around the park on this critter. It was so much fun. When we alighted (a trick in itself) we each wanted our photo taken with the camel. As Gary was just snapping my camera the camel bent down and kissed my cheek! We all just howled with laughter—my wish had come true, just not quite from the species I had imagined.

As time passed I was getting more involved with the church and I loved the friendliness of the members. I was also getting more interested in the World Vision organization. Our church was not just a Sunday thing; we all had responsibilities of one kind or another. All the Sisters take on the role of visiting teaching once a month. We go in pairs to designated houses with an inspiring message.

Actually, the idea is for us to take care of one another's needs and our focus is very much on service. For example, if someone had just come home with a new baby, her visiting teachers would make sure they delivered meals to the family for at least three days. This gives the new parents time to adjust without having to worry about preparing meals. There are many other things as well, but the flipside of this is that we frequently get together at the church for a big meal. Sometimes the men do all the preparations and cooking and then serve the ladies at tables they have decorated with flowers.

Up until now I have had three different "callings," or roles in the church. When I was very new I took on the role of taking care of the missionary meal calendar. These young men love to eat and throughout the month are invited to different homes for supper. I ensured there was always somewhere for them to go. Next I was the single sister's representative for the church, and now, for the past year and a half have taught the adult Sunday school and continue to do this. It takes some preparation each week but I really enjoy it.

That same year I took a more active role with World Vision. I had been to a couple of local meetings and was impressed with what I'd learned. One day I turned around to my family and said, "Oh, by the way, I am going to Mongolia." You could have heard a pin drop. Then one of my offspring said, "What have you done with our mother, and who are you?" Previously I had been nervous just about flying to Victoria, a flight of just one hour and twenty minutes, but here I was, stretching my wings and about to take flight. I had seen an invitation from World Vision looking for volunteers to go on a pilot project to Mongolia, and suddenly I was just filled with a passion to do this. The thought of travelling by myself and changing planes in different countries suddenly seemed like a walk in the park. So I applied and was fortunate enough to be chosen along with nine other people from different parts of Canada. Incidentally, World Vision only knows me as Cynthia. That is also what is on my Facebook page.

Another facet of this trip was that I have a photograph of my mother taken when she was about twenty years old. She was a very beautiful woman. However, she looked more Asian than Caucasian and this had me wondering about my genealogy. Did she look Chinese? No. Did she look Japanese? Again no. Before going to Mongolia I sponsored a little girl whom I would be meeting there. I looked at her photo and nearly fell off my chair. She was the exact image of my mother!

While I was on the trip, everywhere I looked I could see the faces of my aunts and uncles. This was not just my imagination; the similarities were definitely there. The trip itself was so worthwhile. Apart from the opportunity of seeing this beautiful land and experiencing its culture and the warmth of its people in welcoming us, there was the amazing progress of the World Vision projects. They were covering every aspect of helping these people to have a better, healthier lifestyle and eventually become self-sufficient. Basically they had subsisted on the meat and milk of the yaks, but World Vision had brought in huge greenhouses, seeds and the means for growing all kinds of vegetables. There was health care, water wells, schooling, summer camps for children with special needs, nutritional counselling—and the list could go on and on. One especially interesting project was the Parents Income Generating Project. Just about everything here was made from felt, and there was a little gift shop set up with the most remarkable handmade articles. There was everything from slippers to jewellery to embroidered felt bookmarks. An added benefit was the people who were on the trip with me. What a great group. I am still in touch with most of them.

Once I was home I spent the next year promoting what I had seen and learned. With Tara's help I put together a Power Point presentation of some of my photographs and went around to different groups to give presentations. As everything in Mongolia was so different I brought home many things, including some old Buddhist scrolls, and put these items on a display table. After the presentation I had people milling around and asking questions for well more than an hour.

Not only did this experience give me a feeling of satisfaction, I felt empowered and was passionate to do whatever I could. Once home I sponsored another child from Mongolia. Meeting my little girl on the top of a mountain in the middle of nowhere had been one of the most incredibly joyous moments of my life. Another joyous moment came at the end of October that year when my youngest, Dan, and his girlfriend, Jacqueline, moved to Calgary. Now I think I had all but Richard and his family here, although I am aware they will never move. They are too well established where they are. But hey, four out of five ain't bad.

Initially Dan and Jacqueline stayed with me, but when their furniture arrived they moved into a basement suite at Tara's dad's home. From there they eventually rented a house and took in two supported clients, so they are doing really well. I am proud of what they have achieved.

In April 2010 I went on another pilot project with World Vision, this time to Chittagong in Bangladesh. I think that by now my family had gotten the idea that not only was I spreading my wings but I was flying, free as a bird and full of joy. Earlier in the spring I had reconnected with my dear friend Ruth on

Facebook, except that now she was going by her middle name Anna. I was so happy. Leaving St. Marys without knowing where she was had bothered me. It was a loss. Another loss was all the years and studying I put into my anthropology degree. I was in my third year and doing well when we had to move. Still, no more looking back, one has to move forward. Before leaving for Bangladesh, Anna and I sponsored children from the community to which I was going, so I would be able to meet both precious children.

Nothing could have prepared me for the seething mass of humanity that was Chittagong. After the sparsely populated, wide-open spaces of Mongolia the difference was like night and day. However, the needs were still the same. These marginalized people were trying to eke out a living to feed their families, and beggars in the street were a common sight. Because the poverty here was so much more blatant it had a greater effect on me. Also, we were staying in a very fancy hotel and this pointed out the differences even more. Actually, this was more a necessity than a luxury. First and foremost, World Vision keeps its volunteers safe, so the hotel, complete with armed guards and security scanners was for our protection. Secondly, we needed the Internet, as our project involved writing blogs on what we had been doing. This was for the benefit of the sponsors back in Canada. Now remember, I did say this was a pilot project. The system had some rather frustrating glitches that were not sorted out until we arrived back in Canada. So we just did it when we returned. The hotel was also air conditioned, and after being out from eight thirty or nine a.m. to six thirty or sometimes seven at night in 40 degrees Celsius and high humidity, we were happy to cool off. Mind you, I think all the ladies enjoyed wearing the obligatory shalwar kameez outfits with their flowing headscarves. A big joy for me was that one of my companions from the Mongolia trip was here as well, and we were roommates.

Each morning our group would head out to the Patenga District, where we would visit various projects. As in Mongolia, I was amazed at the broad scope of projects and the work that had gone into getting them up and running. World Vision had also been instrumental in helping the women gain empowerment and start their own businesses. These women were showing just what a difference they could make to their families' standard of living. My biggest thrill was meeting my sponsored child, a 10-year-old boy. He was so bright, and I am sure that with continued support he will go far. He wants to be a lawyer.

Before leaving we spent three days working with the local children doing craft and photography workshops, culminating in a big, community party where the children's talents were displayed. Then it was back to the hotel to pack. I loved Mongolia with a passion, but Chittagong affected me far more deeply. Even now I find it hard to reconcile the fact that we have so much when others have so little.

My journey home, including stopovers, was 41 hours long, out of which time I slept for one hour. We went from Chittagong to Dhaka, Dhaka to Dubai, and Dubai to Toronto and then I carried on alone to Calgary. I looked around my beautiful home and could not help but feel just how unnecessary all my "stuff" was. Once settled I did the same as I did after Mongolia and put together a slide presentation, which I showed to various groups. I believe my photographs impacted them greatly. There were many questions and some very thoughtful faces. For some reason my computer access code to the World Vision site was being particularly troublesome and it took some weeks to sort it out from the Toronto end. Meanwhile, any blogs I wanted to send had to first be sent by e-mail to Toronto and then incorporated into the site from there.

That summer Toby and Tara decided to move. They needed a bigger house with four bedrooms and were having one built in a new community called Skyview Ranch. This put them in somewhat of a dilemma as they had a supported neighbour living in the basement apartment of their current home. I was well-established in my home and Toby had just completed finishing my basement. It was painted, carpeted and looked just as I had pictured it to be.

I was visiting with Toby and Tara one day and said, "Whoever gets this house will be lucky because it is gorgeous." They had done many high-end upgrades; their garden was twice the size of any of their neighbours' (with the added advantage that it backed onto and had a gate that led into the park) and had an unobstructed view of the Rocky Mountains. "I wish I could afford it," I said.

This got Toby thinking. If I bought this house, not only would the supported neighbour in the basement not have to move, but Toby would not have to put the house up for sale and I would have a decent income. As far as finances were concerned, I could buy it privately from Toby and Tara in a way I could afford. Wow, could this really be happening to me?

For a few minutes I thought about it, and then I said, "Don't put it up for sale. I'll buy it."

When I give my word, Toby knows he can rely on it and I won't back out. Also, I could see the advantages for me, not the least of which was the insulated garage attached to the house. At my current home I had to park on the street and was finding it difficult to deal with in the winter.

From that point on things moved fast. My house went up

for sale, and on September 15 I moved into this wonderful house that, with my personal touches, is now my home. One of my greatest joys is the view from my windows. All I can see are fields and mountains, and the passing of the seasons all have their own unique quality, just like the seasons of my life. In the spring there are ducks and geese on the pond raising their young, and in the stand of pines outside my fence are all kinds of birds pecking around for food. At night I hear the coyotes howling. And one in particular (I call him Fred) likes to leisurely stroll around the park. He has a distinct black diamond in the fur on his tail, so I can always recognise him.

In November 2010 I was invited to visit Jean and John. They looked a little surprised when I arrived with a laptop slung over my shoulder, but I wanted to show them the photos from my travels. As usual I had a lovely time with them, and for my upcoming birthday they bought me the book *Gold Diggers* by Charlotte Gray. Now Charlotte happens to be Jean's first cousin, and I already have a signed copy of her book about Alexander Graham Bell. What a talented writer she is. Jean was telling me about all the research she had done up in the Yukon for her latest book.

In February 2011 I felt inspired to write this story of my life. My life had taken many twists and turns—some good, some bad—but it all adds up to who we are. I believe we are the sum total of our experiences. What we do with those experiences, whether we resent them or use them as a learning tool, is up to us. I sincerely hope I can look back on my life and am able to say, "Yes, you did all right."

So now, dear reader, the time has come for me to end my tale. Everything in this book is true (at least as far as this old lady's memory serves her) with the exception of changing just four names in order to protect those people's identities. It is now

January 2012, and I am 71 years old. This past year had been one of watching my grandchildren grow and reliving old memories—some that were happy, some that were sad and some that made me long for "the wished for." So now I am content, I am happy, I am me. I am Cynthia.

Manufactured by Amazon.ca
Acheson, AB